SPARKS OF LIGHT

SPARKS OF LIGHT

ESSAYS ON THE WEEKLY TORAH PORTIONS
BASED ON THE PHILOSOPHY OF RAV KOOK

GIDEON WEITZMAN

JASON ARONSON INC.
Northvale, New Jersey
Jerusalem

The author wishes to thank Rabbi Filber of the Machon Al Shem HaRav Tzvi Yehudah Kook, the Rabbi Tzvi Yehudah Kook Institute, for his permission to quote from *Ein Iyah*.

The author wishes to thank Rabbi Aviner for his permission to quote from *Ma'amrei HaRiyah*.

This book was set in 11 pt. Granjon by Alpha Graphics of Pittsfield, NH and printed and bound by Book-mart Press, Inc. of North Bergen, NJ.

Library of Congress Cataloging-in-Publication Data

Weitzman, Gideon.
    Sparks of light: essays on the weekly Torah portions based on the philosophy of Rav Kook / by Gideon Weitzman.
      p.   cm.
    Includes bibliographical references.
    ISBN 0-7657-6080-0
    1. Bible. O. T. Pentateuch—Commentaries. I. Kook, Abraham Isaac, 1865–1935. II. Title.
    BS1225.3.W44 1999
    222'.107—dc21   98–54335

Printed in the United States of America on acid-free paper. For information and catalog write to Jason Aronson Inc., 230 Livingston Street, Northvale, NJ 07647-1726, or visit our website: www.aronson.com

To Rivki,

"Mine and Yours is Hers"
with love and appreciation

Contents

Shemot

Bemidbar

Devarim

Preface

I was very happy to learn that you are planning to publish books in English. The time has come that the holy concepts connected with the vision of Israel and man, that emanate from the Torah, should be publicized in the world in the language of the time that is spoken by the most people who most need to hear these concepts.

(Igrot HaRiyah, Volume IV, Letter 1148)

Rabbi Avraham Yitzchak HaCohen Kook (5635–5695/1865–1935) was one of the greatest Jewish leaders of recent history. He was steeped in Jewish knowledge of all kinds, a master of halacha, Talmud, and Jewish philosophy, and he also had a good knowledge of the general philosophy and science of his day.

Rav Kook was also a prolific writer and a complex thinker who developed a system of understanding the events that were happening to the Jewish people. It was a time of change, Herzl convened the Zionist Congress in Basle, irreligious Zionists were moving to Israel and establishing settlements and kibbutzim. There was a negative reaction from many religious leaders to these young men and women. Darwin's theory and Freud's new science were gaining popularity and many Jews were drawn further away from a traditional lifestyle.

Rav Kook was able to perceive the inner yearnings that accompanied these revolutionary changes. They represented a deep yearning within these young Jews for morality, equality, and justice. They realized that the world was not static but evolved and moved in a positive direction. Rav Kook embraced both Zionism and the young irreligious Zionists. He developed a philosophy that was based on the kabbalistic concept of fusion. The world appears divided; there is a break between heaven and earth, physical and spiritual, politics and religion. But at the heart of all, everything is fused into a cohesive unit. This is true for the individual, the nation, and all of existence.

Rav Kook set about publicizing his theories and spreading his teachings to young thinkers, both religious and secular. This represents the bulk of his voluminous writings.

Rav Kook never wrote a book of commentary on the Torah, but he did create a lens through which we can perceive and better understand the Torah. That is the basis for this book.

The ideas presented here grew out of many classes on the weekly Torah portion given by me in different times and in different forums, in both Hebrew and English. The talks evolved with time and have taken form over a number of years. They are by no means complete and have been given a number of times subsequent to being written down. They continue to evolve and change.

The necessity to write the book grew out of numerous requests from students for more material on the subject. I was approached and asked for a book based on Rav Kook's philosophy dealing with the Torah and could not find another book in English. At my students' request, here is my attempt to set down and write such a volume.

The ideas presented are based on Rav Kook and my own personal understanding of his philosophy. Any deviations from the truth are due to my misunderstanding and should not be blamed on Rav Kook himself.

The translations of verses and sources are my own and may have been adapted in context. In all circumstances, the original text should be consulted. I have attempted to supply full sources for all quotes and ideas.

There are numerous people who helped me along the entire passage of the book's inception and realization. I only mention some by name, but this is by no means a complete list.

First, I would like to thank every student and friend who asked a perceptive question during these talks. Often these questions lead to new avenues of thought and inspired me to adapt and alter my direction and presentation. As these talks often formed the backbone for discussions around our Shabbat table, I must thank all those who graced our Shabbat meals with their presence. This book is as much part of them as it is part of me.

I would like to thank Doron Peretz for constant friendship and support for so many years. He listened to these ideas from the very beginning, and it was he who heard them late on Thursday nights before they were given for the first time on Friday mornings. I could only wish that he will continue to be there in the future, and I look forward to more collaboration with him.

I would like to thank all the staff and students at Yeshivat Beit-El, my home and source of knowledge. Especially deserving of praise is Rav Zalman Baruch

Melamed, my Rosh Yeshivah, mentor, and inspiration. Also, thank you to Nir Yehudah and all those at the Teacher Institute Library who supplied books, material, and computers for my use at any time of day and night. May all the books that have been written there be successful and may you be the facilitators of many more.

I would like to thank Rav Shlomo Aviner for his advice and kind comments at a crucial stage of the writing process. Many of the ideas presented here, I heard from him. Thank you.

My gratitude goes to Rabbi Morey and Deena Schwartz, and to the people at Congregation BIAV in Kansas City, and to all those who are involved with the Kansas City Community Kollel for allowing me to continue my work while working for them. You are a source of pride to the Jewish people and do amazing work. Keep it up.

My thanks go to Arthur Kurzweil and the staff at Jason Aronson Inc. for editing and publishing this work. Also to Stephen Kort for all his help and legal advice.

I am eternally grateful to my parents and family for support and encouragement, even when our paths and ideas differed. Thank you for everything that you have done and continue to do for us as a family.

I thank my three children Le-ora, Yair, and Rachel for not destroying this manuscript and for making me laugh after a long and frustrating day in front of the computer.

I do not have enough words of praise and gratitude for my wife, Rivki. It is to you that I dedicate this book. You are always there for me and allow me to pursue my interests and career, even when it would seem impossible for you to do so. Thank you for that and for so much more.

I thank God that He has enabled me to complete this work and pray that I shall always sit in His house and visit His sanctuary, to learn, teach, keep, and do.

Gideon Weitzman

Introduction

Torah should appear to us as the foundation of all culture, the reason for its existence and continuation, closely connected with the Divine soul, the essence of man, through the Divine image that he is.

(*Ma'amrei HaRiyah*, p. 101)

Israel cannot return to her true nature without wide and deep learning of Torah. Torah that will produce Torah scholars and establishing set times to learn Torah for the entire populus.

(*Orot Hateshuva*, 6:3)

The Torah, with all her opinions, laws, and judgments for the individual and for the nation is the illuminated eyeglass, through which the spiritual level of the nation is perceived.

(*Shabbat Ha'aretz*, Introduction, p. 10)

Every nation has a national consensus and a national identity. In most cases, this is connected with the common destiny that is forged through historical events and a brotherhood of intentions and ideals. Most identities of nations are developed over generations and centuries of soul searching, due to pressures from within and from without. Throughout the generations questions of morality, destiny, and affiliation are raised, dealt with, and incorporated into the nation's constitution, written or otherwise.

In this respect, as in many others, the Jewish people are unique. Their national charter was not the work of a general assembly, and no synod was convened in order to give them a national identity. The national consensus of the Jewish people was not born of history and was not shaped by the passage of time or a myriad of forces. All this is for one very important reason.

Am Yisrael received their national identity in a solitary and extraordinary event that was to change them and the world. When God revealed Himself to us on *Har Sinai* and gave us the Torah, He also gave us our national identity and consensus. Contained within the Torah are the answers to all of our queries concerning morality, destiny, and affiliation. All the intentions and ideology we require are found within the wisdom contained therein, in the words of the Mishnah "Investigate the Torah from all possible angles as it contains everything" (*Avot* 5:22).

The Torah is, therefore, our autobiography; it is our Torah and we are the main players in its drama and moral system. Were I to compose an autobiography, I would be sure to include five sections: my ancestry and family background, the story of my birth, my task in life, what I accomplished. I would round it off with any relevant moral messages that I thought came out of the story. We find that the five books of the Torah perfectly fit into these five categories:

BeReishit—The Ancestral Lineage of the Jewish People.
Shemot—The Birth of the Jewish People.
Vayikra—The Task of the Jewish People.
Bemidbar—What the Jewish People Accomplished.
Devarim—A Recollection of Moral Concepts Within the Torah.

With this knowledge let us proceed to learning how each of these sections is developed in the text of the Torah.

I

BeReishit

Introduction

Our holy forefathers gave us as an inheritance good character traits. We need to realize them and bring them from potential to real force in order to become complete.

(*Ein Iyah, Berachot*, Chapter 2, Note 30)

The basis of zechut *Avot* (the merit of the forefathers that establishes a special relationship between God and the Jewish people) *is due to the fact that our forefathers impressed their own good qualities in the hearts of the children* (that is, the Jewish people). *Even if the children have externally rejected the true way, the inheritance that we have from our forefathers works in such a way that the children will never get to a point that they will be incapable of repairing their sins and being cured.*

(*ibid.*, Chapter 5, Note 55)

Each person should say: 'When will my deeds resemble those of my forefathers, Avraham, Yitzchak, and Ya'akov,' who strove for the idealism that is encompassed within Israel even before it was realized and was only a potential.

(*Igrot HaRiyah*, Volume I, Letter 93)

*B*eReishit is the book of our ancestral lineage. Every autobiographical work starts off with a description of the family background of the author, and this is for a number of reasons.

To paraphrase Lewis Caroll, one can only know the direction to take in the future if one is fully aware of the direction traveled in the past. Only by investigating where we have come from can we decide where to go in the future, wisely and competently. The sages coined the phrase *"ma'aseh avot siman lebanim"*—"the acts of the forefathers are an indication for subsequent generations" (see Ramban on the Torah, *BeReishit* 12:6; and *Midrash Tanchuma Lech Lecha* 9). Through a deeper and broader understanding of the events that occurred to the fathers of the Jewish nation, we can make realistic decisions concerning the future. In the next few pages, we shall attempt to investigate certain key events in the lives of the central characters in the *Book of BeReishit*. In so doing, the hope of the author is that we shall be in a better position to understand where we have come from, in order to decide what we should now aim for.

There is another reason for examining the past generations. Individuals are made up of a wealth of characteristics that they have inherited from their past. These take the form of properties adopted from the surroundings or from genetic makeup, acquired within the body from conception. This is the case not only with biological genes but also with spiritual genes. These spiritual genes do not control our physical appearance but are concerned with the internal workings of our minds and souls.

Just as with biological genes that come from previous generations, in order to investigate them one must retrace their development, so it is with spiritual genes. In order to understand the spiritual genetic makeup of the Jewish people, one must return to the forefathers of the nation and investigate their spiritual genes. After so doing, we can be certain that any traits that we discover in them will be present in all subsequent generations. (It is, of course, possible that the genes will be present but will be invisible to the observer. Even biological genes are occasionally present in a dormant state. Just because something exists, there is no guarantee that it will naturally express itself in every individual of every subsequent generation. In order to ensure that these genes are present and thriving, we have to develop them as we would any other natural skill, by practice and exercise.)

Therefore, when we learn the *Book of BeReishit*, we are investigating the spiritual genes present in our forefathers, in order to discover our huge potential. We can be sure that all that they achieved and converted to being in their nature, we have inherited from them. All that remains is the will to develop our natural skills and to strive to live a life that resembles theirs as closely as possible. The sages said that one should repeat to oneself: "When will my actions resemble those of my forefathers?" (*Midrash Tanna Devei Eliyahu Rabba* 25), and this mentality is supposed to ensure that we always strive for lofty ideals, and, in so doing, develop our innate spiritual potential.

We shall see, in the following pages, certain traits that the fathers of our nation developed and imprinted on our collective conscience: initially, the will and ability to fuse that which is classed holy with that which is viewed to be mundane. Avraham and his family proved to the world that God rules not only over the heaven but also on the earth. Divinity and sanctity can be discovered in all walks of life and it is the task of man to unite heaven and earth.

Avraham felt the huge obligation of universal responsibility and this he also taught to his children and grandchildren. Later, Ya'akov, through necessity, assigned two separate tasks to his family: to continue Avraham's work, on the one hand; and to guard the Torah within, on the other hand.

These are the messages contained in the *Book of BeReishit*, and this is the beginning of our national autobiography. In the following chapters, we will learn about our rich ancestry, and this will give us an inkling of who we are and what we can achieve.

BeReishit
The Break Between Heaven and Earth

Seeing the techelet, *which is similar to the sea, the heavens, and the Divine throne, reminds us of God's commandments and encourages us to remember the holiness of the commandments. The Divine light emanates through all the soul's faculties and is clothed in holy splendor by manifesting itself in the mundane and physical medium of the commandments. This realization should encourage us to act in such a way that God is present in all our actions.*

(*Olat Riyah*, Volume I, p. 5)

The world will be formed; heaven and earth will kiss; and the joy of all being will be evident. So it is with the individual, the nation, the world, and all of existence.

(*Orot*, p. 132)

These two qualities—on the one hand, the drive to infinite expansion, and, on the other hand, the need to specialize and to confine—fuse through the commandments. They fuse the heights of heaven with the depths of the earth, and this is how each soul is enriched. The soul strives to fuse inner spirituality with the world and physicality, in order that the soul of the living God should reside in the world.

(*Olat Riyah*, Volume I, p. 13)

7

In this, the first *parsha* in the Torah, we find an argument between Cain and Hevel (Abel)—the sons of Adam, the first man. This argument was to lead to one of the first sins, the murder by Cain of his brother Hevel.

There is a very interesting midrash that sheds light on the nature of their argument and leaves us even more confused. By examining this and related midrashim, we will come to an understanding of a message about early man's nature and the task of humanity.

The Torah tells us that Cain, who was a farmer, brought an offering of "fruits of the land" to the Lord; whilst Hevel, a shepherd, brought his offering of the choicest sheep. God happily accepted the sacrifice that Hevel brought but rejected Cain's sacrifice.

The midrash (*Midrash Tanchuma, BeReishit* 9) states that Cain's sacrifice consisted of flax, while Hevel's was wool. From this we arrive at the prohibition against wearing combinations of wool and linen, *sha'atnez* (see *Devarim* 22:11). "The Lord said—it is incorrect that the offering of the guilty should be mixed with the offering of the innocent."

The midrash connects two seemingly unconnected portions of the Torah— the story of Cain's brutal murder of Hevel and the prohibition against wearing *sha'atnez*.

In order to make sense of this extraordinary midrash, let us investigate the basis of the argument between Cain and Hevel. The Torah says: "And Cain said to Hevel his brother when they were in the field, and Cain arose and killed Hevel his brother" (*BeReishit* 4:8). The Torah tells us that Cain said something to Hevel, but the content of this conversation is not recorded. In another midrash, this question is addressed and the details of their discussion are given; *BeReishit Rabbah* (22:7) says: "What were they discussing ? They said let us divide up the World. One took the earth; the other took the possessions. The one said, "The land that you are standing on belongs to me." The other said, "The clothes that you are wearing belong to me." The one said, "Take them off (your clothes that belong to me)," and the other said, "Fly (off the earth that belongs to me)." Through this argument "Cain arose and killed Hevel his brother."

The two brothers, seeing that they were incapable of living together in harmony, decided that they must separate and separate the World along with them. They divided the earth from the possessions or, in other words, the earth from that which is above the earth. They tried to divide the earthly, mundane, material matters from matters that are above the earth. Cain and Hevel wanted to separate the spiritual from the physical.

Cain and Hevel discovered that in the ideal world the spiritual and the physical are indivisibly linked; one cannot easily separate them. Indeed, before Adam's first sin, we are told that spiritual and physical worked together towards the lofty aim of serving the Almighty, and that only subsequently did they become opposed to each other. Cain and Hevel found, relates the midrash, that the only way to separate them was through an act of destruction. "Cain arose and killed his brother Hevel." From this moment, the spiritual was torn from the physical. They became two completely separate entities, diametrically opposed to each other, and the world was changed forever.

We can now begin to understand the midrash that linked Cain's shocking crime with the prohibition against wearing wool and linen combinations. The midrash is telling us that *sha'atnez* is a symbol of this severance of the spiritual from the physical and, therefore, it is forbidden. We try to rid ourselves of the scourge of this transgression and, therefore, distance ourselves from combinations that remind us of this worldwide split. We do not wear wool and linen together.

We can now explain some of the laws concerning this mitzvah of *sha'atnez*. In the Temple, the clothes of the *cohanim* (the priests) were made out of a combination of wool and linen, specifically. Every *cohen* had to wear these clothes while doing service in the Temple. Were he to wear any other clothes, his service was considered improper and disqualified. Why did the *cohen* have to wear this combination of wool and linen?

There is an argument in the *Gemara* (*Nedarim* 35b) as to whether the *cohanim* were messengers of the Jewish people or messengers of Heaven. Was the task of the *cohanim* to intercede on behalf of the people before the Lord, seeking atonement for the sins of the people, or were they charged with the task of bringing God's words to the people, acting as messengers of heaven?

The *cohanim* were a link between heaven and earth. In their service in the Temple, they fused spirituality with more mundane physical service. They were both messengers of the Lord *and* messengers of the people. The *cohanim* had reached a very high level of perfection and, therefore, were permitted to wear wool and linen together. They did not have to be concerned that this forbidden *sha'atnez* would create a rift between the spiritual and the physical. Their whole worship was one of complete fusion between these two separate entities, causing the physical and the spiritual to become one. Therefore, in order for the *cohen's* service to be valid, he *must* wear wool and linen together.

We also find in the *Gemara* (*Yevamot* 4a) that there is no prohibition against wearing wool and linen together in the *tzitzit* (the fringes that are tied on each corner of a four cornered garment). One could wear a linen garment and yet tie on wool strands as the *tzitziot*. All this was on one condition, however: that the *tzitzit* contain the *techelet*, the strand of blue dye taken from the *chilazon* (some type of fish or sea creature). If the *techelet* is missing (as it is today for most people, because, according to many halachic authorities, we do not know exactly what the *chilazon* is) it is forbidden to wear *tzitzit* with *sha'atnez*. Why should this one blue thread be so important that it can outweigh the prohibition against wool and linen combinations?

The *Gemara* (*Menachot* 43b) asks: "What is so special about this shade of blue more than any other color? Because the *techelet* is the same color as the sea, and the sea is the same color as the sky, and the sky is like the *Kiseh HaKavod* (the Throne of Divine Glory, that the Lord Himself "sits" on)." Why should the *Gemara* go through this rather circuitous route and not simply say that the blue of the *techelet* comes to remind us of the sky and the *Kiseh HaKavod*? What is the relevance of the fact that the sea is also blue?

This question is compounded by the fact that the Rambam, in his major work, the *Mishneh Torah*, bringing up this halacha writes: "The *techelet* . . . is the colour of heaven," and omits the references to the sea.

Rashi on the *Gemara* explains that there were miracles that were performed for the Jewish people through the sea (such as the splitting of the Red Sea). The *Gemara* tells us that the *techelet* reminds us not only of the heavens and the Divine Ruler but, that through the *techelet*, we are also reminded of the miracles that we saw on the sea. This is the innovation of the *techelet*: it comes to constantly remind us that Divinity is not restricted to the heavens, but that we, *Am Yisrael*, also experienced miracles and revelation through earthly media; we witnessed miracles on the sea. There is no split between heaven and earth; in reality, the spiritual and physical are intrinsically linked. This is the message of the *techelet*. Whoever wears the *techelet* has a constant reminder of the link between the spiritual and the physical, and therefore, has no problem wearing wool and linen together. If we tie our *tzitziot* with *techelet*, we can wear *sha'atnez*.

Another interesting point about *sha'atnez* is that our sages tell us that if one wears this forbidden blend of wool and linen, his prayers will not be answered. The question could be asked: What is the connection between *sha'atnez* and prayer that one seems to counteract the other? We find a halacha concerning prayer that guides us as to what intentions we should have when praying the *Sh'ma* prayer (*Shulchan Aruch, Orach Chayim* 61:6); "We should assume that God is King over the heavens and the earth." Prayer comes to tell us that the Lord has dominion not only over the heavens, but also over the earth. Indeed, our prayers are a collection of supplications for very mundane, earthly things—wealth, health, and success—and that is the essence of our prayers. It would be, therefore, highly inappropriate for us to come before God to request that He rule over heaven and earth in attire that proclaims a split between the spiritual and the physical. Someone who wears *sha'atnez* while praying cannot hope that his prayers will be answered.

We have seen that the Torah impresses upon us the point that Cain and Hevel, and indeed Adam himself, separated the spiritual from the physical through their actions. We shall see how this rift continued until Avraham appeared to mend it and set the task for every Jew to follow his example. We can also fuse these two entities—the physical and the spiritual—together to form a unity that strives towards the lofty ideal of serving our Creator.

Noach
The Continuing Rift

---

*There are situations where the physical world is so developed that the
light of God dims. There is a certain momentum that drives society for
some time even as the value of life slowly disappears. When there is no
spiritual yearning, the society loses its nature. Individual desire and
demand take preference over social harmony, until the society reaches
depression and disillusionment and all order is reversed.*

(*Orot*, p. 103)

*The impulse for sexual relations can ensnare a person and become
stronger than the need for life itself, because it is connected with the
perpetuation of life. On the other hand, when it is used in a holy way,
the same impulse elevates one through the sanctity of the* brit *to the
level of a total* tzaddik.

(*Orot Haḳodesh*, Volume III, p. 298)

*Wine gladdens the hearts of men, and it also gives joy to God uplifting
the body and the physical being to meet the advance of the spirit,
enabling people to perform the necessary tasks with joy and enthusiasm.*

(*Ein Iyah*, *Berachot*, Chapter 6, Note 2)

"There were ten generations between Adam and Noach, and ten generations from Noach to Avraham" (*Avot* 5: 2). These generations were all
those who lived from the initial split between heaven and earth, from the time
of Adam and his children, Cain and Hevel, up until the time that Avraham

mended the break between them. Do we find that these generations strove to mend the rift? Did they try to develop some sort of fusion, or did they contribute to the already existing split and, in fact, enlarge the distance between the two?

The generation directly before the flood definitely did not help to heal the rift. This is evident not only from the punishment that they received, but also from the relevant midrashim dealing with this period. The Torah informs us: "The sons of the important people saw that the daughters of Man were pleasant, and so they took for themselves wives, from all that they chose" (*BeReishit* 6:2). The midrash explains the verse in these words: "When a woman was ready to be married to her husband, the most important person present would sleep with her first. They were rank with adultery, homosexuality, and bestiality. Rav Huna said, in the name of Rebbi, that the generation of the flood were destroyed when they wrote *ketubot*, marriage contracts, between two men and even between man and beast. (The word *gemumsiot* in the midrash is hard to translate and is an extremely rare word, not appearing even once in the whole of the Talmud. The Midrash *Rabba HaMevuar* translates it as we have done so here, which seems to be much more correct than Marcus Jastrow's translation of love songs.) Where one finds prostitution, there one finds chaos in the world that comes to kill good and bad people alike. God forgives all things and is willing to delay punishment on all sins except prostitution" (*BeReishit Rabba* 26:5). We see that this promiscuity was found not only amongst the human populace but had spread to the animal kingdom as well. "God saw the land, and it was corrupt, because all living things had perverted their way on the Earth" (*BeReishit* 6:12). Rashi explains: "Even animals, beasts, and fowl had relationships with other breeds."

The generation was guilty of crimes connected with interpersonal relationships. They were accused of adultery, homosexuality, and bestiality. All of these crimes attack the institution of marriage. The intimate link between a man and a woman is one that can return us to the level of an animal, always on the lookout for new pleasures since the old ones have ceased to thrill. Conversely, this link can elevate us to a new level of sanctity, providing us with love, affection, and the ability to create new life. The choice is in the hands of man to utilize this God-given potential, this intimacy, to come closer to another person, a loved one, and, thus, draw closer to the Lord Himself. We can also misuse this gift and cause pain, anguish, and vulnerability, widening the gulf between ourselves and our Creator. The generation immediately preceding the flood chose to reject the ability to use this tool to fuse heaven and earth. Instead, they corrupted the union of marriage and all human relationships. Their punishment was that they, who had destroyed the world, were forced to watch while the world physically dissolved around them.

So we see that Noach's generation tragically failed in this mission to fuse the spiritual and the physical. What about Noach himself? Did he not succeed in bridging the gap? Did he fuse heaven and earth?

After several months of seclusion, during which time the Lord wiped out all existing life, Noach eventually emerged from the Ark. He immediately set to work to rebuild some sort of civilization. The first thing he did was to offer sacrifices, thanking God for saving him from the flood. "Noach built an altar to God, and he took from all the pure beast and fowl and offered up sacrifices" (*BeReishit* 8:20). This was an important renewal of man's link and communication with the Lord. Indeed, we are told that "God smelled the odour and said, 'I will not curse the land anymore, and I will never again destroy all life'" (*ibid.*, 21).

Directly after this, we find that Noach started the physical work of replanting trees, and so forth. The first tree that he planted was a grape vine. "And Noach started, and he planted a vineyard" (*ibid.*, 9:20). The result was that Noach took the fruits of his labor, drank the wine, and became inebriated; which, in turn, led to one of his children disgracing him. The sages point to Noach's actions as the central cause of this shame. As the midrash says: "He should have devoted the time to planting trees of greater value instead of planting the vineyard" (*BeReishit Rabba* 36:3).

Wine, also, contains the power to turn us into animals and brings with it anger, pride, and decadence; but it also holds the potential to bring us closer to God. We sanctify the *Shabbat* and the festivals over a glass of wine that "elates the heart of Man" (*Tehillim* 104:15). Wine enables us to reveal our inner thoughts (see *Eruvin* 65a, "Wine goes in and secrets come out"). Our inner divinity is often clouded by our physical state, requiring us to partake of wine to uncover this spirituality. The wine can help us to fuse the spiritual with the physical, or it can cause the gap to widen. Noach misused wine, which became the cause of his own degradation. Instead of helping to unite heaven with earth by rebuilding the world, he preferred the immediate physical pleasure. Instead of planting more useful trees, he chose to first plant a vineyard.

The generation preceding the flood, and Noach himself, continued the historical practice of separating the spiritual from the physical. The next generation came up with a novel way of achieving union between heaven and earth. They would build a tower tall enough to reach the heavens, and this would be the ideal bridge between them and God. "Let us build a city and a tower, and its head will reach the heavens" (*BeReishit* 11:4). Their plan seemed perfect, and yet we find that God deemed their actions a serious crime, one worthy of a severe punishment: the dispersion of the nations into different languages. What was the problem with the approach of the people of the tower?

The midrash tells us that one reason they came up with the idea of building this edifice was that they reckoned that the flood was simply a meteorological occurrence. "Every one thousand, six-hundred-and-fifty-six years, the heavens collapse. Let us build a support system to prevent further collapse" (*BeReishit Rabba* 38:6). They saw the world in purely scientific terms. God was relegated to a geographical location in the heavens. It was assumed that, if they could get there, they would find God and achieve the same level as the Lord Himself. If God is in heaven, then let us go there to fight against Him. It is quite reminiscent of Yuri Gagarin's orchestrated comment on first entering space: "I am in the heavens and there is no God, as I cannot see Him." The assumption being that God is some physical presence residing comfortably in the sky; if we build a tower, we can wage war on Him (Rashi on *BeReishit* 11:1). If I travel to outer space, I should meet Him somewhere along the way.

One result of this conception is related in the midrash (*Pirkei DeRabbi Eliezer* 24). "If a man fell off the tower, they did not notice; but were a brick to fall, they sat and wailed, saying: 'When will we find another brick like that one?'" Their life became measured in such material terms that there was no longer value in human life. It had worth only in that it contributed to their scheme to erect the tower. A brick had more worth than a builder; the physical outweighed the spiritual in their clouded vision.

This was a further step away from the goal of fusing heaven and earth, and yet, the Torah later tells us that God Himself did come down to check their work on earth. Their plan seems to have been successful. They planned to get closer to the Lord, and we find that God drew closer to them. The midrash tells us that God came down to the Earth ten times, and this is one of three occasions that appear in the book of *BeReishit*. All of these visits were due to transgressions on Earth (*ibid.*, 14), the one occurring in the Garden of Eden, thanks to Adam and Chava's (Eve) sin of eating from the Tree of Wisdom, and one in S'dom, when God came to see the despicable sins of the people. God's coming to the world to view man's deeds has an ominous connotation in the book of *BeReishit*. Instead of being a fusion of heaven and earth, it signified that the Lord was about to severely punish the people.

The mistake that the builders of the tower made, unfortunately, is a common one. They assumed that in order to fuse heaven and earth, they had to travel to Heaven and force a relationship with God, be it a dialogue or a confrontation. The important thing in their eyes was to initiate contact. The result was a link of sorts, but one initiated by God, and on his terms, which also involved a punishment. Our task is not to search for Divinity by trying physically to reach the outer limits of heaven; we have a more immediate and relevant task. We must search for God here on earth. We can reveal the intrinsic holiness and sanctity that exists, not in far away galaxies but here in the physical world. We must use our ability to have intimate relationships and reproduce in order to uncover the spiritual in this world. We take wine to sanctify and proclaim the festivals and *Shabbat*. We also get married over a cup of wine; one of the blessings that we make at the wedding ceremony is over wine. We must also harness scientific technology to a positive end, to aid health and alleviate suffering. All these emphasize our task: to discover God here on Earth. Once we distance ourselves from the Lord and relegate God to a distant heaven, the result is a preference for the physical over the spiritual. We arrive at a point where bricks take on more importance than man himself.

The person who first strove to mend the rift between heaven and earth was Avraham *Avinu* (Abraham our Forefather). He showed his generation the way to fuse the physical and the spiritual here in this world. He was the first to call God by the name of God of the heavens and the earth. We will see how Avraham was extremely successful in this task, and our prayers are that we should emulate him to reveal Divinity, sanctity, and the Lord Himself here in this World. "Because this thing is very close to you, it is in your mouths and in your hearts to accomplish it" (*Devarim* 30:14).

Lech Lecha
Avraham-Mending the Rift

*Avraham called God 'Lord' and informed the whole world that the
One God created His creatures, and their complete state was included
within the plan of Providence, as was individual concern over every
communal and private ethical act. These were the reason for creation.*

(*Ein Iyah, Berachot*, Chapter 1, Note 77)

*The whole world is waiting for the light of Israel to appear, the clear
light of God's glory, of the people that are to relate His glory [that is,
Israel]. This knowledge comes from Avraham, who blessed God on
high, who influences both the heavens and the earth.*

(*Orot*, p. 22)

The tephillin *on the arm, through their holy action, sweeten all the
natural life forces within the entire existence, specifically within man.
It prepares everything for the higher [Divine] light. Therefore, it is
fitting that we bless "to put on* tephillin" *which symbolizes the
strength that prepares life to accept the higher sanctity.*

(*Olat Riyah*, Volume I, p. 29–30)

In this week's *parsha* we find a story concerning Lot, Avraham's nephew,
who was captured by four fierce kings. Upon hearing of his nephew's plight,
Avraham immediately went to free him, defeated the four kings, and freed
Lot, along with many other captives. This must have been an exceptionally
dangerous mission. We are told that these four kings had beaten five kings

who had risen up to enslave them, and we can learn from this that they were successful warriors. Despite this, Avraham fearlessly ran to save his relative and other unfortunate individuals who had fallen into the hands of these conquerors.

Not only did Avraham successfully repel the four kings and release his nephew from captivity, he also recovered a great amount of physical possessions belonging to Lot and to the five monarchs, one of whom was the King of S'dom. On Avraham's triumphant return from battle, the King of S'dom came out to greet him together with Malki Tzedek, the king of Shalem (most probably a reference to Jerusalem). They brought out, in honor of Avraham, a feast of bread and wine. They praised him, blessed him on his victory, and thanked him for returning their possessions.

The King of S'dom then made Avraham a very generous offer: "You give me the people whom you freed, and you will be at liberty to keep the possessions for yourself" (*BeReishit* 14:21). However, Avraham declined this offer saying: "I swear to God, the Highest Power who rules over Heaven and Earth, that I have taken neither a thread nor a shoelace (from the bounty), and I will not take anything that belongs to you, that you should not say that I have caused Avram to prosper" (*ibid.*, 22–23).

The *Gemara* says on this sentence (*Chulin* 89a) that, on the merit of these words, "his children gained the mitzvah of the thread of *techelet* and the straps of the *tephillin*." Because Avraham did not want to receive any remuneration for his outstanding act of courage and kindness, he merited two new *mitzvot*. He received the blue strand of the *techelet* in the *tzitzit*, and the straps that bind the *tephillin* to the head and the hand.

In addition, we find a midrash that says (*BeReishit Rabba* 39:3): "Rabbi Berachia brought an exegesis on the verse 'we have a young sister'" (*Shir HaShirim* 8:8). This refers to Avraham, who brought together all peoples of the world. Bar Kapara said this refers to Avraham who mended the rip (this is a play on the word sister, *achot* in Hebrew, which can also be explained to mean sew or mend).

The midrash tells us that Avraham's feat was his ability to bring together all of the inhabitants of the world. Avraham managed to influence and convince those around him, and thus, they started to worship the One God together with him. Indeed, on the verse (*BeReishit* 12:5) "And Avram took Sarai, his wife; and Lot, his nephew; and the possessions that they had acquired; and the soul that they made in Charan. And they went to the Land of Cana'an." The sages ask: What is the meaning of "the soul that they made in Charan"— "were all the people of the world to congregate, they would not be able to 'make' even a mosquito, and you say that they made souls in Charan?!" (Quite an appropriate observation in that, to the present day, man has been unable to *create* in the laboratory even the most elementary organisms.) The answer given is that it refers to the souls that they converted from idol worship to their new monotheistic religion. "Avraham converted the men and Sarah converted the women" (*BeReishit Rabba* 39:14). From the large numbers that we see were associated with Avraham's household, we reveal the extent of his success in the mass conversion of an idol-worshipping populace.

Another example that we have of Avraham's success in this task is that, later, Avraham told his servant to swear in the name of "The Lord the God of the Heavens who took me out of my father's house" (*BeReishit* 24:7). The midrash asks: Why suddenly does Avraham talk about the God of the Heavens, when previously he referred to Him constantly as the God of the Heavens and the Earth? Rashi quotes the answer that the midrash gives in slightly different language than the original midrash: "Said Avraham, 'Now, indeed, He is the God of the Heaven and the Earth, because I have introduced this term into the lexicon of the people. However, when He took me out of my father's house, He was the God of the Heavens and not of the Earth. As the world did not know Him, and His name was not recognized in the World." Avraham tells his servant that before he started his mission of informing the populace of the fact that God is not only in the heavens, but that He also has dominion, influence, and relates to the world, the name of the Lord was known, but not as God of the earth, only as God of the heavens. Avraham, however, precedes his words with the statement that, today, everybody is aware of the fact that the Lord is God in the heavens and in the earth.

How was Avraham so successful in his mission? By what method did he convince his neighbors of the veracity of the Jewish religion and the One God? The answer may lie in the second answer offered by the midrash, that of *Bar Kapara*: Avraham mended the rip. He was the one to come and reunite heaven and earth. Avraham's huge success came from living and presenting a new worldview, one that fused the spiritual with the physical. Avraham mended the rift and, in so doing, attracted large numbers of people away from idol worship to truely Divine pursuits.

Idol worship was concerned with the here-and-now, the instant gratification of man's passions. They removed Divinity from life and rejected it as irrelevant to everyday existence. When Avraham returned spirituality to the realm of relevance, it was immediately attractive and was adopted by large numbers of people.

We see that Avraham regarded simple, everyday affairs as holy duty. Welcoming strange idol-worshipping guests became, for him, an important mitzvah, a wonderful opportunity to publicize the name of God and the true path. The *Gemara* (*Sotah* 10a) says the verse: "And Avraham planted an *eshel* in Be'er Sheva, and he called there in the name of the Lord" (*BeReishit* 21:33) should be understood to mean that he caused others to call on the name of the Lord. "How? He would bring to the passersby and to his guests food to eat. After they ate and drank, they wanted to thank and bless him. He said to them: "Do you think that you have partaken of my food? You have eaten from the Lord of the Universe. Thank, praise, and bless the One who created the world."

Avraham's attitude towards fusing the heavens and the earth is also evident in his simple everyday speech. In his conversation with the King of S'dom, Avraham stressed that the Jewish God rules over "heaven and earth." This is not merely a figure of speech, but shows Avraham's true nature and his inner feelings. In the words of the *Gemara*: "Even the everyday comments of the sages require understanding" (*Avodah Zarah* 19b).

We are now in a position to explain the *Gemara* regarding the rewards that Avraham received for his conversation with the King of S'dom. Because he fused the spiritual and the physical in this dialogue and in his entire life, he was rewarded with the mitzvah of *techelet* and the straps of the *tephillin*. We have already discussed the *techelet* as a symbol of this fusion and, therefore, it is an appropriate reward. The second reward was not the *tephillin* themselves but, specifically, the straps. The straps enable us to bind the *tephillin* to the body. Without the straps, the *tephillin* would exist but we would be unable to join them together with the body. The mitzvah of *tephillin* requires the straps, and it would not be sufficient to keep the *tephillin* in their cloth bag. In order to fulfill the Divine will, we must bind them to our arms and head. Avraham, who exemplified this binding of the holy to the worldly body, merited the reward of the straps of the *tephillin*, the ability to fuse the spiritual and the physical.

This was Avraham's task in the world, and he also set this to be one of the basic elements of Judaism. It is a religion that continually fuses the holy and the mundane, the spiritual and the physical, heaven and earth. This is evident when browsing through the *Shulchan Aruch* (the Code of Jewish Law). We find that the halacha deals with such diverse subjects as laws governing the relationship between neighbors, between employer and employee, between suppliers and clients, between family members, between a man and his wife, general education—the list is endless. From the moment that a Jew awakes until he goes to sleep at night (and even when he is asleep), from birth to death and every event in between, the Jew's life is governed and directed by a complete system. It guides his thoughts and actions toward one massive task, that of serving the Creator, the God of heaven and earth.

We have seen that Avraham came to the world to mend the huge rift that had developed between heaven and earth. In so doing, he developed the Jewish credo and created a religion whose major task is to prove to humanity that God exists not only in some distant heaven with no relevance to anything human. On the contrary, God reveals Himself to the world as much through criminal law as through ritual service. Avraham was very successful in this task; indeed, we see that his household swelled with people thirsty to hear this new idea. They readily converted to this new religion.

Thus, Avraham developed the basis for the new way of life and was the "first Jew." We shall see how he spread this message throughout the world and advanced the will and the word of God.

Vayera
Universal Responsibility

The blood of the circumcision proves that, from our inception, we were stamped with our "Jewishness" throughout our existence, without a land and wandering amongst the other nations, through our specifically Jewish blood of circumcision.

(*Igrot HaRiyah*, Volume IV, Letter 1025)

The seed of Avraham received a special level of fastening onto their souls—the mark of circumcision—to change the natural form and prove the incomplete state of nature. This removal is not a subtraction at all; rather it is a completion according to the will and word of God.

(*Olat Riyah*, Volume I, p. 396)

The connection between the body and the soul is beyond human comprehension. Therefore, when God commanded Avraham to circumcise himself, Avraham could have been mistaken into thinking that this was due to a flaw in his soul. In truth, it was to elevate the connection between body and soul.

(*ibid.*)

The *parsha* of *Vayera* opens with the words: "And God appeared to Avraham in the plains of Mamre" (*BeReishit* 18:1). Rashi immediately asks: What is the significance of where Avraham happened to be sitting when the Lord spoke to him? Surely we are far more concerned with the content of the Divine command than the geographical details. Rashi, in order to answer this striking question, brings a midrash from the *Midrash Tanchuma*, and we shall look here at this midrash in its entirety.

> "May God's name be blessed that He rewards all those who are worthy of reward. Avraham had three friends: Aner, Eshkol and Mamre. When the Lord told him to circumcise himself, he went to ask their advice. He went first to Aner, who said 'This is what God told you to do? Do you really want to cripple yourself, that the relatives of the kings that you killed could come and kill you, and you would be unable to escape them?' He left him and went to ask Eshkol. Eshkol told him, 'You are old and if you circumcise yourself, you will lose a lot of blood, and you will be unable to bear it and could die.' Finally, Avraham went to ask Mamre his advice. Said Mamre 'You came to ask advice on this matter?! God saved you from the fiery furnace (in Ur Kasdim), and performed all the miracles, and delivered you from the kings. Without His strength and power, they would have killed you. He saved your whole body, and you come to inquire about one part of your body. You must most definitely do as He commanded.'
>
> "The Lord said 'Because you counseled Avraham to circumcise himself, I will speak to him in your territory.' Therefore, the verse states 'And God appeared to Avraham in the plains of Mamre'" (*Midrash Tanchuma, Vayera* 3).

The midrash, and subsequently Rashi, explain that the seemingly unnecessary detail of where Avraham sat at the time of the revelation comes to teach us of the reward that Mamre received for his positive advice concerning the circumcision of Avraham, his household, and all future descendants.

The question must still be asked: Why did Avraham seek counsel from these nonbelieving friends? Were the Lord to appear to any one of us and command us to perform a particular task, we would surely comply willingly. Yet Avraham, whom we know to have perfect faith in the Almighty, went to ask his companions whether he should fulfill the commandment of the Lord or not. It is also difficult to understand why this particular instruction caused Avraham such conflict and consternation. Avraham had been put to the test so many times and successfully passed so many ordeals. He left his home at a considerably old age to wander in the desert to an unspecified destination at the request of the Lord. He had survived being thrown into a furnace rather than reject his faith, and endured endless suffering—famine, war, and persecution— in the land of Cana'an. Never did he question God's ways or his trials and tribulations, yet suddenly, this edict to circumcise himself caused him to stop and consider the issue and to ask his friends' opinions. Was this a sign of weakness on Avraham's part, an instability in his usually unshakable faith?

Rabbi Eliyahu, the Gaon of Vilna, supplied an answer to this pressing question. He explained that Avraham's concern over this particular *mitzva* emanated from his feelings toward those around him. He understood that his task was not only to serve God, but also to publicize the fact as widely as possible.

Avraham our Patriarch strove as much as possible to convert others. He was extremely successful, through God's help, as it says: 'And the soul that they had *made* in Charan' and see the translation of Onkelos (who translates 'the souls that they caused to keep the Torah.' See also chapter "Avraham—Mending the Rift," p. 20–21). Part of the reason for this success was that the populace, at that time, found it taxing to keep their religion (of idol worship), to burn their children in service to their gods. Avraham brought them the word of the Lord to serve the One God. The service entailed faith and an adherence to the Seven Noachide laws (these are seven laws that all mankind received through Noach. They are prerequisites for the service of God for all gentiles, for example: not to kill, not to have promiscuous sexual relationships, not to steal, not to eat the limbs of a living animal [the prohibition of *ever min hechai*] and not to pervert agriculture by grafting different strains of plants). Through this method, Avraham managed to find a receptive audience for his views. However, now the Lord commanded him, at the old age of 99, to circumcise himself and all the males of his household over 8 days old. Avraham feared that this would cause the gentiles to distance themselves from him and his teachings, that they would no longer flock to him to convert. He preferred to lose his own well-earned Divine reward and to continue to attract converts from all over the world. Therefore, he asked advice from Aner, Eshkol, and Mamre. The first two advised him against this unusual request, but Mamre advised him not to rebel against the Divine commandment. (*Kol Eliyahu al haTorah* on *Vayera*)

The Gaon of Vilna explains this uncharacteristic behavior, in that it was all part of Avraham's role in bringing the Word of God to the people of the world. Avraham felt himself to be a messenger of the Lord, not only for his own family or clan but for humanity as a whole. He had a universal responsibility to teach morality, spirituality, and holiness to all. This was of such importance that he was willing to relinquish his own reward to continue his success in this field, a success that even took priority over keeping God's word and fulfilling His immediate command. So important was Avraham's task that he could not proceed with any commandment that seemed to jeopardize his phenomenal success in convincing the people of the truth of the way of God. He had to investigate whether or not his actions would weaken his wonderful relationship with his gentile neighbors. Who better to ask than his three gentile associates? Therefore, the midrash opens with the information that Avraham had three non-Jewish friends. These were the people that Avraham logically decided to consult regarding the mitzvah of *brit mila* (circumcision).

Aner and Eshkol tended to think that this action would be viewed by most as an unusual type of service, reminiscent, in their minds, of idol worship, and difficult to comply with. They, therefore, advised Avraham against this deed. However, Mamre saw things in a completely different light. He understood that one of the most captivating aspects of Avraham's nature and new way of life was not only the fact that this service was easier than offering one's own offspring to the fire to appease the gods. Most people were attracted to Avraham by something much deeper. Avraham's appeal was his willingness to comply with God's desire, even where it seemed, to the outside observer, illogical and impossible to follow. Yet, despite all of this apparently logical objection, Avraham always complied with God's will without comment or question. This was a very novel approach to Divine service. Avraham had an extremely close relationship with his Creator. God spoke to him regularly and answered his prayers. Avraham, even though he might be in a position to question God's actions and commandments (as he did with regard to the decision to destroy the cities of S'dom and Ammora), never questioned the Lord's intentions. Avraham followed God's directives implicitly, leaving his comfortable house in Charan to go to "the Land that I shall show you" (*BeReishit* 12:1). Later, he was willing to sacrifice his son Yitzchak on an unspecified mountain somewhere in the "land of Moriah" (*BeReishit* 22:2).

Mamre saw that this was what attracted people. They felt Avraham's conviction almost tangibly, witnessed his true belief in the life that he had chosen for himself, and saw the readiness with which he allowed the Lord to shape that life. This act of circumcision, rather than distancing Avraham's potential converts, would act as further proof of Avraham's unwavering allegiance to God's will. God had continually performed miracles for Avraham, and these miracles had helped to convince the surrounding people of the veracity of Avraham's monotheistic way of life. He who had saved Avraham from the furnace and the kings would see to it that the world understood his actions in their true light. This was the continuation of Avraham's covenant with the Lord. This alone would attract further converts. Avraham must circumcise himself because the Lord God had said so.

Avraham followed Mamre's sound advice and Mamre received his just reward, in that God chose to speak to Avraham from Mamre's domain. The continuing conversation between God and his human servant Avraham continued, and it continued as a result of Mamre's advice. Therefore, this was a fitting reward.

We have seen that Avraham felt a deep sense of universal responsibility. He knew that he had the task of spreading the Word of God throughout the world and anything that might weaken this job was, in itself, a danger. However, this universal role could not be at the expense of the ongoing communication with the Creator. Indeed, it is this relationship that gives life and meaning to the whole idea of universal responsibility.

Chayei Sarah
The Father of Many Nations

*The trait of openheartedness—to include the whole world, all of
humanity—belongs to Avraham. When it comes from a recognition of
the special stand of* Am Yisrael, *and from that flows a love of all
people, that is praiseworthy, like Avraham, the father of many nations.*

(*Orot*, p. 169)

*Nationalism is a natural and suitable emotion for a person, similar to
the love of one's own family. Therefore, Avraham and Sarah were
concerned with the welfare and success of their own people. However,
due to their spiritual standing and Divine prophecy, they realized that
a complete individual should not confine himself to worrying only
about his own nation. One should try to bring about redemption for all
of humanity. Therefore, Avraham was the father of many nations, and
this was greater than just the limitation of nationality.*

(*Ein Iyah*, *Berachot*, Chapter 1, Note 174)

*One cannot love the collective unless he first loves every individual;
therefore "Love your neighbor as yourself" is the basis of the Torah and
the rest is just commentary.*

(*ibid.*, Chapter 5, Note 74)

Avraham lived his life and practiced his new religion of Judaism with great
emphasis on the importance of spreading the message of Judaism
throughout the world. It was to affect every person. Judaism is not a way of

life for the Jewish people alone. It has firm guidelines for all the nations of the world. Judaism contains great lessons of morality, utopian societies, and the ultimate Divine experience.

Throughout his life, Avraham strove to teach all of those around him the importance of serving the one God, of living a moral life, and of revealing the holiness in mundane things. The midrash tells us that Avraham, immediately on discovering the truth of the One God's existence, set about convincing his family and all those around him.

> Terach, the father of Avraham, dealt in idol worship and sold idols. Once, he had some errands, and so he left Avraham in charge of the shop. A man came to buy, and Avraham asked him his age. When the reply came, Avraham exclaimed, "Woe to that man that is himself 60 years old and yet worships a day-old idol." The man was very embarrassed, left the idol, and went away.
>
> On another occasion, a woman brought an offering of flour for the idols. Avraham took the flour, smashed all of the idols except the largest, and then placed the hammer in the hand of this idol. On his return, his father was furious and demanded to know who had done this to his idols.
>
> "An amazing thing occurred," said Avraham. "A woman brought some flour as a present for the idols, and when I placed it in front of them, they started to argue amongst themselves. Each one wanted to eat the flour first, and then, the largest of the idols took the hammer and broke all of the others."
>
> His father became more incensed "Why are you lying to me? Do you think that they have the ability to think and move?"
>
> "Listen to what you yourself are saying," answered Avraham (*BeReishit Rabba* 38:13).

Avraham was so confident that he was correct that he set out to persuade his father in a rather drastic fashion, but one that was very successful. He proved to his father the absurdity of worshipping inanimate objects that he himself had fashioned.

Another midrash relates that, after the episode with the idols, Terach was forced to hand his rebellious son over to Nimrod, the ruler of the area, in order that he would deal with him. Avraham, far from being put out by this dangerous situation, continued to argue with Nimrod himself. In order to appreciate Avraham's audacity one needs to understand that Nimrod's name pointed to his nature; the root of his name means *rebel*. The sages tell us that Nimrod knew the Lord and purposely rebelled against him (Rashi on *BeReishit* 10:9). He was known to be ruthless and arrogant, as can be seen by this exchange between him and Avraham.

Nimrod said to Avraham "Do you not know that I rule the world, and that the sun, moon, stars, and men all answer to my beck and call? Yet you have dared to cross me and challenge my faith."

Avraham replied: "My lord the king, since the day of creation, nature has decreed that the sun should rise in the East and set in the West. Why do you not decree that tomorrow it will rise in the West and set in the East? If you can do this, then I will declare that you are the ruler of the world. Another thing, if you really are the ruler of all things, then you must know everyone's inner thoughts. Tell me, what I am I now thinking of?"

Nimrod was shocked by these insolent questions, but Avraham continued.

"You are not the lord of the world, but you are the son of Kush. If you really claim to be all powerful, how is it that you were incapable of saving your own father from death. But, in the same way that you were unable to save him from his inevitable end, so you will not be able to save yourself from death."

Nimrod immediately sentenced Avraham to death by fire (*Tanna Devei Eliyahu Zuta* 25).

The end of the episode is that God saved Avraham from the fiery furnace. By allowing him to be thrown into the furnace and emerge alive, God caused a miracle that would be publicized to all the inhabitants of Ur Kasdim. According to the above midrash, however, Terach, realizing that his son was about to be killed, fled, together with Avraham and all his family, in the direction of Cana'an and reached the area of Charan. From this midrash, we see that Avraham was successful in convincing his father of the veracity of his way of life. According to the more accepted version of the story, the whole populace of Ur Kasdim witnessed the miracle that God performed for Avraham. This must also have served to convince them of the validity of Avraham's monotheistic religion.

From the time that Avraham and his family arrived in Charan, Avraham started to have great success in publicizing God's name to the people of Charan and to the whole world. How was Avraham so successful in spreading the message? We have already seen the pedagogical method that was employed by Avraham, but how did he go about the task in practical terms? What was his method?

The answer may be found in Avraham's name. Originally Avraham was born with the name Avram, and only later God changed his name to Avraham. The verse says "No longer shall you be called Avram, but you will be called Avraham, as I have set you to be the father of many nations" (*BeReishit* 17:5). Rashi explains that this new name is made up of several words put together: *av* meaning father, and *ham*, which is a shortened form of *hamon*, meaning many. From this combination was derived the name *Avraham*, meaning the father of many nations. The *Gemara* states that, before this point, Avraham had been the father of Aram only, and from this moment on, he became also the father of many nations (*Berachot* 13a). If the name Avraham means the father of many nations, then the *Gemara* deduces that the name Avram means *Av* of *Ram*, *Ram* being a shortened form of the place Aram. But there remains a problem with this method of explaining Avraham's name. If God wanted Avraham to cease being the father of Aram and to take on this new role as the father of many nations, HE should have changed his name completely from Avram to Avham. We have already seen Rashi's annotation of the name into two separate parts, *av* and *ham*. Surely God should have changed the name to Avham. Avraham converted from being Avram, the father of Aram, to being Avham, the father of many nations. The name Avraham contains one redundant syllable, *Ra*, in Hebrew, the letter *Reish*. What is the significance of this one letter?

Rashi states "The *reish* that was already present in his name from the time that he had been the father of Aram did not move." What does Rashi mean in this rather cryptic comment?

When God changed Avraham's name, He never intended Avraham to cease being the father of Aram. The *reish* did not move because Avraham remained the father and spiritual guide of his town, Aram. God's intention was that Avraham should now start publicizing the name of the Lord, whilst remaining the father of Aram. More than that, Avraham was only successful in his new role as the father of the whole world because he retained his role as the father of Aram. There is a Talmudic expression: "If you attempt to grab too much, you will find that you have grabbed nothing at all!" (*Yoma* 80a). One who tries to achieve more than is realistically possible does not succeed in fulfilling his potential. The result is that he will achieve nothing. God guided Avraham to start on a reasonable level. His task was to be the father of Aram, to influence the people of Aram and succeed in teaching them the principles of Judaism. Were he to succeed, the result would be that all of the world would hear of this novel faith and would flock to him to study its basis and to convert. This was the secret of Avraham's vast success and wide-ranging influence. The *reish* remained; he always remained the father of Aram and, from this humble stance, he became the father of all the nations.

There is an argument in the midrash as to what constitutes the one major rule of the whole Torah. Can one concentrate the whole of Judaism into one dogmatic principle? Ben Azai said "This is the book of the generations of man" (*BeReishit* 5:1). That is the major principle in the Torah. Rabbi Akiva said "Love your neighbor as you love yourself" (*Vayikra* 19:18). This is the major principle (*BeReishit Rabba* 24:7). We can explain their argument as an extension of what we have just discussed.

Ben Azai chose a verse dealing with all of mankind. All people were created in the image of God, as this verse and the whole of the beginning of the Torah shows. In order to understand and teach the Torah, ideas must be understood in grand, global terms. The Torah is the book of the generations of man from Adam until the end of time; that is the underlying message of the Torah.

Rabbi Akiva has a completely different approach. Of course, the Torah has a worldwide appeal and message, but in order for us to be successful in both understanding its content and spreading its message, we must start at a more realistic point. Let us start by loving our neighbours. In fact, the start precedes even this. In order to be successful in fulfilling this commandment, we must first love ourselves and genuinely believe that we are created in God's image. After we love ourselves, the next stage is to truly love all those around us—our families, friends, and neighbours. From this very strong beginning, we will successfully conquer the whole world with our message of devotion, divinity, and sanctity.

Avraham succeeded by being first, influential over his household; then, his neighbourhood; then, and only then, over the whole existing world. If we grab the right amount, not only will we succeed on this relatively small level, but we will be in an ever-strengthening position to continue to elevate ourselves, those in our immediate vicinity, and the whole world.

Toldot
Yitzchak—Avraham's Successor

From the sanctity of thought and the sanctity of actions that work to fix the holiness of one's nature and will, to the point of holiness of marital relations within one's pure and holy nature, the connection becomes more sanctified, and the family is bound together with totally holy strands that are very strong and cause immense value of life for generations.
(*Orot Hakodesh*, Volume III, p. 299)

The inclination for sexual matters can ensnare a person stronger than the forces that bind him to life itself, because it is connected with the continuation of life of all generations. On the other hand, it can be elevated in holiness to the level of a tzaddik *of all the generations.*
(*ibid.*, p. 298)

When a person does not use his basic instincts for a higher purpose, then it becomes a source of shame to him. But when he utilizes those same instincts using his intellect, they are praiseworthy and splendid, and they show God's praise.
(*Ein Iyah, Berachot*, Chapter 6, Note 42)

Avraham had two sons. The first, Yishmael, was the offspring of the union between Avraham and Hagar. The second was his true heir, Yitzchak, Avraham and Sara's son.

Yitzchak's life very closely mirrored that of Avraham in many ways. They had a number of common experiences that the Torah records. Both Avraham and Yitzchak had two sons, the younger of whom was a *tzaddik* and followed in the ways of his father. Avraham's second son was Yitzchak, and Yitzchak's was Ya'akov, but the oldest, in both cases, left the fold and distressed his father. In Avraham's case, this was Yishmael and in Yitzchak's, it was Esav. Both Avraham and Yitzchak were involved in famines that spread through the land of Cana'an—"And there was a famine in the land, and Avraham descended to Egypt, to dwell there as the famine was very severe" (*BeReishit* 12:10). "And there was another famine in the land apart from the first, in the time of Avraham, and Yitzchak went to Gerar, to Avimelech, the king of the Pilishtim (Philistines)" (*BeReishit* 26:1). In Yitzchak's case, the end of the story was different. "And the Lord appeared to him (Yitzchak) saying do not go to Egypt, but remain in this land that I have told you" (*ibid.*, 2). When faced with a similar situation, Yitzchak decided to pursue a path identical to his father's, to travel to Egypt to escape the drought. He was only prevented from doing so by a Divine command to remain in Cana'an.

Avimelech and his Chief of Staff, Pichol, drew up a pact with the father, and then, later, with the son. "During that time, Avimelech and Pichol, the Chief of Staff, called to Avraham, 'God is with you in all that you do. Now swear in the name of the Lord that you will deal kindly with my descendants as I have shown you kindness'" (*BeReishit* 21:22–23).

Later, "Avimelech and Pichol, the Chief of Staff, traveled from Gerar to see him (Yitzchak). 'We saw that God was with you, and we decided that we should make a pact between us'" (*BeReishit* 26:26, 28). Avraham and Yitzchak named the place where they made this pact Be'er Sheva (see 21:31 and 26:33).

God gave Avraham the power to bless others As the Midrash explains the verse: "All of the peoples of the world will be blessed through you" (*BeReishit* 12:3). Even though God had already promised to bless Avraham, why does the Torah add this extra verse? "The Lord said to Avraham: 'Until now, I had to bless My world. From now on, you have control over the blessings. Whomsoever that you see fit, you may bless'" (*BeReishit Rabba* 39:11). This power was passed on to Yitzchak, "And all of the nations of the world shall be blessed through your offspring" (*BeReishit* 26:4).

Another striking resemblance between the two was in their physical appearance. The *parsha* starts by relating the generations of Yitzchak. "These are the generations of Yitzchak, the son of Avraham. Avraham begat Yitzchak" (*ibid.*, 25:19). The midrash immediately points to a problem with this verse. The Torah lists the generations of Yitzchak and, logically, should start with his offspring, Ya'akov and Esav. Why does the verse initially state that Yitzchak was the son of Avraham? "When Sara was taken in by Paro and Avimelech and became pregnant with Yitzchak, the nations questioned whether Avraham was capable of conceiving a son at the age of 100. It appeared that the son was Paro's or Avimelech's. God instructed the angel in charge of births to mold his features to exactly resemble those of Avraham. It would be obvious to everyone that 'Avraham begat Yitzchak'" (*Tanchuma, Toldot* 1).

One more problematic similarity in the lives of Avraham and Yitzchak is that both told non-Jewish kings that their wives were not, in fact, their wives but their sisters. Avraham used this tactic twice, first during the time of famine and the descent to Egypt. Avraham told his wife "I now know that you are a beautiful woman. When we come to Egypt, they will kill me if they discover that you are my wife. Say that you are my sister" (*BeReishit* 12:11–13). Later, "Avraham declared that Sara his wife was his sister" (*ibid.*, 20:2). We find that Yitzchak, faced with a similar situation, chose a similar path of action. Instead of going to Egypt, he remained in Cana'an but lived in Gerar, the locality of the Pilishtim—"And the locals asked about his wife, and he told them that she was his sister" (*ibid.*, 26:7).

Why did Yitzchak choose this strategy after the rather disastrous results that it had caused during the lifetime of Avraham? "God inflicted Paro and his household because he took Sara" (*ibid.*, 12:17), and then later, "God appeared to Avimelech and said 'You will die because of the woman that you have taken, as she is already married'" (*ibid.*, 20:3). This course of action was the cause of the kings being threatened with Divine punishment. Why would Yitzchak repeat this ploy if it had backfired in the past?

Avraham's major concern was to teach the true service of the One God to the world. This task was so important that Avraham was willing to surrender his own reward, to endanger his own life, in order to be successful. This attribute was passed on to Yitzchak, together with traits of physical likeness and the like. All of Yitzchak's actions must be examined in this light, and for that matter Avraham's repetition of this conduct must also be understood in this vein.

Avraham, and later Yitzchak, strove to teach a lesson in the necessary connection between man and wife. This was so important that, in order to stress the lesson, it was essential that it be repeated three times.

The animalistic urge within man pushes humans to behave like beasts. In the animal kingdom, the natural way of procreation demands the link between one male and one female. No less but also no more. They do not have the capacity to love or develop any sort of romantic connection; the act of mating is a necessity, but the link stops there. When man appeared on the world scene,

the act of fusion between male and female was elevated to the level of enjoyment and dignity for both man and woman. This was a new and much more
exalted level than the animals were capable of achieving. The woman ceased
to be a vessel for the sole purpose of procreation. She started taking an active
part in the romantic side of the connection, and the act of love became a complete partnership between man and wife.

This link was perverted by the sin of Adam and continued (as we have
previously encountered, see the chapter on "Noach—The Continuing Rift").
The midrash tells us that the pharoahs married their sisters and historical find-
ings corroborate this information (See Encyclopedia Britannica, 15th edition,
1997, Volume 18, p. 123, "Egypt"). This was the new level of unleashed passion and erotica that the Egyptians contributed to the world.

When Avraham first left Cana'an and traveled to Egypt, "when they came
close to Egypt. He said to Sara his wife 'I now recognize that you are a beautiful woman'" (*BeReishit* 12:11). Rashi asks the obvious question on this verse:
"Does this mean to say that until now he did not recognize her beauty?" We
know that by this time they had been married for a period of some years. Had
Avraham really never noticed his wife's beauty? There is even a *halacha* that
states that it is forbidden for a couple to marry unless they have seen each other
(*Kiddushin* 41a, and *Shulchan Aruch*, *Even Haezer* 35:1). Even though this injunction may not have legal weight against Avraham, who lived long before
the Jewish people received the Torah, the sentiment expressed by this law is
correct for all times and all people. The physical attraction between man and
wife is essential for a normal and happy marriage. How could Avraham have
ignored his wife's beauty for so long?

The truth is that Avraham had always recognized his wife's beauty, both
her physical beauty and the inner beauty of her spirit. But he had always seen
her, through his own holy eyes, as a complete partner in their home. Indeed,
they had both converted their guests to monotheism, he involved with the
males, while she involved herself with the women (*BeReishit Rabba* 39:14).
There were areas in which he acknowledged her powers as superior to his
own. The midrash tells us that she had greater powers of prophecy than he
(*Midrash Tanchuma*, *Shemot* 1). Theirs was a partnership.

Now they were entering Egypt, where the morality of the inhabitants was
particularly low. In Egypt, women were viewed as objects to satisfy male
passions. Avraham knew it was imperative that he look at his wife through
Egyptian eyes if he meant to comprehend the what way they would see her.
He realized that they would view her in purely erotic and physical terms. They

would see a beautiful woman and would strive to have her in whatever way possible. They would even be willing to kill her husband if necessary.

Avraham realized that here, too, was a golden opportunity to spread a message of world importance. He had the ability to teach, together with Sara, a lesson concerning the link between man and wife. Unlike the Egyptians who married their sisters, Avraham elevated his wife to the level of a sister. She did not exist merely in order to give him pleasure, whether she liked it or not; they were partners in life.

This level that Avraham and Sara achieved is regarded by the kabbalists as an extremely high accomplishment. It is called *Achoti Kalla*, based on the verses in *Shir HaShirim* (the Song of Songs 4, 9,10,12, and so forth) that refer to the connection between God and the Jewish people in terms of husband and bride. Among others, the image of *Achoti Kalla* is employed to signify this deep link.

The message that Avraham sought to convey through this method was gradually understood by those around him. Initially by Paro, and then, subsequently, by Avimelech. There is a distinct progression in the verses and the effectivity of those involved to realize Avraham's true intentions. When Paro took Sara into his house, God plagued him and his household with "great plagues over the matter of Sara, the wife of Avraham" (*BeReishit* 12:17). Paro threw them out of his house and deported them from Egypt. By the time Avraham found himself in similar circumstances in the house of Avimelech, humanity had started to grasp the importance of the connection between man and wife. When Avimelech took Sara, God himself appeared to him and warned him that he must return Sara to her husband. "I know that you are innocent and, therefore, I made sure that you did not sin with her" (*ibid.*, 20:6). Avimelech, on the following morning, questioned Avraham as to the reasons behind his actions. He understood that Avraham must have had a lofty motive for saying such things. Avimelech realized that he had a lot to learn from this individual and his ways. Far from deporting them both, Avimelech offered them the opportunity to settle in his land and later forged a covenant with Avraham. He also requested that Avraham pray for him and for his welfare, recognizing that such things lie in the hands of the Creator.

When Yitzchak came to Avimelech, there was no need for Divine intervention in order for the message to be conveyed. "Avimelech, the king of the Pilishtim, looked through the window and saw Yitzchak and Rivka together in intimacy" (*ibid.*, 26:8). The *Zohar* explains that Avimelech did not literally view them together, as it is imperative to conceal intimacy between man and wife and not publicize it (see *Shulchan Aruch*, *Orach Chayim* 240:6), but rather that he understood the real connection between them. The idea that Avraham, and later, Yitzchak, strove to teach had been successfully adopted by the nations. There was no need to repeat this lesson again and, indeed, we find no repetition of such behavior anywhere else in the *Tanach*.

Avraham and his family gave the world a new perspective on marriage and physical relationships. No longer were woman to be treated merely as objects for man's enjoyment. Both partners were to join in the great plan to serve the Creator through a refined and sanctified relationship.

Vayeitzei
Leah and Rachel, Inside and Outside

There are tzadikkim *who are totally revealed, even though they receive strength from the hidden world. There are* tzadikkim *who are totally hidden, who only influence the world in an oblique way.*

There are other tzadikkim *who wear both crowns, the hidden and the revealed. There are those within whom these two crowns tend to negate each other, and there are others within whom these two crowns totally compliment each other, and they sail in both the land and the sea, in the land and in the heavens.*

There are other tzadikkim *who have fused the two crowns together; the revealed and the hidden have become one entity. They do not belittle either sister, neither the revealed nor the hidden world of Rachel and Leah, because they do not perceive them as two separate entities but rather, one facet.*

(*Orot Hakodesh*, Volume III, p. 348)

The greatness of Torah influences both the hidden secrets of the Torah and the revealed light of Torah. Like Leah and Rachel, who both built the Jewish people.

(*ibid.*, Volume I, p. 29)

Always the revealed and the hidden, Rachel and Leah, without jealousy, both build the house of Israel.

(*Igrot HaRiyah*, Volume III, Letter 753)

Ya'akov also followed in the footsteps of his father and illustrious grand-father. He utilized the God-given opportunities that were presented to him in order to disseminate the teachings of Judaism.

After leaving his parent's house in Be'er Sheva and going to his uncle's abode in Charan, God had appeared to him in Bet El and promised to look after him in Charan. He then continued in the direction of Charan and eventually arrived in the land of Kedem. There, he came across a well and three groups of shep-herds gathered to draw water for their flocks. Ya'akov immediately challenged them as to why they were wasting time in the middle of the day. "Draw water for your sheep and go and take them to graze" (*BeReishit* 29:7).

The midrash explains that Ya'akov wanted to teach them an important lesson in the employer–employee relationship. "He said to them 'If you are employed to guard the sheep, then it is still the middle of the day'" (*BeReishit Rabba* 70:11). The implication being that it is theft to waste the employer's time if one could continue to work within existing conditions. He also had something to tell them about using time wisely—"and if you are self-employed, it is not the time to return from the fields" (*ibid.*). It would be a waste of time to return to town if the sheep could continue to graze. It might also be cruel to the animals, preventing them from eating more just because the shepherds wanted to go home.

Immediately on arriving in Charan, Ya'akov found the opportunity to relate these important ideas that he had learned in his father's and grandfather's house. He saw his universal responsibility in the same way that Avraham had understood his, and Yitzchak after him.

The new religion and way of life that they had discovered and developed had to be preached and spread throughout the world. It was a way of life and understanding that had worldwide relevance, not only for those that prac-ticed it actively but also for all nations. This little lesson that Ya'akov taught the shepherds is a good case in point. Ya'akov manages to illuminate a small but very significant idea. One should be honest in business and, if one is em-ployed to do a specific piece of work, one should do it to the best of one's abili-ties in the given circumstances and not terminate the work before the correct time. Otherwise, one is stealing from the employer. The second lesson is that one should not waste time. Even if the sheep belonged to them, and if they were not stealing by returning home earlier than usual, they were wasting time, and this, too, is considered a crime. It is true, in such a case, that one cannot be held responsible for stealing from an employer, but, just as seriously, one is stealing time from oneself. As time is a precious God-given gift, it could be claimed that one is stealing from the Almighty in these circumstances.

Ya'akov, then, is seen to be the true continuation of the path set out by Avraham and Yitzchak. The Rambam explains how Avraham discovered his Creator and immediately set about to impress this truth on the idol-worshipping public in his vicinity.

> When he (Avraham) knew this truth, he set about challenging the people of Ur Kasdim. He went from place to place publicizing the existence of the One God who is worthy of our worship until he arrived in Cana'an. He convinced those that came to hear him of the truth until thousands joined him and his household, and he wrote books on the subject. Then, he taught Yitzchak, his son, this path, and Yitzchak also taught this way (and continued the work of his father Avraham). Then, Yitzchak taught this path of action to Ya'akov, who continued to teach and publicize the way of God to the world (*Mishneh Torah, Hilchot Avodah Zarra* 1:3).

The Rambam explains that Avraham, Yitzchak, and Ya'akov were all part of a continuous process of discovering God and teaching the word and service of the Lord to the world populace. They held this task to have the utmost importance and saw it as their universal responsibility.

Ya'akov also wanted to teach this principle to his household and primarily to his wives. He observed that his two wives, Leah and Rachel, had very different characteristics. Leah was quiet and reserved, whereas Rachel was outgoing and very practical.

The first time that the Torah introduces Rachel, the verse states: "Rachel came out with the sheep, as she was a shepherd" (*BeReishit* 29:9). It is understandable that Lavan, their father, had no sons and, therefore, sent his daughters out to look after his sheep. But it seemed more appropriate that his oldest daughter would be the natural choice for this responsible task. Why was Rachel, and not Leah, the shepherd? Rachel, in her nature, was connected with the outside world, whilst her sister Leah stayed indoors. Leah is described as having "thin eyes" (*ibid.*, 17), which could be understood to mean that her eyes were sensitive, requiring that she remain inside while Rachel went to work in the fields.

When Ya'akov later called his wives to ask them whether the time was opportune to return to Cana'an, it was Rachel who spoke before her older sister: "And Rachel and Leah answered" (*ibid.*, 31:14).

These differences can be understood on a simple, superficial level; however, in the Kabbala a much deeper significance is found in these diversities between Leah and Rachel. The *Zohar* (the major work of kabbala, traditionally composed by Rabbi Shimon Bar Yochai just after the destruction of the

Second Temple) refers to Rachel as the *Alma D'Itgalya*, the revealed world; whereas Leah represented the *Alma D'Itkasya*, the concealed, hidden world (*Zohar*, 1:154). Rachel was concerned with the physical world; she went out into the world and attempted to influence and change it. On the other hand, Leah was involved with the concealed, spiritual world. She remained at home and guarded the safety and sanctity of the spirit.

Rachel is described as being "good looking and beautiful" (*BeReishit* 29:17), her concern is with developing the outside aspects of her existence, unlike her quiet and sensitive older sister, Leah. She was also the only one of the patriarchs and matriarchs who was buried outside the cave of Machpela. Instead, she was buried on the way to Efrat in a tomb reserved just for her in Beit-Lechem (see *BeReishit* 35:19).

These distinct qualities blend together with Ya'akov's task to continue the dynasty of Avraham and Yitzchak. Ya'akov needed a strong personality to help guard the safety of his new family and the beginnings of the nation of Israel. Leah was ideally suited to this task; and indeed, most of the tribes were her sons or the sons of her maidservant, Zilpa—eight out of twelve sons and a daughter. Rachel's nature was suitable for a different role. She was the perfect choice to continue the main task started by Avraham, Yitzchak, and later, by Ya'akov. She was to assume the role of spreading the Torah outside and to assume the obligation of universal responsibility that they had established. With her nature, Rachel was to excel in this task.

Shlomo, the king, states, in the book of *Mishlei*: "One who grabs a dog's ears enters into an argument that is not his concern" (*Mishlei* 26:17). This may well refer to Rachel, who stole her father's idols when they left his house, on the way back to Yitzchak and Rivka's home in Cana'an (see *Midrash Tanchuma, VaYishlach* 2:2).

Rachel's last action before leaving her father was to steal his idols. This is reminiscent of her husband's grandfather's first action on discovering the One true God, for Avraham also destroyed his father's idols (see Chapter on *Chayai Sarah*, "The Father of Many Nations"). Rachel continues Avraham's teachings, spreading the words of Torah throughout the world and utilizing every opportunity to teach moral and spiritual lessons. Rachel epitomizes the external, revealed world. She saw her task in life in terms very similar to the way Avraham, Yitzchak, and Ya'akov saw their lives.

"Rachel stole her father's idols" (*BeReishit* 31:19), and later, when her father came to search for the idols, she "took them and put them in the saddle of the camel and sat on them" (*ibid.*, 34). All this was carefully planned in order to distance her father as much as possible from forbidden idol worship. Indeed, after she took the idols, we find that Lavan reached a new height of spirituality; God came to him in a dream and spoke to him (*ibid.*, 24). He later drew up an agreement and a peace treaty between himself and Ya'akov, swearing in the name of the Lord (*ibid.*, 50).

Ya'akov inherited the ways of his fathers and continued to preach Judaism and morality at every possible opportunity. His wife, Rachel, was a perfect partner in this task. However, Ya'akov also needed to create a strong spiritual home for the emerging nation that he was to father and, therefore, he also required a wife like Leah. She was firmly rooted in the hidden inner world, the *alma d'itkasya*. With these two wives and his many children, Ya'akov was preparing the strongest possible foundations for the Jewish people. Each tribe was to have a different task, and together, they were to fuse and pool their respective resources to begin the nation of Israel.

Vayishlach
Guarding the Torah, Spreading the Torah

Ya'akov's portion is endless, as his is concentrated in order to contribute more [to the world] and gain strength. The nations shall say: "Let us go to the mountain of God, to the house of the God of Ya'akov" (Yeshiyahu 2:3). *His is the fusion of the two extremes, that of the individual secluding himself in order to give back, eventually, to the collective.*

(*Ein Iyah, Berachot,* Chapter 9, Note 263)

Avraham and Yitzchak called on God's name in a general sense, but they did not found a nation, and their aim was to publicize God's name to the world. Then Ya'akov came and the nation started to flourish as a separate and distinct entity from him, as the time had come to start a nation by establishing a nation apart from the rest of the world.

(*ibid.,* Note 356)

God prepared within Israel two separate forces, one corresponding to the body that strives for the physical preservation of the nation, that is the correct basis in order to realize all of the tasks of the Jewish people. To be a holy nation, one nation in the land as a light to the other nations. On the other hand, a force that would develop the spirit [of Am Yisrael].

(*Ma'amrei HaRiyah,* p. 94)

Ya'akov was presented with an extremely honorable task: namely, to be the father of the Jewish nation. We are called the Children of Israel, Israel being the name that God himself chose for Ya'akov. In our *parsha*, God said to him: "Your name will no longer be Ya'akov, but you will be known as Yisrael" (*BeReishit* 35:10). This would appear to be identical to the change made to his grandfather's name—"You will no longer be called Avram, but Avraham" (*ibid.*, 17:5). However, our sages point out an interesting difference: subsequent to the change of Avraham's name, the Torah never again refers to him as Avram. Indeed, we find an injunction in the *Gemara*: "Anyone who calls Avraham by the name of Avram transgresses a positive commandment" (*Berachot* 13a). On the other hand, the Torah itself interchanges quite freely between the name *Ya'akov* and the name *Yisrael*, even after God Himself changed his name and apparently gave a similar commandment that from then on his name would be Yisrael.

There are, of course, many reasons for this difference but, on the simplest level, it seems to indicate a very significant difference between Avraham and Ya'akov and their respective roles. Avraham was an individual who discovered God on his own merit and chose to follow Him and teach His Torah to the world. God changed Avraham's name and gave him a new task—spreading the Torah to a much wider arena. This was the essence of Avraham's life. However, Ya'akov was the father of the Jewish nation. No longer was the Torah to be the property of single individuals; it was to be the blueprint for setting up the holy nation (See *Shemot* 19:6).

Ya'akov, unlike Avraham, had two separate tasks. He was the father of the nation (and for this purpose he received the name *Yisrael*). He also had the universal responsibility that he had inherited from his father and grandfather (and this is shown through the name *Ya'akov*). The unique quality of Ya'akov–Yisrael is that both of these roles existed side by side. He was responsible for spreading the Torah and, at the same time, for founding and forging the nation. Avraham was concerned entirely with spreading the Torah as was Yitzchak. After Avram accepted the role of Avraham, the Father of Many Nations, he did not have two roles; he never returned to being merely Avram. Therefore, anyone who refers to Avraham as Avram transgresses, since he is, in effect, belittling the role of Avraham in the world. Ya'akov, who strove to juggle and fuse these two roles, remains both Ya'akov and Yisrael.

Ya'akov realized that, in order to successfully accomplish the task of converting the populace and also developing the nation, he had to divide the roles amongst his children. Each could specialize, and they would subsequently work together, each adding their own expertise to the People of Israel.

The division of labor was done according to the natural inclination of each son and, eventually, each tribe. We learned in last week's *parsha* that Ya'akov's wives had differing temperaments and that each excelled in a specific area: Rachel was involved in the outside world, in the *alma d'itgalya*; whereas Leah represented the inner, hidden world, the *alma d'itkasya*. In light of this, Rachel and her children were ideally suited to the role of going out into the world to spread the Torah, whilst the children of Leah were to safeguard the Torah on the inside, within *Am Yisrael*.

As the Rambam writes: Avraham taught Yitzchak, who in turn passed on his teachings to Ya'akov, "and our forefather Ya'akov taught all of his sons. He set Levi (the son of Leah) apart and appointed him to sit and guard the commandments. This continued amongst the children of Ya'akov until they formed a nation in the world that knew God" (*Mishneh Torah, Hilchot Avodah Zarra* 1:3).

Therefore, we see two strands emerging in the house of Ya'akov. Yosef, who fully understood and adopted the quality of universal responsibility to spread the Torah, and the other brothers, who personified the role of the national responsibility of guarding the Torah.

Our *parsha* contains a good example how the brothers' approaches differed from those of Yosef and their father Ya'akov. Sh'chem saw Dina, the daughter of Leah, and he took her, raped her, and wanted to marry her. Ya'akov, upon hearing of this terrible incident, remained silent (*BeReishit* 34:5) and awaited his sons' return from their work in the fields. Conceivably Ya'akov saw here another opportunity to teach an important moral lesson with regard to marriage and the prohibition against rape.

However, when Dina's brothers came home, they tricked Sh'chem and the entire town into circumcising themselves. They then used the opportunity of the townspeople's pain to enter the town and kill the inhabitants. Ya'akov was furious with them and even reminded them of his anger at the very end of his life, when he gathered all of his family together to bless them individually and collectively (*BeReishit* 49:5–7). On this auspicious occasion Ya'akov found it fit to remind them of this major transgression, showing how shocked he was by an incident he held to be indicative of the nature of these sons.

His opposition to their actions in Sh'chem was on two separate levels. "Through their anger, they killed men. Cursed is their anger" (*BeReishit* 49: 6,7—part of his blessing to Shimon and Levi just before he passed away). But he also rebuked them with the words: "You have made me look ugly and embarrassed me in the eyes of the local inhabitants" (*ibid.*, 34:30). Ya'akov's second concern was how the people would judge his sons' actions, that their actions would make Ya'akov "ugly" in the eyes of the people. The direct result of this would the people's unwillingness to come and drink from the spiritual fountain that Ya'akov represented. This was of primary importance to Ya'akov since he saw himself continuing the great work started by his predecessors, spreading the Torah and its moral teachings to all people. Were the nations to hear of Shimon and Levi's reaction to Sh'chem's albeit despicable crime, they would tend to view Ya'akov and the whole Torah as just another collection of barbaric customs, no different from those of the then-current idol-worshipping religions.

Yet God performed a miracle and, even after this event, the Torah states: "They traveled and all of the surrounding towns were filled with fear of God" (*ibid.*, 35:5). The populace still feared the Lord and flocked to Ya'akov to hear his words of wisdom, and this was most certainly a miracle.

When Ya'akov challenged his sons, accusing them of actions that might prevent the continuation of the work of teaching the moral lesson of his forefathers to the world, they simply replied: "Can he (Sh'chem) make a prostitute out of our sister?" (*ibid.*, 34:31). Instead of seeing the universal task of saving the world, they saw the national task of strengthening the Jewish people. If someone thought that they could rise up against the Jewish people, defile them, and treat them any way they wanted, they would learn that there was a force to be reckoned with. They could not rape Jewish daughters and get away with it. This was the task that the children of Leah took upon themselves, to safeguard the Jewish people and, in so doing, to protect the Torah itself. In their eyes this was of utmost importance, beyond teaching the Torah to the world. They disagreed with the children of Rachel, and even with their father, on this point. The Torah calls them "the sons of Ya'akov, Shimon and Levi, the brothers of Dina" (*ibid.*, 25). Rashi immediately asks why the Torah refers to them as the sons of Ya'akov. This is common knowledge and it seems unnecessary to repeat this information. Even though they were Ya'akov's sons, they acted "like people who were not his sons" (Rashi ad loc.). Shimon and Levi acted in the manner they saw fit, in keeping with their role of preserving the Jewish people and the Torah at all costs. This was, after all, the task that Ya'akov himself gave to Levi and his brothers when, in the words of the Rambam, "he set Levi apart and appointed him to sit and guard the commandments" (*Mishneh Torah, Hilchot Avodah Zarra* 1:3, see above). Yet this behavior was contrary to the way Ya'akov had chosen for himself, and also very different from the conduct of Yosef and the children of Rachel.

Ya'akov was the father of the nation of Israel and, in this role, he forged two separate and essential camps within his house. He understood that this was the only way that he could successfully found and strengthen the nation. However, we shall see that this caused tension and a rift between the brothers. Each was to develop a separate role that would ultimately save the Jewish people and enable them to conquer every eventuality that would befall them in the future.

Vayeshev
Yosef and his Brothers— Irreconcilable Differences

"The God of Avraham, the God of Yitzchak, and the God of Ya'akov,"
each one acquired his own particular level in his service to God. But,
even though they each had a different level, there was still total unity of
purpose in worshipping God Almighty.

(*Olat Riyah*, Volume I, p. 269)

Israel has been given two tasks; we need to accept God's word for
ourselves and to act in order to inform the world of the sovereignty of
the God of Israel.

(*Ein Iyah, Berachot*, Chapter 1, Note 1)

We love the ethical responsibility toward the rest of the Universe, in the
same way that we love ourselves [Am Yisrael], *and even more than we*
love ourselves.

(*Orot*, p. 139)

In last week's *parsha* we learned of the all-important task assigned to Ya'akov–Yisrael: to forge the Jewish nation. No longer was this to be a collection of individuals, but a nation.

The major difference between these two is that an individual acts alone, is an island, and can develop his own skill. Indeed, each of the forefathers had added his own expertise and natural abilities to the job of serving the Creator in this world. Therefore, we learn that each of them composed one of the three daily prayers. The *Gemara* (*Berachot* 26b) relates: "The forefathers established the daily prayers." Avraham was responsible for *Shacharit*, the morning prayer, according to the verse "and Avraham rose early in the morning and went to his designated place" (*BeReishit* 19:27). Yitzchak established *Mincha*, the afternoon service, from the verse "and Yitzchak went out to converse (with God) toward evening" (*ibid.*, 24:63). Ya'akov instituted *Arvit*, the evening prayer, as it says "and he came to 'the place' and he slept there" (*ibid.*, 28:11). Each developed their personal skill and contributed this to the special relationship between himself and God.

We say in our prayers, at the outset of the *Amida*, the standing prayer, which is the central part of every one of our services, "the God of Avraham, the God of Yitzchak, and the God of Ya'akov." Why did the members of the Great Assembly, who composed the wording of our prayers, not simply say: "the God of Avraham, Yitzchak, and Ya'akov"? This alludes to the fact that each of the forefathers, by contributing his own part to the worship of the Lord, acquired a close relationship to Him on his own merit. God was not close to Yitzchak only because he was the son of Avraham, but in his own right, and the same is true of Ya'akov. Therefore, the prayer is worded "the God of Avraham, the God of Yitzchak, and the God of Ya'akov."

When dealing with a national entity, each person is different. As the *Gemara* states regarding the Jewish people, "in the same way that they all look different one from the other, so are their opinions different from each other" (*Berachot* 58a). This is reminiscent of the famous joke: "Two Jews, three opinions." The nation must be forged of many different personalities. The myriad preferences and skills will lead to a stronger and broader people.

Ya'akov wisely divided the necessary tasks for national and international preservation and development amongst his sons. Each was to mature in a certain way to contribute his own natural skills to the Jewish people. The sons of Leah were suited to preserve the Torah within *Am Yisrael*, whereas the children of Rachel were to continue the work of Avraham, Yitzchak, and Ya'akov, spreading the Torah throughout the world.

Yosef, the elder son of Rachel, felt that he had the responsibility to correct any misdemeanor that he saw in the outside world, including the faults of his brothers and his family. The Torah tells us that: "Yosef told his father the bad things that he witnessed in his brothers" (*BeReishit* 37:2). The *Talmud Yerushalmi* explains these words in the following way: "He said that they ate *ever min hechai* (the limb of a living animal), or that they mistreated the sons of Bilha and Zilpa, the maidservants of Ya'akov and used them like their servants, or that they befriended the daughters of the surrounding Cana'anites"

(*Peah* 1:1). He dreamed dreams that seemed to predict that he was to have a rosy future and would rise in station above his brothers and even above his parents. Again, he felt compelled to relate the dreams in the most public fashion possible. "And he told his father and his brothers" (*BeReishit* 37:10).

He also felt a closeness to the sons of the maidservants, as Rashi explains the verse "and he was friendly to the children of Bilha and Zilpa" (*ibid.*, 2), "his brothers humiliated them, but he drew them close." Yosef took his responsibility as the son in charge of spreading the Torah and as the representative of the *alma d'itgalya*, the revealed world, very seriously.

This charge was to cost him dearly. All of Yosef's actions were contrary to the way of thinking that his brothers had adopted. They hated him for being the way he was. "They were incapable of speaking to him cordially" (*ibid.*, 5). However, Ya'akov loved Yosef, seeing in him a reflection of himself, and made him heir to his path of universal responsibility.

The rift between Yosef and his brothers came to a head on the first opportunity that they had to harm him. When Yitzchak sent Yosef to Sh'chem to check on his brother's welfare, they watched him from a distance and conspired to deal with him once and for all. "Here comes the dreamer. Let us kill him and throw him into a pit, and we shall say that he was devoured by a wild animal, and then what will become of his dreams?" (*ibid.*, 19–20). Instead of killing him, they eventually threw him into "an empty well with no water in it" (*ibid.*, 24). The *Gemara* explains the superfluous words "even though it was empty of water it did contain snakes and scorpions" (*Shabbat* 22a). The significance of this exegesis is understood when one considers that the *Gemara*, in another place (*Yevamot* 121a), states that if someone fell into a pit of lions and wild animals, he did not necessarily die. But were he to fall into a pit of snakes and scorpions, his wife can remarry without requiring witnesses that he actually died. That is because these animals kill at the slightest provocation and, therefore, this unfortunate individual definitely died inside the well containing the snakes and scorpions. Yosef's brothers threw him to certain death in the aforementioned well.

The prophet Amos relates the Divine prophesy that makes up the *haftara* of this week's *parsha*, which opens with God's words to the Jewish people. "Thrice did Yisrael sin and for their fourth sin I cannot forgive them, that they sold a poor *tzaddik* (righteous man) for shoes" (*Amos* 2:6). This is a reference to the actions of Yosef's brothers in selling him to slavery in Egypt. But what of these shoes? The *Targum* translates this to mean "they sold him because of his chosen path." The brothers wanted to do away with Yosef because of his background and his life's mission to spread the Torah. This mission was so diametrically opposed to their way of thinking that they felt the natural thing to do was to try and stop him, even if it meant that he were harmed or even killed in the process.

The midrash declares: "In the same way that the snake is deadly, so is Egypt a deadly place; in the same way that the snake is not straight, so is Egypt devious and crooked" (*Shemot Rabba* 9:3). The *Gemara* relates that surrounding the mountain of Sinai are scorpions (*Babba Batra* 74a), and this has been explained as a reference to the nations of the world, eager to learn of the secrets of the Torah from Sinai. With this knowledge, we can now explain in greater depth the actions of the brothers.

Yosef epitomized the *alma d'itgalya*; he was the one chosen in his generation to spread the Torah to the nations. He publicized this fact to his brothers as well, not hesitating to relate his dreams, to tell his father of his brothers' misdemeanors, and to draw the sons of the maidservants closer to the Torah. The brothers strengthened the *alma d'itkasya*, the hidden world; they ensured that the Torah was kept alive within the confines of *Am Yisrael*. These two approaches seemed opposed to each other, and the brothers could not bear the company of their younger brother, Yosef. So they decided to put him to the ultimate test; they threw him to certain death at the hands of the murderous and cunning Egyptians—"and then what will become of his dreams." Ironically, at the hands of those Egyptians, the very people that Yosef thought to educate with morality and Divinity, he would surely die or assimilate. It was indeed certain death. This would also prove the brothers' point: that the task of spreading the Torah to the outside world was so fraught with danger that it was best abandoned, that the primary task should be to teach the Torah inside, to the Jewish people themselves.

But there was a flaw in the brothers' plan. True, for a son of Leah, for someone concerned with the inner world, to go and live among the Egyptians would certainly lead to annihilation. But Yosef was made of different mettle; he came from the other side, from the revealed world. We are to witness that far from vanishing in Egypt, Yosef thrived. Additionally, in so doing, he saved the Jewish people, and this was to lead to the fusion of the tasks of the children of Leah and the children of Rachel.

Ya'akov's house held two opposing camps, each with a task in the Divine plan for *Am Yisrael*. This caused such friction that Yosef and his brothers were at ideological loggerheads. The brothers tried to keep Yosef from fulfilling his dangerous mission, but this was to lead to his prospering, specifically, in Egypt and the salvation of the whole nation.

Miketz
Yosef in Egypt—the Ultimate Jewish Survival

*Yosef developed the ability to enhance his inner soul and was not
affected by all of the powers around him that strove to cause him to
deviate from the path of completion and justice. He recognized his
inner integrity due to his overcoming his base desires. Therefore, no one
else could have an adverse affect over him, as he had chosen the right
path.*

(*Ein Iyah, Berachot*, Chapter 3, Note 37)

*Yosef saved the Jewish people in a physical way. He was swallowed up
among the nations and he knew seventy languages. However, he still
knew the power of holiness.*

(*Ma'amrei HaRiyah*, p. 95)

*Sometimes it is possible that the very things that are bad turn out to
cause good events to occur. For example, the situation that resulted in
the capture and sale of Yosef caused his dramatic rise.*

(*Ein Iyah, Berachot*, Chapter 9, Note 58)

"These are the generations of Ya'akov; Yosef" (*BeReishit* 37:2). Far from
stating the obvious, the intention in the verse is that, in the same manner that Yitzchak's life reflected many aspects of his father Avraham's life,
so it was with Yosef and Ya'akov—many similarities are observed between
the two. "All that occurred in Ya'akov's life was repeated by Yosef. In the same

way that the brother of the former wanted to kill him, so did the latter's brothers' plan to kill him. Both were hated," and so forth (*BeReishit Rabba* 84:6). These are the two examples quoted by Rashi, but the midrash itself contains many other similarities: "Both were rich, both were accompanied by angels, both were exalted through dreams; they both died in Egypt and their bones were brought for burial in the land of Yisrael," and so forth). Maybe the most striking thing about the two was the physical resemblance that Yosef had to his father, Ya'akov (see *Midrash Tanchuma*, *Vayeshev* 5; and Rashi on the aforementioned verse). This is reminiscent of the link between Avraham and his son Yitzchak. Yet Yosef also inherited many of the qualities of his mother, Rachel. She is described as being "handsome and goodlooking" (*BeReishit* 29:17) and so is her son Yosef (*ibid.*, 39:6). In the same way that Rachel died before her older sister (*ibid.*, 35:19) so did Yosef pass away before his brothers, even though they were older than he (*Sota* 13b, "Why did Yosef die before his brothers?").

Yosef was blessed with the qualities of both of his illustrious parents, and this was to be to his advantage in the task assigned to him. He had to descend to Egypt, succeed and survive there, and lay the foundation that was to enable the Jewish people to arrive there. Due to his work, they were eventually to leave, receive the Torah, and re-enter the land of Israel as a nation. Indeed the *Gemara* informs us that at one point during this ordeal in Egypt, Yosef was about to sin with the wife of Potifar. He had even entered her chamber for just this purpose, when the image of his father appeared to him and reprimanded him for this action (*Sotah* 36b). This apparition helped him; he managed to control himself and not sin. This *Gemara* teaches us that Yosef took with him to Egypt not only the physical traits that he acquired from his father but also his father's way of life. It spurred him on, in his most difficult and solitary moments, to succeed.

Yosef continued the work of Ya'akov and Rachel and was the representative, in his time, of the *alma d'itgalya*, the revealed world. From the moment he arrived in Egypt and was sold as a slave to Potifar, "God was with Yosef" (*BeReishit* 39:2). "God blessed the Egyptian's house because of Yosef" (*ibid.*, 5). When Potifar became enraged with Yosef and threw him into prison, because of trumped up charges and false accusations made by his wife, "God was with [Yosef] and caused his endeavors to succeed" (*ibid.*, 23). As for his own efforts, he was careful to exploit any opportunity to publicize God's name. When the servants of Paro turned to him in search of an explanation for their dreams, Yosef replied, "God supplies the answer" (*ibid.*, 40:8). When Paro summoned him to interpret his own troubling and mysterious dreams, Yosef told him, "God will answer" (*ibid.*, 41:16). After delivering his Divinely in-spired explanation, he did not forget to add "this is correct, and it is a mes-sage from God" (*ibid.*, 32). Even when Potifar's wife attempted to seduce him, he refused: "How could I sin to the Lord?" (*ibid.*, 39:9). Yosef mentioned the Lord's name and His merciful acts wherever and whenever he could. He never seemed put out by all that happened to him, even though he was relatively young, just 33 years old, when he was brought before Paro, the most power-ful leader of his time. His custom of assigning everything to God greatly af-fected those in his vicinity. Potifar saw that God accompanied Yosef, and willingly placed all of his own affairs in Yosef's hands so they might flourish (see *ibid.*, 39:3, 6). Paro himself referred to Yosef as possessing "the spirit of the Lord" (*ibid.*, 41:38) and freely admitted that "since God has informed you all of this" (*ibid.*, 39). Yosef, therefore, had tremendous success, convincing the Egyptian heathens of God's existence and influence over the world. This is proven by their responses to him in the name of the Lord Himself.

Apart from continuing the work of all those who felt universal responsi-bility and therefore publicized the name of God to the whole world, Yosef also carried on the tradition of teaching important moral lessons. We find that Yosef restructured the economy of Egypt. He encouraged Paro to restructure food distribution, by interpreting Paro's dreams. Again, later in the *Book of BeReishit*, the actual process of distribution is explained. The people initially sold their belongings to pay for the food that they purchased from Yosef. When this did not suffice, he sold them food in lieu of their estates and their persons. In light of these acquisitions, Yosef made it law in Egypt that the populace would pay the Paro a set tax of one fifth of their income. The Torah says, "Yosef made this a law in Egypt until the present day" (*ibid.*, 47:26). The significance of this verse is that this law was not only enacted during Yosef's lifetime or during the years of the famine, but became part of Egypt's finan-cial structure for all times. Yosef's influence over the Egyptians stretched not only to his own lifetime but also well beyond his death. Even when the Egyp-tians persecuted the Jewish people, their culture was influenced by Yosef.

Yosef saw this change in fiscal policy as adding a moral dimension to Egypt's attitude to government and the sanctity thereof. Not only did he al-ter their taxation system but, more significantly, their moral attitude.

Another example of Yosef teaching the Egyptians an important moral les-son is found in the midrash. When the Egyptians came to buy food from Yosef, he requested that they first circumcise themselves (*BeReishit Rabba* 91:5. See also Rashi on *BeReishit* 41:55). The *Yafe Toar* explains that the rationale be-hind Yosef's action was intended to curb lecherous behaviour. This was even more urgent as Yosef knew that his brothers would eventually come and join him in Egypt. The decadent behavior would greatly affect and harm them, much more than it would affect him.

Throughout his time in Egypt, Yosef lived and worked amongst the Egyptians themselves, and one would assume that this would influence him. One would suppose that, with the passage of time, he would become more and more like them, at least in his external physical appearance. However, nothing could be further from the truth. He is described by Potifar's wife as "a Jewish lad" (*BeReishit* 39:14). Again, he is described in similar terms by Paro's butler (*ibid.*, 41:12). We see that Yosef was not at all influenced by his surroundings but remained "a Jewish lad." The word used in both cases to describe Yosef is *Ivri*, which is reminiscent of Avraham, who was described in the midrash as Avraham the *Ivri*. The midrash explains: "The whole world was on one side and he was alone on the opposing side" (*BeReishit Rabba* 41), thus using the word *Ivri* in the sense of *side*. This quality was relevant both to Avraham, who challenged the contemporary thinking of his time, and to Yosef, who succeeded in changing the moral structure of Egypt.

Yosef, throughout his time in Egypt, lived amongst the Egyptians themselves and yet remained the same "Jewish lad" that he was before he came into close contact with them. This is very indicative of the children of Rachel, those that are connected to the revealed world, or *alma d'itgalya*. This is in great contrast to the children of Leah, those who represent the *alma d'itkasya*, the hidden world. Indeed, when the rest of Yosef's family descended to Egypt to escape the famine in Cana'an, they settled in a separate area, in Goshen, away from Egyptian life and the Egyptians themselves. "Yehuda (the son of Leah) was sent down first to Yosef, to Goshen, to arrange things before him (Ya'akov and the rest of his household)" (*BeReishit* 46:28). According to the midrash, Yehuda went to Egypt in order to "establish schools to teach the rest of the tribes" (*Midrash Tanchuma, Vayigash* 11). This was suddenly of primary importance. Before the scene was ready for the descent of Ya'akov's other sons, the children of Leah, provisions had to be made for educating their children and ensuring that they would not be influenced by the surrounding corrupt society.

Yosef was sold into slavery in Egypt by his brothers, who assumed that they were actually sending him to certain spiritual death. However, that was because they saw things through their own eyes, through the eyes of the *alma d'itkasya*. But Yosef was the son of Rachel and came from the *alma d'itgalya*. In this capacity, he not only survived, but rose above his status as a slave to become the vice president of the Egyptian empire and succeeded in teaching them a few important moral lessons in the process. Yosef understood that his situation was generated by God, and this gave him the energy required to continue and to succeed. His first words to his brothers, after eventually revealing his true identity, were: "God sent me before you to feed you. God sent me here to rescue you and to revive you. You did not send me here but God Himself, that I might become a minister in Paro's government" (*BeReishit* 45:5–8). This was a great responsibility and we have seen that Yosef fulfilled it to the best of his abilities.

The separate ways of Yosef and his brothers were about to merge and fuse. In order for this to occur, there had to first be a play-off between them, which we will see in next week's *parsha*.

Vayigash
Synthesis between the Revealed and the Hidden Worlds

*The intention of choosing the kingdom of David was in order to fuse
the two parts of the nation. It was not sufficient that they did not
negate each other, rather they were to fuse and to compliment each
other. The sages said in a midrash that David is described as being red
with beautiful eyes. He had all of the necessary elements for fighting
and establishing a kingdom coupled with spiritual elevation.*

(*Ma'amrei HaRiyah*, p. 95)

*Through the fusion of two forces together, they both improve. The
physical force becomes more subtle and holy as it draws nearer to the
specific sanctity of the Jewish people. The spiritual force is strengthened
in a physical sense until it is capable of having expression in Israel and
thus influence the entire world.*

(*ibid.*)

Har Sinai *is the source of the Torah and, through the Torah, Israel has
the power to guide the world to the ways of God. However, until we
are perfect, the other nations afflict Israel as they received the Torah
[but did not keep it]. But, within them, they are ready to receive the
responsibility of the Torah.*

(*ibid.*, p. 444)

W e have already seen, throughout the past few weeks, that Ya'akov's two sets of sons followed diverging, individual paths. On the one hand, Yosef and the children of Ya'akov's second wife Rachel were concerned with the *alma d'itgalya*, the revealed world. In this capacity, they were involved with teaching and spreading the moral and Divine messages contained within the Torah to the whole world. Rachel tried to distance her father from his idol worship, and Yosef went to Egypt to spread Divinity and spirituality there, in the heart of the decadent society of the time.

On the other hand, Ya'akov's first wife, Leah, and her offspring were firmly planted in the *alma d'itkasya*, the hidden, inner world. Their task was one of guarding the sanctity of the Torah within the Jewish people. They also taught the Torah but, instead of teaching the nations of the world, they confined their efforts and concentrated on spreading the Torah to the Jewish nation. As we have already explained, both are essential to building a nation.

Both are important and each contains an intrinsic danger. The way of Yosef is potentially devastating for the individual. He is exposed to many influences and persuasions, many of which are foreign. They threaten to envelop him and, instead of influencing the world, the descendant of Rachel achieves the complete opposite and is himself influenced by his hostile surroundings. Indeed, the prophet Hoshea prophesied that "Ephraim (the son of Yosef) will assimilate amongst the nations" (*Hoshea* 7:8). However, there is also a danger in the way of Leah's children. True, there is no fear of outside influences corrupting the Torah and the nation, but the Jewish people also have a responsibility to bring the word of God to the world. Without the path of Yosef, the Torah becomes confined and exclusive.

It seems obvious, therefore, that at some stage of history the divergent paths should fuse and we should find that they work in conjunction to fulfill these two essential tasks.

Before seeing when this may be, it should be noted that these distinctive characteristics are not reserved only for the immediate descendants of Rachel and Leah, but run through the entire *Tanach*. Let us examine just a few examples. The tribe of Levi were descended from Leah. Their task in the wilderness, and later in Israel, was to work in the *Beit Hamikdash*, the Temple. Both the *Cohanim*, who worked in the Temple with the sacrifices, and the *Leviim*, who were more involved in the service and the liturgical aspects of the Temple, were from the tribe of Levi. The Temple itself was almost entirely covered over and this was very suitable for the tribe of Levi. Their whole Divine service was hidden from view and was in the realm of the *alma d'itkasya*. When the nation of Yisrael entered the land of Israel, the land was divided amongst the tribes, each receiving a distinct portion. The Temple fell between the areas of two tribes. Most of the *Beit Hamikdash* fell into the portion of the tribe of Yehuda, from the children of Leah, who were well-suited to dwell in the area of the Temple that was connected to the *alma d'itkasya*. But the *Gemara* tells us that the Temple should really have fallen into the portion of Binyamin, from the children of Rachel, but a strip of land left Yehuda, entered into the portion of Binyamin, and swallowed up the altar in the Temple (*Yoma* 12a). Geographically, Binyamin should have had the Temple in their portion of the land and yet, it fell to the tribe of Yehuda instead. Indeed, the *Gemara* informs us that this intrusion from Yehuda caused Binyamin a great deal of anguish. In light of the fact that the Temple was covered and in the realm of the *alma d'itkasya*, it is perfectly understood why the Temple could not fall to the tribe of Binyamin, even if it required a geographical twist to ensure this. Binyamin, with his responsibility to the whole world and his connection to the *alma d'itgalya*, was unsuited to guarding the sanctity of the holy Temple.

Another example is to be found in the kings of Israel. The first king to be anointed was Shaul, who was descended from Binyamin. The *Tanach* recalls his lineage all the way back to Binyamin to stress his connection with the way of life of Binyamin and the children of Rachel (*Shmuel* I, 9:1–2). He was the king from the revealed, open world and this was perhaps a contributing factor to his downfall. He was unable to bring himself to rise above his inclination to spread the Torah throughout the world and was unable to follow the Divine command when it stood in the way of this ideal, in his own viewpoint. He was a human king, and this was essential at the outset of the monarchy in Israel, but God established the permanent house of the monarchy on more Divine individuals. The next king was David, from the tribe of Yehuda, the son of Leah, and it was from his house that all subsequent kings were to come. In the words of the Rambam: "The descendants of David constitute the permanent monarchy and if a king will arise from the rest of Israel, his reign will terminate eventually, and his sons will not be crowned" (*Mishneh Torah, Hilchot Melachim* 1:9). The monarchy was to be based on the children of Leah in the *alma d'itkasya* and was to serve the interests of the Jewish people and guard the Torah within.

David's son, Shlomo, was the next king and he was punished for his love of foreign women. "In his old age, Shlomo's wives lead him astray to idol worship" (*Melachim* I 11:4). The *Gemara* explains that they tried to seduce him to idolatry unsuccessfully, or alternatively, that he should have prevented them from their own idol worship, and because he was lax to do so, it was considered that he himself sinned (*Shabbat* 56b). But the plain text suggests that Shlomo's downfall was through these foreign women that he married and brought into his palace. How could Shlomo love these women to the extent that it would lead to his downfall as the king of Israel?

It was generally accepted that one of the best ways to draw a pact between foreign powers was through marriage. The children of kings would marry and this would seal the friendship between the two kings involved. Shlomo tried a similar strategy, marrying as many of the daughters of the surrounding monarchs as possible in order to draw them into a closer relationship with him. In so doing, Shlomo also hoped to gain a further victory, not in military terms but on the spiritual front. If he was on good terms with all of these kings on a personal level, they would also be encouraged to visit him in Yerushalayim and come closer to the word of God. This was a public relations exercise that seems to be much more suited to a descendant of Rachel than to one, like Shlomo, from the tribe of Yehuda, the children of Leah. This was the ruin of Shlomo; he tried to fulfill the task of a scion of Rachel and this caused his downfall.

There were, in history, those special individuals who were successful in crossing the boundaries, and even though their lineage was from Leah, they acted as representatives of the *alma d'itgalya* and triumphed. Moshe is a classic example. He was from the tribe of Levi, the son of Leah, and was therefore connected to the *alma d'itkasya*, and yet, we see several examples of his spreading the Torah to the peoples of the world. His father-in-law was Yitro, a Midiyanite priest who according to the midrash, had worshipped every existing form of idol before meeting Moshe (*Mechilta*; and see Rashi on *Shemot* 18:11). Even so, Moshe so successfully drew him close to the Torah and to God that his name was changed to Reuel, meaning "friend of God." On another occasion, God refers to *Am Yisrael* as "your people" (*Shemot* 32:7) to Moshe, implying that the Jewish people belonged to Moshe and not to God. The midrash on this verse relates that "when we were in Egypt, I (God) said to take out my people, but I said not to take out all of those that came to convert and join the Jewish people. However, you (Moshe) were humble and said that one must always accept those that want to draw close. I knew what they were capable of doing, such as worshipping the Golden Calf, and told you not to accept them, but you went against My words and converted them" (*Shemot Rabba* 42:6). Moshe was willing to go against the Lord's instructions to spread the Torah to the world. This was an action connected with the *alma d'itgalya*, and yet Moshe was successful in this task.

With regard to the synthesis of the two worlds, we find, in this week's *haftara*, the prophet Yechezkel prophesied "take a wooden rod and inscribe on it to Yehuda, and on another rod write to Yosef. Bring them together and they will fuse together in your hands" (*Yechezkel* 37:16,17). There definitely will be a synthesis between the paths of Yosef and the children of Leah, the *alma d'itgalya* will fuse with the *alma d'itkasya*. When will this be and what will bring it about?

In the *Gemara*, we find that one of the sages of the Talmud, Rabba Bar Bar Hanna, went on many mysterious and wonderful journeys that contained deep moral lessons. On one such occasion he visited *Har Sinai* and found it surrounded by scorpions that resembled white donkeys (*Babba Batra* 13a).

Rav Kook explains this esoteric text in the following way: *Har Sinai* is the source of the Torah and the nations are drawn to this source in order to learn the elements of the Torah. However, they find that the Jewish people, themselves, are spiritually removed from the Torah, and so they become frustrated. Instead of drawing close to God and His people, they tend to revert to intimidating them. The mountain was surrounded by scorpions who terrorized the Torah and its recipients. But they resemble white donkeys; they have an intrinsic purity and are willing to accept the yoke of the Torah and the Jewish People. It is up to us to rectify this situation. It depends on our willingness to correct our deeds and draw close to the Torah ourselves. If we do so, and we are indeed capable of this, then, instead of having to endanger ourselves by going out to the world, it will be obvious to all that are willing to listen that we have many important moral and spiritual lessons to teach the world. We will teach the world through example, and influence through actions. Our prayer is that we will succeed and will witness in our days the rebuilding of the Temple, "My house will be a house of prayer for all of the nations" (*Yeshiyahu* 56:7).

Vayechi
Ephrayim and Menashe—
Jewish Continuity in Egypt

Whoever puts all of his effort into sticking to the right path, the evil eye has no power over him. Yosef developed this trait in himself, and his sons received it from him due to his merit.

(*Ein Iyah, Berachot*, Chapter 3, Note 37)

We find in Yosef a great spiritual strength through his trials—a handsome young slave, his soul was strong enough to emit the cry of "How can I commit this crime toward God?!" It was strong enough to reject any influences from his earthly master, and he bequeathed this strength to his children.

(*ibid.*, Chapter 9, Note 62)

The basis for the nation and her future depends on education. It is already known from many sources that education affects all [society], and we see this in practice.

(*Ma'amrei HaRiyah*, p. 229)

This week's *parsha* opens with Ya'akov drawing close to his death. Before his demise, he called to his sons in order to give them a final blessing and to relate to them certain prophesies with regard to the future.

Before summoning all his sons, Yosef called for his two oldest sons in order to give them a special, personal blessing. Ya'akov uttered the words that were to become part of a very special ceremony performed on a weekly basis in the Jewish home.

Ya'akov had assured Yosef that his sons would be included amongst the tribes and would receive a portion of the land of Israel as a result.

"Your two sons who were born in Egypt prior to my arrival in Egypt belong to me. Ephrayim and Menashe will be like Reuven and Shimon" (*BeReishit* 48:5). "Israel will bless (their children) by likening them to your children, thus: May you be like Ephrayim and Menashe" (*ibid.*, 20). Every Friday night, Jewish fathers bless their sons in this format that was laid down by our forefather Ya'akov. They bless them that they should strive to resemble Ephrayim and Menashe, whilst their daughters receive the blessing, "May you be like Sara, Rivka, Rachel, and Leah."

The ceremony itself is sublime and deeply moving. It is an inspiration for children to receive this special blessing from their parents on this most elegant and spiritual occasion. The daughters of the household receive a call to resemble our matriarchs who were all special individuals in their own right and who gave birth to the Jewish people. On the other hand, the sons are blessed with aspirations to be like Ephrayim and Menashe. Surely it would be more suitable to bless our children to be like Yehuda, the tribe of the kings, or Levi, the priests. What was so special about Ephrayim and Menashe that they became the ideal Jewish figures?

The text contains very little information about them and, indeed, we really know nothing of them apart from them being the sons of Yosef who were born and bred in Egypt.

That is the clue. Even though they were born in Egypt, Ya'akov included them in the count of his sons. They were "like Reuven and Shimon." What is the significance of Ya'akov's promise to Yosef? After all, logically, Ephrayim and Menashe had no claim to be included in the role call of the tribes, since they were from the next generation and were the only members of their generation to be included in the tribes, all the rest of the tribes being sons of Ya'akov and not his grandchildren.

Ya'akov made a very important statement about Yosef's sons. They grew up in Egyptian high society in the palaces of the Egyptian aristocracy. They did not have the privilege of a Jewish environment or intensive Jewish schooling, as there were no Jewish schools in Egypt until Yehuda founded the first one immediately preceding the descent to Egypt. This situation must have affected Ephrayim and Menashe, and we would assume that it put them at a great disadvantage when their cousins came to Egypt. They must have been recognizably Egyptian in dress and conduct, or at least so we would imagine. Ya'akov assured Yosef that this was not the case. Ephrayim and Menashe were as much Ya'akov's offspring as any of his biological sons who had received a Jewish education and grown up in the best Jewish environment available at the time. Yosef's sons may indeed have grown up in Egypt, but they were indistinguishable from the rest of the family; they were "like Reuven and Shimon."

For this reason, throughout the ages, fathers have blessed their children: "May you be like Ephrayim and Menashe." With this we confer on our children our hopes that they will emulate these two spiritual giants. It is relatively easy to be righteous when one is in a conducive environment (it is not easy and still requires a lot of work and devotion, but it is *relatively* easy). Many alumni of *yeshivot* and Jewish schools were deeply religious while learning in these institutions, and yet found themselves, a short time after, not performing their religious duty as they themselves would have liked. The pressures of everyday life and the constant need to justify one's actions in a hostile society often cause one to relax the religious fervor that one previously felt and to cease practicing Judaism.

Ephrayim and Menashe never bowed to these pressures and retained their religious passion even against the background of Egyptian decadence. They proved themselves worthy of inclusion within the tribes. Our blessing to our children is that they remain righteous even in the most difficult and uncompromising circumstances, and this is truly a very special *bracha*.

Yosef succeeded in passing on the Judaism that he received in his father's home to his sons, even though his sons never witnessed Judaism as practiced in their grandfather's house until he came to join them in Egypt. This is actually appropriate for a son of Rachel, connected to the *alma d'itgalya*, the revealed, open world—the capacity to enter the public arena and remain unscathed religiously.

This is not a way of life for the large majority who are strongly influenced by their surroundings. It was not by chance that Rachel, who was chosen to be an "ambassador" for Judaism, had only two sons who followed in her footsteps, while Leah gave birth to half of the twelve tribes, and her children were those that continued to strengthen the Torah amongst the nation of Israel. The prophet tells us that "Avraham was an individual" (*Yechezkel* 33:24). Avraham was active in his own way and this was very suitable for him and his family, including his son and grandson; this is obvious from the large success that they enjoyed. This course of action, however, is reserved for individuals. It is not the practice for an entire nation. Only special, strong characters can succeed in entering into public life and resisting the temptation to follow the crowd and become like them. Yosef succeeded, and this was evident in his sons.

How was Yosef successful? Maybe there is a lesson here for us and our own children in these troubled times of assimilation. What was Yosef's secret for Jewish continuity?

The answer is that he had no secret. As previously seen, Yosef spoke to all with whom he came into contact in the name of God. To Paro, to his jailer and fellow inmates, and even to Potifar's wife as she tried to seduce him. Those individuals, upon hearing the name of the Lord from Yosef, answered him also in the name of God. If Yosef's behavior had the power to affect the decadent Egyptians, how much more would they affect and influence his own sons. Yosef always remembered that God sent him to Egypt and gave him an important mission there, and this information he carefully passed on to his sons. Thus, they retained their faith in God.

When Yosef eventually revealed himself to his brothers, he initially spoke to them in Hebrew and then showed them that he was circumcised. One of the commentators on Rashi explains that he used these two signs because "the circumcision was proof that the bond of brotherhood between them had not been broken. The fact that he spoke to them in Hebrew showed them that he never attempted to hide the fact that he was Jewish and came from Israel" (*Ikar Siftei Chachamim* on Rashi, *BeReishit* 45:12). Indeed, he is referred to as "a Jewish lad." He did not believe that one could be a Jew only at home, and he publicized his Judaism as much as possible. This also had the desired effect that his children followed the example that he set for them.

The *Gemara* tells us that on one occasion, after a meal, one of the Talmudic sages said, "Ya'akov our forefather did not die." To which the obvious question is asked: "But he was embalmed and buried. How can you say that he did not die?" "As long as his children are alive, it is as though he himself is still alive" (*Ta'anit* 5b). Ya'akov merited, through Yosef's tenacity to his faith, to see his grandchildren follow the path that he taught his own children. The whole time that his ideals and morals were upheld, it was as though he himself continued to live through Ephrayim and Menashe.

We are also the children of Israel. The whole time that we continue to survive, live, and teach the ideals that he brought to the world, we continue to give Ya'akov, Yitzchak, and Avraham eternal life. It is a big responsibility but it promises great rewards. Our prayer is that we shall always continue to represent them honorably and succeed for "as long as his children are alive, it is as though he himself is alive."

II

Shemot

Introduction

There are two essential elements required for one to be free; physical freedom of the body from slavery, slavery that forces one's Divine image to be subjugated to other forces that constrict its value. This freedom is dependent on the other freedom, that of the soul.

(*Olat Riyah*, Volume II, p. 244)

The difference between a slave and a free man is not only one of external status, that one is enslaved by someone else, and the other is not. We can find a clever slave whose spirit is free and, on the contrary, we can find free men who have the spirit of a slave. Freedom is being true to one's own internal, intrinsic nature.

(*ibid.*, p. 245)

Had God taken us out of Paro's slavery but left us in Egypt, we would have remained slaves to Paro in Egypt. Egypt is an impure land and it emphasizes the impurity within us. Therefore, God took us out of Egypt so that we might be capable of receiving the Torah and holiness.

(*ibid.*, p. 268)

The *Book of Shemot* is the book that relates the birth of the Jewish people. We would assume that such an account would start on a glorious note. The nation would be born into the wonderful tradition that had been established by Avraham, Yitzchak, Ya'akov, and their families. It would be an earth-shattering birth that would be noted by the entire world. A few wise men bearing gifts, blessings, and the respect of the nations would not go amiss.

Yet when we do open the real *Book of Shemot*, we find a very different scene awaiting us.

The family of Ya'akov, the Jews of the day, were not in their land and natural habitat. They were residing in Egypt due to a famine in their own land. If this was not enough, the ruler of Egypt decided to afflict them and turn them into his slaves. The Jews toiled hard under this task master and his people, building for them store houses and pyramids.

Perhaps the worst slavery of all was that eventually, after decades of servitude, the children of Ya'akov were enslaved mentally and spiritually. They lost their spiritual nature and their will to be free. When this happened, then they were really slaves.

When this occurred the exodus was an immediate imperative. This was the start of our birth. The term *Am*, nation, with reference to the Jewish people, was first coined in Egypt by Paro (*Shemot* 1:9). This was the start of Jewish nationhood and national birth. The birth was only complete, however, after we left Egypt and met God.

We are a nation that met the Lord and continue to do so. During the following weeks, we shall learn how.

In order to achieve this, God required a facilitator, a great leader. He had to be able to fuse the people together and infuse them with the will to be free. He then had to bring them to the level that they would be suitable to meet the Almighty.

The ideal choice was Moshe, and we shall see the qualities that he possessed in due course. If the *Book of BeReishit* was rich with characters and individuals, the *Book of Shemot* centers around one figure, Moshe. Moshe was the initiator of the exodus from Egypt. He staged a theological discussion with Paro, took us out of Egypt, and facilitated the meeting with God. He also ensured that the meeting would continue.

Moshe oversaw the birth of *Am Yisrael* and led them until his death. He carried them throughout his life "in his breast, as a nurse carries an infant" (*Bemidbar* 11:12). He was even willing to forego his own reward on our behalf. At a crucial moment, when the nation had sinned against God, the Lord offered Moshe the following proposal: "I have seen this difficult people. Let Me destroy them and I will establish your children as a great nation" (*Shemot* 32:9,10).

This was a golden opportunity. It was indeed true that *Am Yisrael* were a "stiff-necked" nation that had tormented God and Moshe even before leaving Egypt. Moshe now had the chance to reestablish the link between God and the Jewish people from scratch. Instead of the current band of unruly ex-slaves, he could take his own children and start afresh.

However, Moshe argued that they were His subjects and "His people." The original relationship between us and God had to continue despite all the problems that were involved. His answer to God's offer came back: "The people have indeed committed a terrible sin and made golden images. But forgive them, and if not, then strike me out of Your book" (*ibid.*, 31,32). Moshe felt so much responsibility to *Am Yisrael* that he forced God to forgive them. He countered with the "threat" that he would be willing to give up his rightful place in the Torah if the Lord would not pardon them.

Far from rejecting *Am Yisrael*, Moshe carried them in his heart. He knew that he was their leader, and that his role was to bring them into the world. He was not more important than them. If *Am Yisrael* were to be destroyed, if the relationship between the Jewish people were to cease, God forbid, he would have no relevance.

So the *Book of Shemot* is the book of Moshe and his struggle to cause *Am Yisrael* to be born. Our birth was not comprised of a one-off, chance meeting with God. We were born in order to continue meeting God on a regular basis. Through the medium of the *Book of Shemot*, we shall learn how this is possible. Hopefully, this will also teach us something not only of the Jewish past, but of relevance to the Jewish future as well.

Shemot
Moshe, The Ultimate Jewish Leader

Moshe rested on the merit of others; he was born with good and holy qualities to holy and righteous parents. He was worthy by his elevated nature, but he added total completion, to a much higher degree than he would have reached, based purely on his natural pedigree.

(*Ein Iyah, Berachot*, Chapter 1, Note 144)

The ruler of each generation should attempt to understand each and every individual, and through helping every person, he will elevate the entire status of the congregation. The generation is comprised of diverse individuals and each one should be catered to according to his needs.

(*ibid.*, Chapter 4, Note 22)

To lead the nation one needs to be concerned not only with the present situation, but also with the state that the nation will attain in the future and for eternity. Perfect leadership has to establish the future of the nation.

(*ibid.*, Chapter 5, Note 31)

If the *Book of Shemot* is the book of the birth of the Jewish people, then Moshe was our midwife. He was the one who took us out of Egypt, and brought the Torah from the heavens down to the earth and gave it to the Jewish people. He spent forty days and nights together with the Creator on our behalf in order to learn the Torah and later relay it to the Jews in the wilderness.

What were the qualities that enabled Moshe to fulfill his task, and why was he chosen by God for this all-important and responsible position? The answer is found partially in this week's *parsha* and in the rest of the *Book of Shemot*.

Initially, Moshe proved to possess certain key qualities of any successful Jewish leader. Due to this, God revealed Himself to him and taught him certain other crucial principles that we shall see presently. This study is important within itself in understanding Moshe the man, and, as in our studies of *BeReishit* and the characters contained therein, this gives us an opening into a deeper spiritual world that one can, and should, aspire to reach. With this particular study of the characteristics of the classic Jewish leader, we profit further by receiving the blueprint for all future leaders that are to follow Moshe. When choosing a leader or grooming potential leadership within our communities, we must look for certain traits and develop a specific outlook on the whole concept of leadership.

Yocheved, Moshe's mother, placed him in a basket in the Nile in order to save him from the murderous decree of Paro to drown all Jewish males. He was eventually found by Paro's daughter during a stroll on the banks of the river. Immediately, on discovery, Moshe's older sister Miriyam appeared and informed Paro's daughter that she was willing to supply her with a Jewish wet-nurse for this newfound baby. This appearance was, of course, planned, as she had lain in wait for her brother to be discovered. The *Gemara* tells us that the reason she was able to offer her mother's services as Moshe's wet-nurse was that Paro's daughter took him to all the available Egyptian ladies and still he refused to nurse, as he was in line to converse with the Lord and the Egyptian milk was impure (*Sotah* 12b). In order to prevent his starvation, Paro's daughter was forced to give him over to his biological mother (although she did not know that Yocheved was his real mother) in order to nurse "kosher" milk.

This, therefore, was the first sign of greatness. Moshe was intrinsically pure, and this was a requirement for any leader, a natural purity and sense of holy purpose.

Moshe was taken by the daughter of Paro and grew up in his palace. There he learnt about Egyptian history and culture and was, in his outward appearance, an Egyptian prince. When he eventually was forced to flee to Midiyan, the locals referred to him as an Egyptian man (*Shemot* 2:19), and he did not correct them but remained in the guise of the noble Egyptian. We see that Moshe felt at home within the Egyptian establishment. When he returned to Egypt to save the Jewish people, he had no qualms about approaching Paro and demanding freedom for his people, even though the rest of the elders were reluctant to enter the palace and consequently departed before he faced Paro (see *Midrash Tanchuma, Shemot* 24). Yet, with all that, Moshe made it his business to leave the palace and go to view for himself the welfare of his nation. "He went out to his brothers and saw their suffering" (*Shemot* 2:11). Rashi explains that he saw their anguish and made it his duty to feel their pain (Rashi ad loc.).

Moshe did not ignore his brothers, even though he himself was not affected by the evil decree and had obtained a degree of impunity, having grown up as an Egyptian prince. In this, he resembled God Himself, who vowed "I am with him (Israel) in his suffering" (*Tehillim* 91:15). This feeling of empathy with the community is essential for any communal leader.

Moshe's humility was legendary: "Moshe was very humble, more than anyone on earth" (*Bemidbar* 12:3). There could be no suspicion that he accepted the position of leader for any ulterior, personal motives. He himself initially rejected the post and tried to "prove" to God that he was unworthy. It was only as a result of God forcing him that, eventually, he agreed, on the condition that Aharon, his brother, joined forces with him.

All of these qualities made Moshe the perfect choice to lead the Jewish people from slavery to freedom and give them their national identity. In addition, God taught him various lessons with regard to leadership through the medium of the burning bush and the signs that he gave Moshe to take to Egypt. These hold many lessons for any future potential leaders.

The first sign was God's name. "I will come to the children of Israel and tell them that the God of your fathers sent me here, and they will ask Your name. What will I tell them?" asked Moshe. "I will be what I will be" (*Shemot* 3:14), came the reply. Within this cryptic answer lies a deep message. Rabbi Charlap explains that most often a leader sees the situation as it appears to him at the present. He views the level of the nation as they currently stand. The leader perceives the current deficiency of the people.

God taught Moshe that in order to bring about a drastic change, one must be a visionary and be able to conceive of abstract futures and rise above the present. "I will be what I will be" and not what I may appear at the moment.

The next thing that God instructed Moshe was that, on arriving in Egypt, he was to gather the elders and tell them of his Divine mission. It is essential that a leader respect the hierarchy of the community and have a sense of historical pride. In Judaism, old people are respected as having wisdom and life experience; the word for elder, *zaken*, is an acronym for "one who has acquired wisdom." Therefore, Moshe initially consulted the elders of the people.

Moshe was to take the elders and go to Paro and demand: "We want to go for a three day journey into the desert to sacrifice to the Lord our God" (*ibid.*,

18). Rabbi Charlap asks that, since surely God was capable of taking them out of Egypt completely, why did they initially request to make just a three day trip, and not demand that he free them from slavery? He answers that the demand was directed as much to the Jews as to Paro. God wanted Moshe to stir up the people to desire their own freedom; if they were capable of desiring this, albeit, minor freedom, then they would be ready for redemption. A large part of slavery is developing a slave mentality; and when this happens, the slave can no longer comprehend concepts like freedom and personal responsibility.

God told Moshe that, in order to succeed in freeing the Jewish people, he must first quash this slave mentality. In order to do this, he had to create a situation wherein the people would wake up by themselves. He would act as a facilitator to this change in mentality. A leader must change the attitude of his congregation to think positively but, if he wants this to be a real change, he must enable them to make the change by themselves, as it were, without him having to change their minds for them.

Moshe was still skeptical about the success of this mission. "They will not believe me, or listen to me and will claim that God never appeared to me." God replied: "'Throw down (your stick) to the ground,' and it became a snake" (*ibid.*, 4:3). The midrash explains the significance of the snake in the following way: "You (Moshe) spoke evil against My sons (in saying that they will not believe you) in the same way that the snake spoke evil. My children will believe, as they are inherent believers" (*Tanchuma, Shemot* 23). The snake was sent as a punishment to Moshe, since he had spoken evil of the Jews, and we find a link between evil speech, *lashon hara*, and the snake.

God indicated to Moshe that even though the people were on a low spiritual level, it was forbidden to speak evil of them. They were inherent believers and all that it would take was a skillful leader to turn this potential belief into a vibrant feeling. "'Stretch out your hand and grab the snake's tail.' He did so and it returned to a staff in his palm" (*ibid.*, 4). If you can learn the sensitive area of the people, you will be able to convert them into a disciplined and obedient nation.

Moshe was then instructed to place his hand inside his shirt next to his heart. On removing his hand, he found that it was "leprous as snow" (*ibid.*, 6). According to the midrash, this was also a punishment for his evil speech against *Am Yisrael*. Interestingly, the leprosy was white as snow. This is reminiscent of the verse "if your sins will be red, I will whiten them like snow" (*Yeshiyahu* 1:18). Snow is pure white and is a symbol of purity. Even within the impurity of leprosy there was an intrinsic whiteness and purity. Moshe had to believe in that purity in order to believe in the mission to save the people. But again, this was only a potential purity. How was he to bring this out in the Jewish people? "'Return your hand to your heart.' He removed his hand from his heart and behold it had returned to its original healthy condition" (*ibid.*, 7). If he were capable of bringing them close to his heart, then he would successfully return them to their pure and perfect state.

So we have seen the qualities that God gave to Moshe the leader and, in so doing, we have learned some of the qualities that every leader must possess. He must have intrinsic purity, feel empathy with the congregation, and be humble. He must be a visionary, learn how to delegate tasks and responsibility, and encourage the people to strive for greater heights of their own accord. More than anything else, he must believe in the power of his flock and in their purity. His task is then to bring out their natural abilities and spirituality, to develop them so that they can come as close as possible to God.

Our prayer is that we shall merit such great leaders and encourage the growth of others so that we, too, shall reach our potential and serve God to the highest degree.

Vaera
The Plagues and God's Existence

The rays of the light of God fill all of the worlds and vitalize them from the source of life itself. This is what gives strength to the souls, the angels, to every living creature to feel within it consciousness of life.

(*Orot Hakodesh*, Volume II, p. 329)

"King"; the general sovereignty over the entire world, the controlled governing of all the component parts, all encompassing, justice found in all parts of the world.

(*Olat Riyah*, Volume I, p. 1)

We deal with individual laws and precepts, yet we know that all of the ways of the Torah are the ways of God; they emanate from the highest source of all life. We have to link the laws with God, that is to link the lower individual Torah with the higher all-encompassing Torah.

(*Orot Hatorah*, Chapter 3, Paragraph 1)

On seder night, the first night of Pesach, in all Jewish homes, we read the Haggadah. Therein we read the story of the freedom of the Jewish people from slavery in Egypt, the same story that is dealt with in the following few weeks' *parshiot*.

In the Haggadah, we read the list of the ten plagues that God brought onto the Egyptians. These were sent both as punishment for enslaving *Am Yisrael* and as a persuasion to free them. After the list of plagues, the Haggadah states: "Rabbi Yehuda used to assign the plagues abbreviations—*DeZaCh, ADaSh,*

BeAChaV." These are the first letters of the Hebrew names of the ten plagues:
Dam, blood; Zephardea, frogs; and so forth.

Is there any other significance in Rabbi Yehuda's novel way of presenting
the plagues beyond the simple fact that it was a memory aid? Through our
investigation throughout the next few weeks, we shall see that Rabbi Yehuda
is alluding to the subtle but significant differences between the plagues. Each
of these three groups of plagues represents a moral message of worldwide
importance that God chose to teach *Am Yisrael* and the Egyptians. When
Moshe and his brother Aharon came to Paro, they said: "Thus says the Lord,
God of Israel, send out My people and they will worship Me in the wilderness" (*Shemot* 5:1). Paro answered "Who is God that I should listen to Him
and release *Am Yisrael*? I do not know of God and I also have no intention of
freeing Israel" (*ibid.*, 2).

Paro raised three objections to Moshe and Aharon's demand: God does not
exist. There is no such thing as the God of Israel, and He has no power over
me. "Who is God?" He simply does not exist. "That I should listen to Him and
release *Am Yisrael*." God does not differentiate between one group of people and
another. Why should I release my Jewish slaves? "I have no intention of freeing Israel." He has no power over me, claimed Paro in his audacity. God dealt
with each of these three claims with a different set of plagues, as we shall see.

Paro's first objection was that God simply does not exist and, therefore,
Moshe and Aharon's Divine message to release *Am Yisrael* had no relevance.
The midrash explains that Paro instructed his servants to bring him all the
encyclopedias of their gods. He searched through them yet did not find a
mention of any God of Israel (see *Midrash Tanchuma, Vaera* 5; and *Otzar
HaMidrashim*, Eizenstein Edition, p. 356). According to the idol-worshipping
Egyptians, God did not exist because they could not see Him and, addition-
ally, they had no reliable record of His existence.

Their objection was also to the presence of any sort of spirituality or Divinity on earth or in human things. Moshe came with a claim that God had
appeared to him. This sort of occurrence was diametrically opposed to the
theology of Egypt. God existed in the heavens and had no interaction with
humans and their behaviour. One's task was to attempt to appease the gods
as much as was humanly possible, but Man could hope for no more.

Moshe came to Egypt with a tumultuous claim, that God had spoken to
him and instructed him in his human, everyday life. Paro completely rejected
this charge and stated that God did not exist in Egyptian scriptures and, thus,
had no reality at all. God, therefore, chose to bring down upon Paro and Egypt
plagues that would act as fitting punishments and would also serve to certify

His existence in the world. As the verse affirms: "Egypt will learn that I am God, when I will stretch out My hand on them and take out My people from amongst them" (*Shemot* 7:5).

"Go to Paro in the morning and face him on the banks of the Nile. Tell him, 'The God of the Jews has sent me to inform you that you must free My people.' So said the Lord. You will learn that I am God. I will smite the river and the Nile's waters will turn into blood" (*ibid.*, 15–17). The location of this confrontation is pertinent. The midrash explains the significance: "Paro set himself up to be a deity who did not need to fulfill bodily functions. Therefore, in the early morning, he would go to the banks of the Nile and relieve himself, away from the eyes of his subjects. God said to Moshe that he should go and face him there" (*Tanchuma*, *Vaera* 14). We also know that the Egyptians worshipped the Nile as a deity, since it supplied them with sustenance (see Rashi on *Shemot* 7:17). This meeting between Moshe, Aharon, and Paro was timed to attack the existing gods of Egypt—the Nile, and Paro himself—and to introduce him to the real God and Divine power. God decided to "attack their gods first and then the people" (*Shemot Rabba* 9:9), all this to prove His existence.

Moshe's task was to turn the waters of the Nile, their god, into blood, and, in so doing, to shake the tenets of their faith in the Nile and its power to feed them. But not only the waters of the Nile changed into blood. "All the waters of Egypt, their rivers, their pools, and their reservoirs, every body of water turned to blood. Even in the wood and the stone" (*Shemot* 7:19). Rashi explains that even the water component of inanimate objects changed into blood (Rashi ad loc.). The hand of God was revealed not only in the natural bodies of water, the rivers and seas, but also in the man-made reservoirs and lakes. Divinity was evident also in the vessels that they had fashioned themselves in the Egyptians houses. Clearly, God was very much connected to the physical world, contrary to popular opinion in Egypt. This was the beginning of the first lesson that Egypt was to learn.

The next plague was to be frogs that emerged from the Nile and entered "your house, bedroom, and bed. Into your servants' house, your nation, and your ovens. Inside you, your people, and your servants" (*ibid.*, 28–29). The frogs covered the whole of Egypt, entering every possible nook and cranny. The Torah stresses several places that the frogs entered and these have significance as part of the lesson on the presence of God.

In Judaism, spirituality covers every single area of life. There are laws governing one's conduct at home, in the bedroom, and even in the most intimate situations, in bed. Unlike idol worship that relegated God to the Temple and assigned Him a few religious rites, true Divinity is concerned with man's entire existence. More than this, in Egypt, religion was reserved for the high echelons of society and was not accessible to the masses. Paro was a god and religion had no say in national affairs. The frogs attacked every strata of society, from Paro down to the servants. Both national and individual attention was focused on this plague. Indeed, halacha also governs national policy. The king, far from being a deity, has a responsibility to write a special *Sefer Torah* that goes with him on his state visits and public affairs (see *Devarim* 17:18). He must never forget that he is the messenger of the Lord and must also be bound by the halachic system.

Throughout these first two plagues, the sorcerers of Egypt scoffed at Moshe and Aharon's feats of magic, and successfully repeated their tricks, using magic and witchcraft. "They assumed that it was just another case of witchcraft" (*Shemot Rabba* 10:6). Paro, therefore, remained unimpressed by these plagues and even retorted "You are attempting to convince Egypt with magic? We are the experts in magic" (Rashi on *Shemot* 7:22).

The last plague in this group was designed to convince even the magicians of Egypt, and therefore, Paro himself. "Aharon stretched out his hand and hit the dust and it became lice that attacked the people and the animals. All of Egypt was filled with the lice" (*Shemot* 8:13). On this occasion, the Egyptian sorcerers were incapable of creating such infinitesimal creatures. The *Gemara* states: "The phantoms have no control over tiny entities" (*Sanhedrin* 67b). Idolatry concerns itself only with large events—weather, war, and the like. On the other hand, God is concerned with every single thing that occurs throughout the universe and never leaves the world to its own devices. "Every single blade of grass has a force in the heavens that controls its growth." (*BeReishit Rabba* 10:6). Even the miniscule lice were under Divine control and this outwitted the magicians. They were forced to admit "This is the finger of God" (*Shemot* 8:15).

Paro was punished "measure for measure" (*Shabbat* 105b). "You said, 'Who is God?' In the future you will be forced to admit 'God is faithful' (*Shemot* 9:27)" (*Shemot Rabba* 5:18).

When these magicians came to the realization of God's existence and supremacy, then the first message that God strove to teach Egypt was complete. The time was ripe to move onto the next group of plagues and the next lesson.

This lesson was as much directed at the Jews as at the Egyptians. Even though we take for granted the fact of God's existence and are "natural believers," we often tend to neglect this knowledge. We rely on natural events and trends and ignore the fact that God controls our daily events and circumstances. Even the magicians admitted that the tiny lice were due to the finger of God. How much more do we have the responsibility to recognize God's hand in the world?

Bo

Boils and Divine Providence

Israel, as a special nation, blessed with a depth of sanctity and a desire for Divinity, influences all the other nations, to sensitize the national soul of every nation, and to bring them closer to a higher and more Divine stature.

(*Orot*, p. 151)

Very soon the mask will be drawn from the world and all will know that we are the people of God, that God deals with us well. All those that rise and say that God has abandoned us will fall.

(*Orot HaRiyah*, p. 62)

One should know that God's kindness and compassion reach all His creation. However, individuals are chosen, be they people or individual nations, that the good may reach all beings through them.

(*Ein Iyah*, *Berachot*, Chapter 5, Note 102)

We saw last week that the first three plagues of blood, frogs, and lice were sent in order to teach the eternal truth of God's existence. The Egyptians themselves were forced to accept God's presence in the world. They also learned that Divinity is not confined to religious ceremony but involves everything on earth. God reveals Himself even in inanimate objects, on both a private and a national level.

The next three plagues were sent to deal with the next objection that Paro raised to Moshe and Aharon's "preposterous" demand that he release *Am Yisrael* from slavery in Egypt. He replied to them: "Who is God that I should

listen to Him and release *Am Yisrael?*" (*Shemot* 5:2). He refused to recognize
God's existence, and then, subsequently, refused to accept that God was the
"God of the Jews." In his lexicon, there was no such thing as a god of a specific group. Gods controlled the weather, fought wars, and controlled the
heavens, but how was it possible that Moshe and Aharon were correct in their
belief that God sided with one nation against another? As previously discussed, in the eyes of the idol worshipper, god has no dominion over the world
in any sort of specific or controlled manner and, therefore, it is ridiculous to
attempt to assign a nation some sort of claim to any god.

This is very similar in nature to the claim of the philosopher in the work
by Rabbi Yehuda HaLevi, *The Book of the Kuzari*. The book relates that the
king of the Kuzaris had visions that sent him off on a religious quest. He asked
various representatives of several religions what they stood for; eventually,
he found his way to Judaism and converted along with his entire nation. Most
of the book is involved with his discussions with his Jewish mentor and is,
essentially, a theology of Judaism. At the outset, the king approaches a philosopher to inquire what he has to say on the subject of divinity and religion.

"God is above the individual, as individuals are given to change and He is
unchangeable. Therefore, God does not know you and definitely has no in-
terest in your thought and actions. He neither hears your prayers nor sees your
movements. God is the ultimate designer of the world but He does not purposely create individual people" (*Sefer Kuzari* 1:1).

According to this view, God may have created the Universe but, subsequently, He left it to its own devices and has no direct interaction with His
world. In this view, there is no place for terms like "God of the Jews," and
this was indeed Paro's opinion. Even were he to accept that God existed, he
still asked: "Who is God that I should listen to Him and release *Am Yisrael?*"
He refused to comply with Moshe and Aharon's demand to release *Am Yisrael*,
just as he refused to accept the fact of God's intimate relationship with the
world.

God, therefore, brought upon Egypt the next three plagues in order to stress
this fact. *ADaSh*, in Rabbi Yehuda's system, was to teach this principle.

"So says the Lord, send out My people to serve Me. But if you refuse, I will
punish you with wild animals. I will isolate the land of Goshen that is inhabited by My people, and they will not be afflicted with this plague, in order
that you will learn that I am God on earth. I will separate My nation and your
people" (*Shemot* 8:17–18). The plague was to strike the Egyptians exclusively
and not affect the Jewish population at all. In so doing, God would teach that
He was both involved in the internal workings of the world and that He over-

saw every single detail therein. He deals with Israel, providing them with specific supervision and monitoring their actions. He was indeed the God of the Jews and would bring devastation on any nation that would harm and enslave His children. "Tell Paro that the Lord says that Israelites are My first-born son." We were to receive preferential treatment and Providence.

"If you continue to refuse to release them and still enslave them, then God's hand will strike your flocks with a severe epidemic. God will set the flocks of Israel apart from the Egyptian animals, and none of the Jewish animals will die" (*ibid.*, 9:2–4). Indeed, this happened. "All the flocks of Egypt died, but not one Jewish animal was affected" (*ibid.*, 6). Paro, this time, started to suspect that he was up against something and took the time to go and check if indeed none of the Jewish animals were affected. "Paro sent a messenger, and he discovered that none of the Jewish animals had died" (*ibid.*, 7).

This incensed Paro; he now knew that he was beaten and that God did control the world in a careful and supervised manner. He became so annoyed that he continued to refuse exit for the Jews. This was against the advice of his advisers and ministers, but he had found himself in a position that he could not win, and so he fought until the bitter end.

God sent one more plague in order to force the fact of His Divine Providence. He afflicted the Egyptians with boils and other skin diseases. They were so severe that "the magicians were unable to face Moshe" (*ibid.*, 11). This can be understood in two possible ways. They may have been unable to stand before Moshe and Aharon from a lack of physical strength. Or the reason that they were unable to face Moshe and any other Jew was a much deeper one. They were extremely embarrassed by their own haughty conduct. They had waged war on the Creator of the Universe and, from the start, had no hope of success. Their pride had initially gotten the better of them and they had pitted their witchcraft against God. Slowly, they understood the ultimate truth. God not only exists but He supervises the events concerning His children and takes special care of *Am Yisrael*. The magicians were unable to stand up to the Jews, whom they had punished throughout their time in Egypt. This is the last time that we hear of the sorcerers of Egypt. Indeed, the only time that we encounter the Egyptians again is when they implore Paro to release the Jews. "The servants of Paro said to him: 'How much longer will they continue to be a trap for us? Release them and let them serve their God. Do you not realize that Egypt is lost?'" (*ibid.*, 10:7).

This group of plagues had achieved their purpose. They had proven to the world that God is omnipotent and monitors every action in the world. There exists such a thing as Divine Providence. The Jews remained unaffected by the plagues, unlike their Egyptian neighbours. The scene was now set for God to unleash upon Egypt the last set of plagues and deliver the final message.

This basic idea is central to Judaism. We have already seen it written in the midrash that God controls the growth of every single plant. How much more must He protect and care for humans (see *BeReishit Rabba* 10:6)? We are commanded to believe that God watches our every action and that even our thoughts are monitored. This leads us to the belief in reward and punishment for our actions; even though performing the commandments simply in order to receive the reward is disapproved of (see *Avot* 1:3, "Do not worship as servants that await reward, but serve as if there were no reward at all"), there always is either a reward or punishment for every action.

Indeed, in the *Kuzari*, the king eventually comes to a Jewish *Chaver* (wise man), after having spoken with representatives of the other religions. Assuming that the Jew will try to convince him of the truth of the Jewish religion, he is surprised at the Jew's response.

"I believe in the God of Avraham, Yitzchak, and Ya'akov, who took the Jewish people out of Egypt using a string of miracles" (*Sefer Kuzari* 1:11). The *Chaver* decided to try a novel approach. Instead of a program of persuasion, he simply laid out his own beliefs. He did not say that he believed in God Who created the world, but rather in God Who took us out of Egypt. This was in direct contrast to the words of the philosopher. Judaism's major credo is that God is God of the heavens and the earth Who guards us and watches us constantly.

This lesson was made clear to Paro and his servants. Let us never forget it.

B'shalach
The All Powerful God

The true image is that God cannot be constricted to the confines of physical attributes.

(*Ein Iyah*, *Berachot*, Chapter 5, Note 101)

Knowledge brings with it will, which in turn brings ability.
Knowledge, will, and ability are always intertwined. In a place where we would find infinite knowledge, there we find infinite will and also infinite ability.

(*Orot Hakodesh*, Volume III, p. 87)

God's ability is not confined to any standard and is unfathomable by human terms.

(*Ein Iyah*, *Berachot*, Chapter 5, Note 122)

In the past two weeks, we saw the way that God dealt with the heresy of the Egyptians and their ruler, Paro. He brought them certain plagues that were to teach them the all-important lessons that God exists and maintains an intimate relationship with the world. This ties in with the statement made by Rabbi Yehuda in the Haggadah of the Pesach seder. After the list of the ten plagues, Rabbi Yehuda comes up with the abbreviation "*DeZaCh ADaSh BeAChaV.*" We have already explained that Rabbi Yehuda divided up the plagues in this manner in order to draw attention to the fact that each of these three groups was sent to teach another principle of faith—namely, God's existence and His relationship with the world.

The scene was now set for the final lot of plagues and the last message of Divinity. Paro objected to Moshe and Aharon's demand to release the Jewish

people on three accounts. "Who is God that I should listen to Him and release *Am Yisrael*? I do not know of God and I also have no intention of freeing Israel" (*Shemot* 5:2). According to Paro and his advisers in Egypt, God
did not exist, had no connection with the world, and finally, even if they were
to accept the existence of God, He had no power over them, the mighty Egyptian empire.

This last criticism was to be addressed in the final group of plagues. Prior
to this, let us try to understand the rationale behind this claim. How could
the Egyptians really believe that they were stronger and more powerful than
the Creator?

Egypt was the superpower of the day. They were at the forefront of all of
the contemporary advances in science, the arts, and technology. They had
succeeded in building the pyramids, a feat of engineering that remains unex-
plained until the present day. They were also successful on the battlefield and
had captured many slaves whom they forced to work for them. None of these
slaves had ever escaped, a fact recorded by the midrash: "No slave had ever
escaped from Egypt until then" (*Mechilta* 81; see Rashi on *Shemot* 18:9). They
must have felt unstoppable. They were in control of the world's resources and
finances; who could have any authority over them? Definitely not an unseen
and unknown force that these Jewish slaves had conjured up to free them.

God, therefore, chose to teach the Egyptians a lesson that would have re-
percussions throughout the world, in order to teach the world a few lessons
in Divinity and Providence. When the Egyptian empire fell, it was an event
of such force that the effect was felt throughout the world. Yitro, Moshe's
father-in-law, converted on hearing of their downfall. "Yitro, the priest of
Midiyan, heard all that the Lord had done to Moshe and to Israel, His people,
that God had taken them out of Egypt" (*Shemot* 18:1). Rahav, the prostitute
who took in the two spies that Yehoshua sent to spy out the land, helped them.
As she explained: "I know that God has given you this land, and all of its inhabitants are in awe of you. We have heard that God dried out the Red Sea
before you when you escaped from Egypt. When we heard about this we
became weak and lost our morale" (*Yehoshua* 2:9–11). The news of the defeat
of Egypt certainly had a great affect on the surrounding nations. The reason
for this was that God had chosen to bring down on the Egyptians specific
plagues to teach these moral lessons in an unchallengeable way. This was also
His intention in the last set of three plagues—hail, locusts, and darkness. God
proved Paro's claim to be wrong. He was indeed all-powerful and could and
would destroy the Egyptian nation.

"This time I will send all of My plagues upon you, so that you will learn that I am unique in the world. For this reason, I have spared you thus far, in order to show you My strength and to publicize My name throughout the world. Tomorrow, I will bring a severe hail storm, unlike anything experienced by Egypt from its founding until the present day" (*Shemot* 9:14–16). The hail was intended to teach the world that God is all-powerful, and to do so required some very special hail. "Within the hail was fire, and it was heavier than anything that had been previously witnessed in Egypt" (*ibid.*, 24). The midrash explains that the fire and the water "made peace" in order to fulfill God's will (See *Tanchuma, Vaera* 14; and Rashi on *Shemot* 9:24).

The next plague of the locust was also extraordinary and supernatural. "Said God to Moshe: 'I have hardened Paro's heart in order to bring these plagues upon him. In order that you may relate these events to your children and grandchildren, and know that I am God. Tomorrow, I will bring locusts to their land. They will cover all the earth and the land will become invisible. They will fill their houses and your servants' houses, and all of Egypt. Such a thing has never been witnessed before'" (*Shemot* 10:1–6). "The locusts were extremely heavy, unlike anything that had been before or that will ever be" (*ibid.*, 14). God changed nature in order to prove to the Egyptians and to the world that He was all-powerful.

He did a similar thing with the several days of darkness, the next plague. "There will be darkness throughout Egypt, and the darkness will be tangible" (*ibid.*, 21). "It was so thick that it became tangible" (Rashi ad loc.; based on *Shemot Rabba* 14:1–3). "People were unable to see each other or even to stand." (*Shemot* 10:23). "During the last three days of darkness, whoever was sitting could not stand up and whoever was standing could not sit down; if someone was in a bowing position, they could not straighten up" (*Midrash Tanchuma, Bo* 3). God created a new type of darkness as part of His grand plan to prove that He is all-powerful.

In the last plague, all three lessons were combined. The death of the first-born Egyptian children was to show that God exists, carefully monitors the world, and is all-powerful. God Himself smote the first-born children: "I will go out into Egypt. All of the first-born will die, from the first-born of Paro down to the first-born of his slaves, and even the first-born of their animals. There will be great anguish in Egypt that will eclipse anything that they have witnessed so far, and there will never be such a thing again. However, all of Israel will be saved; not so much as a dog will bark at them, so that you may see that God distinguishes between Egypt and Israel" (*Shemot* 11:4–7). All of the elements of the previous plagues were now present: God's existence, His Providence, and the all-powerful Creator. This finally convinced Paro. He released the Jewish people from their slavery and even requested that they pray for his salvation (See *ibid.*, 12:32).

This Divine plan was not only directed toward Paro and the Egyptians and not only at the world's inhabitants-at-large. The primary concern of the Almighty was that His people, *Am Yisrael*, learn that He exists, is all-powerful, and could and would change nature in order to help them. They also had to learn that God had a different relationship with them than with any other nation. Until they learned these lessons, they could not achieve any degree of freedom. True, they would physically leave Egypt, but they would remain enslaved.

In order to free the Jewish people, God had to arrange a final meeting that would show *Am Yisrael* all the elements of the Divine lessons directed to the Egyptians. This event was the splitting of the Red Sea.

Am Yisrael, on leaving the grasp of their Egyptian lords, escaped in the general direction of the land of Israel. After a number of days, they encountered the Red Sea, where, on looking back, they espied the remains of the Egyptian army in pursuit of them. They immediately panicked and cried to God, believing that they were soon to be slaughtered. This was a completely illogical conclusion since they numbered around two million people, whereas the Egyptians were, at most, a couple of thousand (in *Shemot* 14:7 we find that Paro managed to gather six hundred chariots, and we may deduce that he also had other soldiers, but the total number must have been in the range that we mentioned). This proves that Israel was still imbued with their slave mentality. On the banks of the sea, they were to shed off this stigma and start to grow into a nation.

"God will fight for you and you will reap the benefits" (*ibid.*, 14:14). This was the lesson of God's existence. "The angel that protected them went behind them and separated them into the camp of Egypt and the camp of Israel, and they remained separated throughout the night" (*ibid.*, 19–20). The midrash stresses that the Egyptians were punished individually and each received his just desserts but no more. "Those that had tortured the Jews were punished and thrown around like straw. Those who had been less cruel were treated like stones, and the best of them like lead" (*Mechilta, B'shalach* 5). This was evidence of the Providence of God. "The water was a wall on the right and the left of the Jewish people" (*Shemot* 14:22). This was completely in contrast to the usual fluid nature of water and was proof that God was capable of controlling nature and was all-powerful. After this tremendous demonstration of the Divine and His powers, the Jews were capable of throwing off their slavery and believing in God—"Israel saw the great hand of God, and they feared God and believed in Him and in Moshe His servant" (*ibid.*, 31). This caused an outpouring of faith that took the form of the song of praise that they sang on the banks of the Red Sea.

The lessons God chose to teach the world were complete and the Jewish People were now ready to receive the Torah and forge a nation, *Am Yisrael*.

Yitro
The Birth of the Nation

It has already been pointed out that drawing close to Sinai without giving the Torah is irrelevant. But the special nature of Har Sinai *was that, by standing on it before the sanctity that God placed there, the Jewish people were elevated.*

(*Hagada Shel Pesach*, p. 83)

There was a great change that came over the Jewish people and the world through receiving the Torah on Har Sinai, *in the desert.*

(*Ma'amrei HaRiyah*, p. 168)

Elated Divinity, that we strive to reach, to be swallowed, to be collected into its light, descends to us, to the world and amongst us. We find it and bask in its glory, we find peace and tranquillity. Sometimes it grasps us, a lightening bolt from on high, a ray of the Divine that is beyond our comprehension. The heavens open and we see God.

(*Orot*, p. 120)

This week's *parsha* contains the most critical and significant event of the whole of the *Book of Shemot*. In this week's *parsha*, we, the Jewish people, received the Ten Commandments on *Har Sinai*. Because of the importance of this event, there is a custom to stand during the verses relating the Ten Commandments, even amongst those who do not have the practice of standing during the rest of the reading of the Torah (See *Hamoadim BeHalachah, R' Zevin,* p. 326).

In light of this, we can see several discrepancies. The Torah assigns many more verses to the preparations leading up to receiving the Ten Commandments than to the actual commandments themselves. Furthermore, it is the custom on the Seder night to sing a famous melody called *"Dayeinu,"* "It would have been enough for us." This song relates all of the many miracles that God performed for us, from the plagues until entering into the land of Israel and building the Holy Temple. Each line says that had God only performed some of the miracles, that would have been enough, and we would be eternally indebted to Him for so doing. How much more do we owe Him praise, thanks, and devotion for performing the multitude of miracles He did.

In this song, we find a very unusual and surprising stanza: "If He had brought us to *Har Sinai* and yet had not given us the Torah, *Dayeinu*, it would have been enough." The obvious objection to this line is that it certainly would not have been enough. We had gone to all that trouble to prepare ourselves and be worthy of receiving the Torah. God Himself had brought all of the plagues on the Egyptians in order to free us from their slavery and, on His command, we had just trekked through the desert for seven weeks, encountering danger in the form of the Egyptian army and the tribe of Amalek on the way. Surely, the purpose of all this was to ensure that we receive the Torah. What would be the rationale behind coming to *Har Sinai* and not receiving the Torah? Yet every year Jews gather together on the first night of Pesach and recite the praise of God—that if He had only brought us to *Har Sinai* but not given us the Torah, that would have been plenty; we would be satisfied. It would be like preparing for an examination and not being examined.

There would seem to be some deeper meaning to the whole event than just the element of receiving the Torah. Indeed, there are two separate concepts connected with this event. One is *"kabalat haTorah,"* receiving the words of Torah in the form of the two stone tablets, "the work of the Lord written by God" (*Shemot* 32:16). The other is *"ma'amad Har Sinai,"* the whole incident of *Har Sinai*. What is the significance of *ma'amad Har Sinai*?

The relevance of *kabalat haTorah* is obvious. The Torah is our book of law and our eternal guidebook of life. Without the Torah, there would be no *Am Yisrael*. But what of the events surrounding *kabalat haTorah*? What of *ma'amad Har Sinai*?

The answer lies in the greater message of the *Book of Shemot*. The book is the recollection of the birth of *Am Yisrael* and is the second chapter in our autobiography, after the *Book of BeReishit*, that dealt with our ancestry. The *Book of Shemot* centers around our birth as a nation. It started when we left Egypt. Indeed, the first person to refer to us using the term *Am*, nation, was Paro. "He said to his nation, 'Notice that the nation of *Bnei Yisrael* is larger and stronger than us'" (*Shemot* 1:9). There is a school of thought that the Jewish people is born out of strife and what defines us is the existence of anti-Semitism. The *Book of Shemot* does not conclude with Egyptian anti-Semitism, however. This was the beginning of the nation, but it is not what defines us as an *Am*.

In order to become a nation, we also had to receive the Torah, our national identity and consensus. This occurred on *Har Sinai* and is called *kabalat haTorah*, but together with this, we were also part of *ma'amad Har Sinai*. This was essential in our birth as a nation. What happened there was that we not only received the Torah, but also met God face to face. He spoke to us, related the first two commandments to us, and through this, we were born as a nation. We do not believe in God because a prophet told us that He exists, but because we met Him and conversed with Him. This was the force that forged us as a nation. We are a nation that has met the Almighty.

In order to be ready for this tremendous event, we had to prepare: "Purify yourselves and wash your clothing. Be prepared for three days from now, because then God will descend onto *Har Sinai* before the whole nation" (*ibid.*, 19:10–11). Meeting God requires thought and preparation and cannot be approached with haste. The preparation may actually take longer than the meeting itself and, therefore, we find that the account of the arrangements surrounding *ma'amad Har Sinai* is lengthier than *kabalat haTorah* itself, in a similar way that one would be pedantic concerning the arrangements surrounding a short meeting with an important government minister. One would spend a longer time and invest more thought in the clothes, words, and atmosphere of the meeting. So, too, did *Am Yisrael* ensure that every detail had been taken care of several days prior to the grand meeting itself.

Upon meeting God, we became a special nation. We needed the Torah in order to guide us in our task in the world. Even without the Torah, this event would have been extremely inspiring and uplifting. We can truly say that it would have been enough.

Had we had *ma'amad Har Sinai* and personally met God as an entire nation, that would have satisfied us. How much more so when that came coupled with *kabalat haTorah*. Often just meeting a great person can have an impact, even if nothing else is achieved. This author remembers going as a young yeshiva student to hear the lectures of Torah giants, even if he was incapable of really understanding the topic or the language. I came out inspired by the personality that I had met, even though the lecture had been over my head. This type of analogy can give us an inkling of the tremendous effect of meeting the Creator and hearing Him proclaim: "I am the Lord your God" (*ibid.*, 20:2).

This meeting with God was so tangible and inspiring that the Torah tells us that "the whole nation saw the voices" (*ibid.*, 15). This is far from being a typographical error; the people really saw the voice of God. Sight is a much more reliable sense than hearing; in order to ensure that one is perceiving the truth, one has to see it for themselves. When the people made a golden calf, during Moshe's time on *Har Sinai* learning the Torah from God, He instructed Moshe to "go down because your people have become corrupt" (*ibid.*, 32:7). Only on reaching the camp and seeing the severity of the situation, did Moshe "throw down the tablets and break them" (*ibid.*, 19). Only when Moshe perceived with his own eyes, did he fully comprehend, even though God had informed him of what they had done.

The new nation that was born at the foot of *Har Sinai* saw God's voice in the most tangible way possible and their senses were elevated. They saw things that are impossible to see in a normal situation. "God made the invisible visible" (*Midrash Shmuel* 9). The nation knew God in a complete and unshakable fashion; they had seen Him and had fully comprehended His commandments. They understood true Divinity and the existence of God through an event that was to forge them as a nation. In so doing, they had overtaken the great Egyptian empire that had tried to wage war on the Lord and had suffered a devastating and embarrassing defeat. The Jews had been lowly slaves in Egypt only weeks before, and yet, in these forty nine days, they had succeeded in reaching the highest level of human achievement. They had met God and He had given them His Torah. *Am Yisrael* was born.

One could object that this has no relevance to us. True, this was the birth of the nation, but we are supposed to be learning about our own history as a nation. We could say: "I was not there and did not meet God, so where does all of this leave me?"

Our sages say that all of the souls of the Jewish people were present at Har Sinai and participated in *ma'amad Har Sinai* (*Shabbat* 146a). We were all there, every single one of us.

That still only has value if one really feels that they were there and spoke personally to God. If not, the meeting between man and God seems to have been a rare and singular event with tremendous theological significance, but no more.

In the coming weeks, we shall see that the meeting between us and our Maker is far from finished. We maintain an ongoing, intimate relationship with Him.

We became a nation when we met God. We remain a nation that has met Him, and we have the opportunity to continue to meet Him.

Mishpatim
Between Man and Man, and Man and God

The most original and pure form of teshuvah *(repentance) is learning civil law. This area rectifies the stumbling of the heart and establishes Divine justice on its strongest basis. It removes any doubt from the soul as it illuminates practical life.*

(*Orot Hateshuva*, Chapter 13, Paragraph 5)

The laws, the laws of God's Torah, distinguish us from every other nation. Holiness acts on us in an internal fashion. Justice and civil law are holy of holies to the Jewish people and they carry God's name. Seeking God through the administration of justice remains a peculiarity of Israel.

(*Orot*, p. 21)

All of the Torah, ethics, mitzvot, *deeds, and study come to clear the path to enable the great love of God to spread, to cover all walks of life in all their boundaries.*

(*Orot Hakodesh*, Volume IV, p. 389)

This week's *parsha* strikes us as a huge anticlimax. Only last week we read how the Jewish people stood on *Har Sinai*, met the Lord face to face, and received the Torah. We would assume that the Torah would continue this lofty account of our history.

Yet, on reviewing this week's *parsha*, we find that it deals with mundane laws of damages and court procedure. Is this all that remains to be learned after the inspiring events of *ma'amad Har Sinai*? Is this the only significance of *ḳabalat haTorah*?

We can also be permitted to ask another question. The *Book of Shemot* is supposed to be the account of our birth as a nation, as *Am Yisrael*. What is the connection with these civil laws? It is true that they are part of the heritage and moral lessons of the Jewish people and our Torah, but what part do they play in our birth?

The obvious answer to the first question is that we are being taught that the Torah cannot remain in the heavens but must come down to earth. "The Torah is not in the heavens" (*Devarim* 30:12). The Torah contains the thunder and lightning that were present when the people received the Torah on Har Sinai, but it does not linger on these supernatural phenomena. The Torah must deal with human events and even with the less pleasant aspects of human existence. Therefore, immediately after the amazing and awesome events on Har Sinai, the Torah presents a list of legal and civil obligations. Yet our second question still remains unanswered.

In last week's *parsha*, we discussed the fact that *Am Yisrael* is a nation that met with God, and we added that we continue to meet with Him. The question is: Where can we meet God today? The answer to this question also supplies us with an answer to the previous question of the relevance of the list of civil law in our *parsha* of this week.

We can meet God in the courtrooms of the *Beit Din* and in the legal process. The legal system of the Torah is so intricate, it would require a Divine legislator to compose it.

More than this, it understands the human psyche so completely. It trains us to deal fairly and decently with every human, no matter what he is accused of or what, indeed, he may be guilty of doing. The Torah here is teaching us that all are created in the image of God (See *Avot* 3:14). We will examine a few examples and investigate the moral consequences.

The *parsha* opens with the injunction concerning the buying and freeing of a Jewish slave. "When you buy a Jewish slave" (*Shemot* 21:2). The sages explain that this refers to a slave who was a thief, who was caught and was unable to repay his theft (See Rashi ad loc.; and *Shemot* 22:2). In such a case, the *Bet Din* have the option to sell him as a slave and use the money gained to pay off his debt. This is the Torah's solution to the problem of theft in society. Instead of putting the offender in prison, where he will be punished but not corrected, he is sent to live with a decent family until he has readjusted.

Far from being a primitive command, this path is the precursor to modern rehabilitation methods.

The thief was thus exposed to a different type of family than he was used to and learned to take his role and responsibility to the rest of society more seriously. In order to guard the slave's rights, guidelines were laid down as to the conduct between master and servant. The master was forbidden to injure the slave. Were he to beat and injure the slave, then the master was forced to free him (*ibid*., 21:26). The desire of the Torah and the Creator was that this unfortunate individual would adjust his ways. He would be positively influenced by the time spent with the family that purchased him. This stage was always intended to be temporary, and the slave was compelled to see it as such. "If the slave says 'I refuse to go free,' then his master must take the slave to the doorpost and pierce his ear, and he will serve him forever" (*ibid*., 5–6). The sages even explained the word "forever" as a temporary one, "until the jubilee year" (*Kiddushin* 21b).

This unusual ceremony of the piercing of the slave's ear was designed to teach us that we are forbidden to remain slaves to man. We must strive to become servants of the Lord. "The ear that heard on *Har Sinai* 'the children of Israel are My servants' (*Vayikra* 25:55) and went and acquired for himself another master, will be pierced" (*Kiddushin* 22b).

The Torah recognizes the state of society and that, occasionally, it is necessary to amend certain cases. These are the exceptions to the rule that we are the servants of God. But extraordinary cases must never become the norm. The hope is also that, in so doing, the Torah will eradicate, as much as possible, such instances of theft.

The *parsha* contains another example of our concern for every person, even the thief. "If one steals a cow or sheep and slaughters or sells it, he must repay five times the worth of the cow and four times the value of the sheep" (*Shemot* 21:37).

The *Gemara* explains the discrepancy between the repayment for the cow and that of the sheep. "The cattle that the thief lead on its own feet, he pays five times its value; whereas the thief carried the sheep on his back and, therefore, he pays only four times the price" (*Babba Kamma* 79b).

Because the thief had to exert extra effort to transport the sheep, the Torah exempts him from extra payment. The Torah recognizes the rights of the thief and respects his effort. Even though he must pay and his crime is inexcusable, his fine is less than in the other cases.

Throughout the verses, we find that the Torah extols us to be responsible not only for our own actions but also for those of the animals and objects in our possession. The Torah finds guilty the owner of the ox that gores another ox or person (See *Shemot* 21:28–32, 35–36). The Torah relates at length the different cases of one put in charge of another's possessions. If an object is damaged under his care, he is liable to the owner (*ibid.*, 22 6–14).

One is not only responsible for damage caused by livestock. The damaged caused by inanimate objects in his care is also one's responsibility. If someone digs a hole and leaves it uncovered, he is responsible for the consequences. Were someone or something to be harmed as a result, he would have to pay damages (*ibid.*, 21:33). Even if he lit a fire in his own courtyard and the flames spread and damaged a neighbour's field, he is responsible (*ibid.*, 22:5).

The Torah teaches us responsibility for our actions and the actions of those around us, living or otherwise.

The examples of Divine logic and justice contained within this week's *parsha* are almost endless and fill the difficult tractates of the order of *Nezikin* in the Oral Law.

All of these laws are placed in the *Book of Shemot* to impress upon us the fact that we are capable of meeting God through the administration of Talmudic justice. The judges are referred to as *Elohim* (See 21:6, and Rashi ad loc.), literally translated as *God*. The judges are messengers of the Lord and are commanded to "pursue justice" (*Devarim* 16:20). In so doing, they provide a sanctuary for God in the world.

The *Gemara* instructs us that whoever wants to be a *Hasid* (a righteous individual) should keep the commandments related to damages and civil law (*Babba Kamma* 30a). The term *hasid* implies not only observance of the laws between man and man, but also those between man and God. The *Gemara* offers a novel approach to the whole subject of civil law. These laws are not only to safeguard society and its members. They are a way of communicating with God, and indeed, one cannot reach a spiritual level without mastering these laws.

God chooses to communicate with us through civil justice. This is the arena of our continuing conversation with Him. It would be inconceivable that halacha would function without this element of Divine revelation. So, too, is it impossible to communicate with God without the essential factor of an adherence to halacha.

The *Book of Shemot* is the book of our national birth. This involves a meeting and communication with God. In light of this, it is perfectly natural that the *parsha* of *Mishpatim* is contained in *Shemot* and not placed elsewhere in the Torah.

The meeting with God has not finished but continues to this day in the process of Divine justice. One who wants to meet God has only to visit the judges, *Elohim*.

Only after meeting God in the court room can we develop a relationship in a more recognizable liturgical form.

In next week's *parsha*, we will find another arena that affords a meeting with God.

Teruma
Make Me a Temple and I Will Dwell Amongst You

The service of God and the knowledge of God that occurs outside of the Temple and seems not to be dependent on the Temple; however, God decreed that through the sanctity of the Temple all acts are elevated beyond limits. Therefore, the Temple is called the House of Prayer, as even prayer that is acceptable anywhere is more acceptable in the Temple and through its sanctity.

(*Ein Iyah, Berachot*, Chapter 1, Note 8)

In the world, the Higher Intelligence, the Divine Power that illuminates the world, is the basis of all miracles.

(*Orot Hakodesh*, Volume 1, p. 232)

Prayer is only complete with the realization that the soul is in a constant state of prayer. She takes flight and seeks her Beloved continuously. During actual prayer, the constant soul prayer is revealed. This is the glory of prayer.

(*Olat Riyah*, Forward, p. 11)

The *Book of Shemot* does not end with our receiving the Torah even though in our system of the Torah as our history the *Book of Shemot* represents the section on our national birth. The nation came into being when we received the Torah. If this is the case, then the *parsha* containing the story of receiving the Torah (that is, *Yitro*), would be a fitting end to the *Book of Shemot*.

The *parsha* of *Yitro*, however, appears only half way through the *Book of Shemot*. We find that the *Book of Shemot* continues well after the *parsha* of *Yitro*.

Last week we explained the relevance of the intricate laws of *Mishpatim* in this system. This week's *parsha* also deals with a subject that seems to be out of place in the book of our birth as *Am Yisrael*.

From this week's *parsha* on to the end of the *Book of Shemot*, the major subject is building the sanctuary in the wilderness. After receiving the Torah, God instructed Moshe to construct a sanctuary. This was to be the precursor to the Temple, which would eventually be built in Jerusalem. Until the Jewish people entered the land of Israel, they were to build a temporary sanctuary. This was made of wood and animal skins and was "collapsible." When the Jewish people trekked through the desert, they carried this sanctuary with them. When they camped, they erected the building, and it was the central point of the camp.

The construction of the sanctuary, called the *Mishkan*, was no simple feat. It required a high level of engineering and practical building skills. The *Mishkan* was filled with ornate vessels used in the Divine service, and these were extremely intricate. The menorah, the candelabra, was to be fashioned out of a single piece of gold. It was forbidden to construct the branches and then, later, attach them onto the body of the menorah. Also, the branches had to be hollow inside. The body and branches were decorated with flowers and cups of different descriptions. The *Gemara* relates that this was so complicated that Moshe was incapable of making such a vessel. Eventually, God Himself had to show him how it was to be done (*Menachot* 29a).

At first sight, it would seem that the account of the *Mishkan* has no relevance to the *Book of Shemot*. It is more pertinent to the *Book of Vayikra*, that is referred to as *Torat Hacohanim*, the *Law of the Priests*. In *Vayikra*, we find the details of the sacrifices and service in the *Mishkan* and temple performed by the *cohanim*.

Why is it that the construction of the *Mishkan* appears in *Shemot*, the book of the birth of *Am Yisrael*?

The answer lies in the singular events that distinguish the Jewish people. We are a nation that met God, and He gave us our national identity. This was initially on *Har Sinai* through the medium of *ma'amad Har Sinai*. This meeting was not a singular event, but is an ongoing relationship with the Lord. We saw, last week, that the relationship and Divine Meeting continues through the civil laws and the judges.

That is the relevance of the *Mishkan* and the *Beit Hamikdash*, the Temple, to the *Book of Shemot*. Apart from the levitical side of the temple, the *Mishkan* served as a forum where we could continue the eternal meeting with the Almighty.

When God commanded the Jewish people to build the *Mishkan*, He said: "Build Me a sanctuary and I will dwell amongst them" (*Shemot* 25:8). The simple translation of this verse is that God will dwell in the sanctuaries that we build. The midrash translates the verse slightly differently: "I will come down and dwell amongst you" (*Tanchuma, Naso* 19). The midrash explains the term "amongst them" as referring not to the sanctuaries but to the people themselves.

If *Am Yisrael* builds a sanctuary for God on earth, then they are promised that God will descend and live amongst them. Not only will He dwell in the Temple but, through the Temple, He will dwell amongst *Am Yisrael* themselves.

Our continued meeting with the Lord continued through the channel of the *Mishkan*. The daily service in the *Mishkan* was a constant process of Divine Revelation. Indeed, the mishnah relates that there were ten miracles that always occurred in the temple, from the lack of flies to the absence of rain that threatened to extinguish the altar fires (See *Avot* 5:5). These miracles were not confined to the temple itself, but spread to the whole of Jerusalem. "No one ever lacked a place to stay in Yerushalayim" (*ibid.*).

A miracle is, in essence, a means of Divine Revelation. The mishnah tells us that the temple itself acted as a source of Divine Revelation and a way of meeting the Creator. This meeting was less tangible than *ma'amad Har Sinai*, the revelation on Sinai, but the advantage was that it was constant. These miracles were always present in the Temple and were easily observed by the nation.

This is all well and good, but this manner of Divine encounter has also passed from the world. We have no temple and no miracles, no sanctuary and no *Mishkan*. Where can one seek this kind of deep connection with the Creator today?

The *Gemara* tells us that our daily prayers act as a substitute for the daily sacrifices and service in the *Beit Hamikdash* (See *Berachot* 26b). The prayers are our daily opportunity to meet and converse with God. The sages told us that one should turn physically and mentally toward Jerusalem and the site of the Temple during these prayers (*ibid.*, 30a). If one is incapable of physically turning toward the Temple, "one should direct his heart toward the Holy of Holies" (*ibid.*, 28b). The *Mishnah Berura* explains this instruction in the following way: "One should imagine in his heart that he is standing in the Temple within the Holy of Holies" (*Orach Chayim* 94:1, Note 2).

A person should pray with the intention that, during his prayers, he is actually present in the Temple, in the holiest of all places. Such prayer will certainly serve as a forum to meet God. Prayer should not become a rote repetition of words, but a meaningful dialogue with the Creator.

The Rebbe of Kotzk said of the verse "make Me a sanctuary and I will dwell amongst them": "If you build sanctuaries within yourselves, then I will dwell in them."

If we succeed in transporting ourselves, through our prayers, to the innermost sanctuaries and meeting God, then He will come and fill those holy places and dwell amongst us. Then we will fill our lives with spirituality and meet God every single day.

Tetzaveh
The Cohen's Clothes

*The soul is filled with letters imbued with the light of life, with
knowledge and will. From these living letters, every level of life is filled
with light. When one comes to perform a mitzvah, it is saturated with
the lustre of life of all the worlds; it is filled with great and powerful
letters. The light of the Living God resides in all its glory in each
mitzvah. When we come to perform a mitzvah, all the living letters
that are within us increase; we become strengthened through the
Divine light and the Torah.*

*Justice, the central pillar upon which the entire structure [of the
Torah] rests, is the essential essence of life, "the justice of the children
of Israel." It is the essential desire that resides in the soul of the
Messiah, that he will reveal the light of justice, the light that prevents
all wars and bloodshed. The justice of the Jewish people was on the
heart of Aharon, the essence of the spiritual letters of all the children of
Israel, that were illuminated in the* Urim *and* Tumim.

(*Orot*, p. 11–12)

*Man is greater than the animals due to his clothing. The honor that is
drawn from his clothing pushes Man to recognize his intellectual
greatness. Therefore, one should treat clothing with respect.*

(*Ein Iyah*, *Berachot*, Chapter 9, Note 258)

As part of the commandments surrounding the construction of the *Mishkan*, the sanctuary, this week's *parsha* deals not with the building itself but with the contents. The tribe of Levi were assigned the task of daily service in the *Mishkan*, and later in the *Beit Hamikdash*, the permanent Temple in Jerusalem. The tribe of Levi were divided into two groups, the Leviim and the *cohanim*. The Leviim were assigned the task of singing the songs of exaltation surrounding the sacrifices. The *cohanim* performed the service centered around the sacrifices themselves.

The work of the tribe of Levi is described in detail in the *Book of Vayikra*, otherwise known as *Torat Hacohanim*, the *Book of the Priests*.

This week the Torah relates details of the clothing that the *cohanim* had to wear. As part of the program of constructing the *Mishkan*, the House of God, Moshe also gathered materials and manpower to produce these intricate clothes.

These clothes were essential for the service in the *Mishkan* and, later, in the *Beit Hamikdash*, the Temple. The *Gemara* states "were (a *cohen*) to serve without one of the priestly clothes, his service is invalid" (*Zevachim* 17b). Even more, "so long as they wear these clothes, their priesthood is upon them; but without those clothes, their priesthood is not upon them" (*ibid.*).

The clothes were more than just a uniform or a convenience; they were an intrinsic part of the service itself. Indeed, the *cohanim* were ordained into this task through the clothes. On the verse "Draw your brother Aharon and his family near, from amongst the children of Israel to be *cohanim* to Me" (*Shemot* 28:3), Rashi says: "You will sanctify him and make him a *cohen* through the clothes" (ad loc.). The clothes were the symbol which designated the *cohen* as a fully serving member of his tribe. Without them, he could not function as a *cohen*, and definitely not as *Cohen Gadol*, high priest.

Clothes very much make the man. The Torah takes the subject of clothing very seriously; we find constant reminders to respect clothing and not trivialize its importance or worth.

"Every Torah scholar who wears stained clothing is punishable by the death penalty" (*Shabbat* 114a). This is because "the clothes of a person are his pride and glory" (*Shemot Rabba* 18:5). The Torah scholar represents the Torah; it is unsuitable for him to sully and dishonor the Torah by wearing dirty clothes.

On the other hand, "anyone who wears the cloak of a Torah scholar and yet is not a Torah scholar himself, is prevented from entering the domain of God" (*Babba Batra* 98a). It is not enough to just wear the clothes and assume that they will cause immediate change. Clothing is a representation of inner feeling and is a very good indication of a person's thoughts. Only a true *talmid chacham* can wear the clothing associated with this status. Anyone impersonating a Torah scholar is not only incapable of truly representing the Torah but also breaks his own link with the Giver of the Torah.

In the writings of the Gaon of Vilna and others, it is said that clothes are a symbol of one's character traits. When the Torah refers to clothing (specifically, in the *Book of Mishlei,* "Proverbs") the intention is to focus on *midot,* qualities of character (See the explanation of the Gra on *Mishlei* 6:27, et al.).

All this is very interesting and explains, to some degree, why the Torah puts such emphasis on the *cohen*'s clothes. What of the connection with the rest of the *Book of Shemot,* what of the meeting with God? Can we find an opportunity to meet the Creator through the medium of the priestly clothes?

There are many Divine Revelations associated with the garments of the *cohen.* It is pertinent to examine just one significant example.

One of the items worn only by the *Cohen Gadol* was the *choshen,* the breastplate. This was composed of a gold breastplate with twelve gems embedded in it. These gems were inscribed with the names of the tribes of *Bnei Yisrael,* one jewel per tribe. The whole *choshen,* therefore, was comprised of stones inscribed with letters. This *choshen* was tied to the chest of the *Cohen Gadol* using strands of *techelet,* the blue thread used in *tzitzit.*

The amazing thing about this *choshen* was that when *Am Yisrael* had a question of deep national importance, they would ask the breastplate to guide them. The answer would appear in a miraculous way through the letters inscribed on the gems of the *choshen.* Certain letters would light up and these composed the answer to the question posed. This cosmic computer was called the *Urim* and *Tumim.*

The task of the *cohen* was to interpret the answer. Since the letters appeared in no specific order or sequence, they could be read in a number of ways; it was up to the *cohen* to decipher the genuine meaning. Even though this may appear to be simple, it was no mean feat, and we find that there were occasions in history when the system failed, as a result of the interpretation of the *cohen.*

During the time that the *Mishkan* was in Shilo, the *Cohen Gadol,* Eli, once saw a woman enter the Temple and pray. Instead of praying out loud, she simply mouthed the words and no sound was heard. Eli suspected that something was up and asked an explanation from the *Urim* and *Tumim.* The letters ה, כ, ר and ש appeared. Eli read them as the word *shicorah,* drunken woman, and accused the woman of coming to the Temple drunk. "How long do you intend to be drunk?" (*Shmuel* I 1:14). However, this was a mistaken interpretation and should have been read as *kashera,* meaning that the woman was pure and her intentions were honorable. Her name was Chanah and her prayers were directed to God to grant her a child. Eventually, those prayers were answered and her son was Shmuel, who was to anoint Shaul the first king of Israel and herald a new era in Jewish history.

Another occasion was during the period of the *shoftim*, the judges. The nation wanted to punish the tribe of Binyamin for despicable crimes. They congregated in Shilo, the site of the Temple, for this purpose and inquired of the *Urim* and *Tumim* as to what action they should take. "Who should be the first in battle against Binyamin?" they asked. To which the reply came back: "Yehuda should go first" (*Shoftim* 20:18). However, when Yehuda went into battle, they were severely beaten. Eventually, the people realized that they had asked the wrong question. Only when they asked "Should we continue to war against our brothers Binyamin or should we stop fighting?" (*ibid.*, 28) and received a positive answer were they successful in battle.

Not only must the interpretation be exact, but the question, the input, has to be precise and poised in the proper spirit of solemnity.

The *Urim* and *Tumim* could not work without being attached to the chest of the *cohen*. It was impossible to receive an answer unless they were worn by the *cohen*. Therefore, it was essential that the *cohen* and the *choshen* be bound together. This *choshen* offered an ideal opportunity to meet God and was part of the grand meeting between us and our Maker that is described in the *Book of Shemot*.

The *choshen* was attached to the *cohen* by strands of *techelet*. We have already seen that the *techelet* is a symbol of the link between heaven and earth. Nowhere do we have a greater example of this link than in the *Urim* and *Tumim* and its attachment to the *cohen*. It was, therefore, appropriate that they should be bound together by the *techelet* in order to show that, together, they were a living link between us and God, between heaven and earth.

In the same way that God chose to reveal Himself to *Am Yisrael* during *ma'amad Sinai*, so, too, did He reveal Himself through the preservation of halacha and Divine justice.

The conversation between the Creator and His subjects continued in the *Beit Hamikdash* and in the clothes of the *Cohen Gadol*. Each era benefits from this communication in a manner that perfectly befits the time and circumstances, once through prophecy, later through Divine service in the *Beit Hamikdash* and through the *cohanim*. At another stage, the arena for interaction was the dynamic of halacha, the *Beit Hamidrash*, the study house, and the *Beit Din*, the law courts.

Each generation has their particular form of dialogue.

The eternal meeting between *Am Yisrael* and God continues and must continue.

Ki Tisah
The Golden Calf—
Apparent Regression

*Good will and the desire to draw near to God are commendable, but
what can pure will achieve? Therefore, as long as the will does not soar
to the heights of Divine knowledge, it is incapable of having a
successful expression in life. If this will is denied contact with the
higher light, it tends toward an impure source that is vulnerable to the
venom of the snake (the evil inclination), even though it is full of good
intentions and sparks of sanctity. From the greatest heights it is liable to
plunge to the deepest depths.*

(*Orot*, p. 36)

*The desire to draw closer to God occasionally, in itself, leads to
idolatry, but the person immediately feels that they have veered off the
true path.*

(*Ma'amrei HaRiyah*, p. 492)

*During the Second Temple period the sages noted the strength of the
inclination toward idolatry, and they purged that inclination. The
natural desire for spirituality was curtailed and weakened.*

(*ibid.*)

This week's *parsha* focuses on the ultimate sin of the Jewish people. This
refers to the *Chet Haegel*, the sin of the Golden Calf. Rashi explains that
every single calamity that has befallen *Am Yisrael* is, in some way, punishment

for the sin of the Golden Calf (Rashi on *Shemot* 32:34). It was not just another terrible sin, but the worst possible crime. It was a rejection of God and of Moshe. "The people saw that Moshe tarried in descending from the mountain. They congregated around Aharon and said to him: 'Make us a god that will lead us, as we have no idea what has happened to this man Moshe, who took us out of Egypt'" (*Shemot* 32:1) .They demanded that Aharon "make a divinity" that would be a leader and guide for the people. This was a rejection of the Divine leadership that they had received up to this moment. The reason they gave was that Moshe had disappeared without a trace. They did not possess the patience to wait for him to return from his sojourn on the mountain in conversation with the Lord. They rejected both God and His servant Moshe.

How is it possible that an entire nation that had met God face to face on *Har Sinai* were capable of idol-worship? Not only did they bow down to the idol that they had made, but this whole episode occurred a mere forty days after the events on *Har Sinai*. How was it possible that *Am Yisrael* fell from the highest possible spiritual heights to an idolatrous low in less than two months?

The question is compounded by examining another section of the *Tanach*. In the latter days of King Shlomo's reign, Yerovam revolted against the monarchy and the king's son, Rechavam. After the death of Shlomo, he established a separate kingdom in Sh'chem. The only problem with this was that he knew the people would persist in visiting the Temple during the holidays. If they continued their pilgrimage, then he, Yerovam, had lost his exclusive hold over the people, and they would still be linked emotionally to the *Beit Hamikdash* and the kingdom of Rechavam. In order to resolve this, he set up two golden calves on the way to Yerushalayim, one in Beit-El and one in the area of the tribe of Dan. "He (Yerovam) said to them (his citizens): 'you no longer need to go up to Yerushalayim. Here is your god, Israel, that brought you out of Egypt'" (*Melachim* I 12:28). This is a rather extraordinary statement in itself, yet it is even more unusual in context of the history of the original Golden Calf.

When the Golden Calf was formed in this week's *parsha* the people said "This is your god that brought you out of Egypt" (*Shemot* 32:4). In light of this, Yerovam's actions seem to be insane. He built a Golden Calf using a formula similar to the one used by his, and his audience's, predecessors. Yet the results of the original Golden Calf must have been well known to all present. The Golden Calf was the source of all strife and misery. Surely, there must have been more appropriate models for Yerovam to imitate than the Golden Calf. Yet he built a Golden Calf and assured his subjects that this was the god that had saved them in the past, the implication being that the same god would save them in the future.

We, therefore, see that the sin of Yerovam and the *Chet Haegel* are strongly linked together. If we are able to understand the intentions and the motives behind one of them, they would give us an insight into the meaning of the other.

In the *Kuzari*, Rabbi Yehuda Halevi explains the events of the Golden Calf in the following way: "The nation never intended or imagined that this action was against the desire of the Creator. On the contrary, it emanated from a strong desire to worship God. They, therefore, came to Aharon with their request. Aharon wanted to reveal their inner desire and, therefore, helped them" (*Sefer Kuzari* 1:97).

The motive behind the Calf was the wish to serve God. After Moshe disappeared from the sight of the nation, they sought a replacement, an expression for their religious fervor. The Golden Calf was not, then, a simple case of idol worship in which the individual forms an idol and believes in the power of his handiwork. The idol worshipper believes that his success, or lack of it, is dependent on the idol that he has formed. Therefore, he is careful to appease the god in order that it will fulfill his requests and desires. The Golden Calf was completely different. The nation never believed that this statue had intrinsic powers of its own. They still believed in God and wanted to serve Him to the best of their abilities. They did seek, however, a go-between, a physical representation of God. For this purpose, they built the Golden Calf. It was to act as an intermediary between *Am Yisrael* and their Maker.

They did not reject God, far from it. The building of the Calf emanated from their desire to serve God and enhance their spirituality. They did not even reject Moshe, as such. They felt that they had passed the stage of human leadership and were entering a new stage in which they would be lead directly by a deity. They had "matured" from the leadership of "this man, Moshe" (*Shemot* 32:1). From now on, they sought divine guidance, be it from God the Almighty, or alternatively, a physical, "divine" intermediary.

That is not to say that the people did not sin and were not liable for their crime. However, it does mean that their transgression was less severe than it initially appeared. "The people sinned in that they made a physical likeness of God, something that was forbidden. They assigned some sort of divinity to their handiwork" (*Sefer Kuzari, ibid.*). This is not in anyway a simple sin since it transgresses one of the Ten Commandments. However, it is much less severe than it originally seemed and was not idolatry in the classical sense.

So we have learned that the Golden Calf was a sin, but one that had its roots firmly planted in spirituality and a desire to attain greater spiritual competence. This sheds light on Yerovam's actions. Yerovam specifically reminded the nation of the past Golden Calf and awakened within them that same motive. He pushed them once more to strive to draw closer to God. He tried to assure them that this time they would reach a different conclusion. He would direct their religious fervor toward God and not away from Him. This, Yerovam claimed, was more important than physically ascending to the *Beit Hamikdash* in Jerusalem.

Yerovam also sinned. Religious fervor is a good thing, but unless it is directed in the right way, it can lead an entire generation astray. The only legitimate way of expressing such desire is through the Temple and service therein. Only the Torah contains the instructions that enable us to attain true religious experience. Through halachic methods alone can we hope to meet God. Any deviation from this path is a sin that can distance us from God instead of drawing us closer to Him.

That was the sin of the *Chet Haegel*, and Yerovam himself fell into the same trap. Moshe alone had the ability to return the people to true Divine service. It was he who constructed the *Mishkan* that was designed for this purpose.

Indeed, the original Golden Calf was born out of the Divine meeting, amazing though this may sound. The people were so enthused with *ma'amad Har Sinai* that they felt a need to continue the meeting. In this, they were correct. Yet they were misguided into believing that this could occur through a medium other than God.

It is very hard for us to comprehend the rationale behind idol worship. How is it that seemingly great, intelligent people could have worshipped idols fashioned by their own hands? The *Gemara* supplies something of an answer. It relates that, on one occasion, Rav Ashi announced to his students that, on the next day, they would learn about "Menashe, our friend." Menashe was the most deviant of kings. It is recorded of him: "Menashe also spilled innocent blood until he had filled Yerushalayim from wall to wall, apart from the fact that he caused Yehudah to sin and do evil in God's eyes" (*Melachim* II 21:16). He was guilty of murder, idol worship, and leading the people astray. Rav Ashi, therefore, had no qualms about referring to him as "our friend" in a cynical way.

Menashe however, was far from pleased. "Menashe appeared to him in a dream. 'You call me your friend. If you are so clever, tell me, where does one cut the bread after making the blessing *'hamotzi lechem min ha'aretz?'* ["who brings forth bread from the ground," the blessing on bread.] Rav Ashi was forced to reply that he did not know. 'You do not even know the answer to such a simple question and yet you dare to call me your friend!' Rav Ashi was confused. 'If you are so clever, how come you worshipped idolatry?' Rav Ashi asked. Menashe replied in the dream: 'If you had been there, you would have picked up your coattails and run after idols.' On the morrow, Rav Ashi had learned his lesson and had a different attitude to Menashe. 'Let us learn about our teacher, Menashe.'" (*Sanhedrin* 102b).

The *Gemara* teaches us an important lesson with regard to the psychological circumstances surrounding idolatry. In a particular generation, it was common practice to worship idols—so much so, that even great people like Rav Ashi or Menashe would be drawn to such customs. We can explain this in the same way as *The Kuzari*. A generation that is close to God is also susceptible to idolatry. The wind of spirituality blows through the nation; either it is directed to the service of God or elsewhere.

Meeting God is not so simple and must be done through exact and specific methods. As long as the meeting continues, we must be aware of these guidelines and adhere to them. If we do not, then the result could well be that, instead of serving God, we will end up serving a Golden Calf.

Vayakhel
The Foundation of the *Mishkan*

It is impossible to assess and define the essence of Am Yisrael *on an ordinary scale. It contains everything within it and all is founded on her devotion to God.*

(*Orot*, p. 138)

The light of God is Knesset Yisrael (*the congregation of Israel*), *the Jewish ideal that dwells within the nation. It is this that forms her into one nation throughout her generations.*

(*ibid.*, p. 140)

The fusion of Knesset Yisrael *and God is through the identification of the will of the nation that appears in the national soul, with the will of God for all of existence. As these two become more and more similar, so the fusion is enhanced.*

(*ibid.*, p. 141)

This week's *parsha* deals with the actual construction of the *Mishkan*, the sanctuary. After several weeks dealing with the specific details of the plans for the sanctuary and the vessels within it, the nation gathered the materials and started the process of construction.

Moshe appointed a man by the name of Betzalel to be in charge of the whole project. Moshe oversaw the work and made sure that it continued according to plan and copied exactly the will of the Creator.

The scene must have been very exciting as the whole of *Am Yisrael* was enrolled in this task. It was at the center of the camp and became the focus of the entire nation's attention. So much so, that God had to remind them that, even though they were performing a mitzvah in constructing the *Mishkan*, they were not to neglect other important commandments; *Shabbat*, for example. The midrash explains that the *parsha* opens with Moshe reminding the people of the mitzvah of *Shabbat* for this purpose. They should not make the mistake of assuming that the building of the *Mishkan* was so important that it took precedent over *Shabbat* and other *mitzvot* (*Mechilta, Vayakhel* 1).

Such was the spirit of the people that all other activity was postponed. The construction of the *Mishkan* was seen as being of utmost importance.

Within the description of the *Mishkan*, we learn that the sides were constructed of wooden planks. These planks were joined together and made up the walls of the sanctuary. In order that the entire wall not collapse, the planks were inserted into silver blocks called *adanim*.

These *adanim* were forged from the half-shekel pieces that *Am Yisrael* gave to Moshe as part of the census that God commanded him to count. "When you count *Am Yisrael*, each person will give a ransom to God, and no plague will come upon them through this census" (*Shemot* 30:12). It is forbidden to count the Jewish people in the ordinary way. If one were to count them one by one, then a calamity would befall them. Instead, they were to each give a half-shekel coin. These were then collected. Moshe counted the coins and thus discovered the number of *Am Yisrael*. After the census was complete, the coins were gathered, melted down, and forged to make the *adanim* that supported the walls of the *Mishkan*.

King David ignored this warning with disastrous results. David was determined to count the people against the advice of his closest advisor, Yoav, the Chief of Staff. After performing the census, David realized that he had sinned, and he repented. God sent the prophet Gad to tell him that he was to be punished. In a rather unusual passage, the prophet gives David the option of choosing one of three punishments that he would suffer as a result of his sin. He could choose either seven years of famine, defeat in battle for three months, or three days of pestilence in the land. David chose the last option and this was duly sent from heaven as a punishment. During the plague, 77,000 people died. Finally, God Himself stopped the plague before the results were even more devastating (See *Shmuel* II 24).

What was so terrible about counting *Am Yisrael* that it could bring such horrific results?

The reason that a leader would want to count his people was in order to learn how much force he controlled. This was usually connected with military strength. Battles were fought and won on the basis of numerical might.

The larger the army, the greater the chances of winning in battle and, therefore, the more power it held.

The Torah teaches us that the Jewish people are different. Our strength is not in numbers. "God did not feel affection for you and choose you due to your great numbers. In fact, you are the smallest of nations" (*Devarim* 7:7). We did not attain our status as the people of God because we were the strongest and largest nation. That is not our strong point and numbers are irrelevant to us. Why then did God choose us?

"You are a holy people. God chose you to be His chosen people from all of the world's nations through His love for you and because of His covenant that He swore to your forefathers. You must surely know that God is a faithful God, who keeps His covenant and is merciful to those that keep His commandments for a thousand generations" (*ibid.*, 6, 8–9).

God chose us to be His special holy nation since we are the continuation of the covenant that God made with Avraham, Yitzchak, and Ya'akov. The rest is unimportant. Even though we are an infinitesimal nation numerically, our importance in the arena of world history far outweighs our numbers.

We cannot count *Am Yisrael*. It is impossible to give such a concept a numerical value. The only way that we can comprehend their numbers is by collecting half-shekel coins and counting them.

The coins went to support the *Mishkan* and formed the foundation of the Temple, the House of God. That is the true strength of *Am Yisrael*. We are the foundations of the House of God in this world. Through our existence, God has a house and a place to dwell in the physical world. Such is our strength and our task in the world. "Build Me a sanctuary and I will dwell amongst them" (*Shemot* 25:8). This can be understood as referring not only to the actual *Beit Hamikdash* or *Mishkan*, but also to the Temple of our nationhood. God dwells within *Am Yisrael*. This fact cannot be relegated to number and figures. It is forbidden to count the Jewish people.

We have learnt that the *Book of Shemot* is in essence the book of the birth of Israel. This birth is through a continuous process of meeting God. This occurred on *Har Sinai*, through the halacha, and in the Temple. Here we have discovered the ultimate way of meeting God. If we look at *Am Yisrael*, we are, in fact, viewing God Himself.

"God, the Torah, and Yisrael are all one entity," states the *Zohar* (*Acharei Mot* 73a). We are indivisible from our Maker and must be viewed in conjunction with Him.

When we encounter *Am Yisrael*, we meet God. We are His chosen people, and we are the foundation of His earthly existence. The Temple is built on us. We are the house of God.

P'Kudei
Moshe's Sanctuary

*Moshe, our teacher, had lofty ideals within his own life and a
perfection that was distinct from the Jewish people. He was, therefore,
capable of establishing an entire nation like Israel. Due to his great
love of the Jewish people, he agreed that all his perfection would be
channeled toward improving the nation, and he did not seek any glory
for himself except that of the glory of the nation of Israel.*

(*Ein Iyah, Berachot*, Chapter 5, Note 60)

*There is a very high state, that of Moshe, the true and trustworthy
shepherd, whose heart and mind were only concerned with his human
flock.*

(*Orot Hakodesh*, Volume III, p. 202)

*Like the intensity of the Sun's rays, the abundance of light shines on us.
We find within us light and life of a whole world, essentially Moshe,
who was directed to the light of the world, the light of life, and the
Torah of life, the love of kindness, and the building of worlds.*

(*Olat Riyah*, Volume II, p. 159)

The *Book of Shemot* is drawing to a close. In this, the last *parsha* of the
book, we find an account of the dedication of the *Mishkan*, the Sanctuary. It is quite logical that this account should appear here, as the end of the
Book of Shemot is concerned with the construction of the *Mishkan*.

Throughout our studies of these *parshiot*, we have stressed their relevance
to the rest of the *Book of Shemot*. It will be recalled that in the system of the

autobiography of *Am Yisrael*, the *Book of Shemot* represents the section relating the birth of the Jewish people. Our birth was achieved through the special acts of meeting God that we merited, not once, but in a continuous and
permanent way. We met God face to face during *ma'amad Har Sinai* and continue to meet Him to the present day through a variety of medium.

We do not believe that religious experience is a once in a lifetime occurrence. In our system, it is a way of life. Our whole life is a process of Divine
revelation and "religious experience." King Shlomo instructs us to "know
Him in all your endeavors" (*Mishlei* 3:6). It is not enough to meet God only in
the synagogue or through religious ritual; one must strive to inject Divinity
into his everyday life. God exists as much in the law courts as He does in the
Temple. History is as much a process of Divine revelation and Providence as
is prayer and liturgical practice.

And so we arrive at the last *parsha* of the book. Within it, we find an account of the dedication of the *Mishkan*. At the conclusion of the construction
of the edifice that was to be the House of God, the Temple was to be sanctified. In order for the building to function in the role of sanctuary, it had to be
dedicated. The vessels and the Cohanim were anointed and prepared for the
Divine service.

Most interestingly, the account of the dedication of the *Mishkan* appears
three separate times in the Torah. Once here, again in the *Book of Vayikra*,
and yet again in the *Book of Bemidbar*. Obviously, the Torah does not contain
unnecessary repetition, so each account must have a reason. The Torah shows
us the different facets of the *Mishkan* and the *Beit Hamikdash*. Each time the
Torah repeats the story of the dedication of the *Mishkan*, it is in order to teach
us a different aspect of the Temple service.

We shall deal with each one as we come to it in the course of the *parshiot*.
Here we have to understand the relevance of the account of the dedication of
the *Mishkan* to the *Book of Shemot*.

As we have stated several times, the *Beit Hamikdash* afforded a continuation of the Divine Meeting between God and His people. This is the essence of the whole *Book of Shemot*. The book concludes, therefore, with the
account of the dedication and the beginning of the active service of the
Mishkan.

The Temple was the ideal medium through which *Am Yisrael* would continue to meet God face to face throughout history. Indeed, we have the mitzvah
of *Aliya Leregel*, a pilgrimage to the Temple three times a year during the three
"foot festivals" of Pesach, Shavuot, and Succot. The mitzvah requires that the
whole family and the entire Jewish people make a trip to Jerusalem in order

to "see and be seen" by the Almighty (See *Chagiga* 2a; and Rashi ad loc., "everyone is obliged in the mitzvah of seeing").

The festival took on a completely different connotation in the time of the *Beit Hamikdash* than it does today. It was the time to go and meet God, and all went. "Men, women, children, even the stranger in your midst" (*Devarim* 31:12). The *Gemara* asks for what purpose did the children come? After all, they were incapable of truly comprehending the greatness of the occasion. The answer is given: "to give a reward to those that brought them," that is, their parents (*Chagiga* 3a). One of the commentators on the *Gemara* explains that the purpose of bringing the small children was in order to enthuse them with the whole event. The hope was that they would be so in awe that they would be inspired to worship throughout their adult lives (See *Maharasha, Chiddushei Aggadot*, ad loc.).

It must have been an awe inspiring occasion to witness all of *Am Yisrael* arrive in the Temple in order to see and be seen.

When they arrived in the Temple, the *Gemara* relates what they saw. "They would roll back the curtain that separated the Holy of Holies from the rest of the Temple. They would be shown the *ceruvim* (cherubs) that were above the Ark. The *ceruvim* were hugging each other. They saw that they were loved by God, like the love of a man and a woman" (*Yoma* 54a). The *ceruvim* were formed in the image of children; one, male, and the other, female. They were placed above the *aron habrit*, the Ark of the Covenant, that contained the two tablets that Moshe received on *Har Sinai*. The *ceruvim* embraced each other like man and wife. This was an expression of God's love for His people; one of the *ceruvim* represented *Am Yisrael*; the other, God Himself. The embrace signified the close relationship between the nation and God. When *Am Yisrael* came to Yerushalayim three times a year, they came to see God. They witnessed the embrace of the *ceruvim* and saw their favor in God's eyes.

This is the side of the *Beit Hamikdash* that the Torah stresses in the *Book of Shemot*. In the story of the birth of the Jewish people that is the *Book of Shemot*, the most dominant character is Moshe. He toiled constantly on our behalf and compelled us to be born. He facilitated the meeting with God by bringing us out of Egypt. He prepared us, prior to seeing God on *Har Sinai*, and related to us the contents of the Torah. It was Moshe who initiated the construction of the *Mishkan* and appointed the team that was to build it.

It is highly appropriate, then, that in this week's *parsha*, the person chosen to erect the *Mishkan* was Moshe. It was his "baby," not only in the physical sense, but also in that it enabled the eternal meeting between *Am Yisrael* and God to continue. And continue it would, long after the death of Moshe, similar to a child outliving its parents and midwife. "God said to Moshe: 'On the first day of the first month, you will erect the *Mishkan*'" (*Shemot* 40:12).

Even more significant is the fact that Moshe and his descendants were not *cohanim*. However, during the initial week of dedication of the *Mishkan*, Aharon and his sons were not yet sanctified to act as *cohanim*. This presented a problem, as the service in the *Mishkan* required a *cohen*. The *Gemara* solves the predicament by stating that during that first week Moshe acted as the *Cohen Gadol* (See *Zevachim* 101b, and Rashi on *Vayikra* 8:28). This was the ultimate accolade that God awarded Moshe. The *Book of Shemot* concludes with him serving in "his" sanctuary as the *Cohen Gadol*, albeit only for one week.

With this, the *Book of Shemot* closes. The meeting with God was established as a habitual occurrence. This was Moshe's great achievement, and he saw it through from the early stages until its conclusion. He took a group of slaves who were not even certain that they wanted to leave Egypt and achieve freedom. He organized them, freed them, and, several weeks later, brought them to a sufficient spiritual level so that they could meet God face to face. But this solitary encounter was not enough, and his mission was not complete until he established the possibility of meeting God in the spirit of the people. He brought them the halacha that enabled further interaction between *Am Yisrael* and their Maker. Finally, he built and erected the *Mishkan*, the forerunner of the *Beit Hamikdash*, that was to be the most vibrant source of union between People and Deity.

Moshe facilitated the birth of the Jewish people. The nation was now ready to realize its role in the world as a messenger of God's word to humanity.

With this *Shemot* ends and *Vayikra* begins.

III

Vayikra

Introduction

Am Yisrael are the cohanim *of God in this world.*

(*Ein Iyah, Berachot,* Chapter 1, Note 1)

There are those who mistakenly think that peace can only be achieved by everyone having the same idea. When they see Torah scholars engaged in differing opinions and arguing about the Torah, they think this causes the opposite of peace. In truth, peace can only be achieved by having a plethora of peace, when every side will have its place according to its value. By amassing all of the different opinions, even those ideas that seem to contradict each other, the light of truth and justice will become clear.

(*Olat Riyah,* Volume I, p. 330)

It is a very bad sign for a party or a specific group to think that it has a monopoly on the source of life, on all wisdom and justice, and to see any other opinion as meaningless and insignificant.

(*Igrot HaRiyah,* Volume I, Letter 18)

*V*ayikra, the third book of the Torah, deals with the task of *Am Yisrael* in the world. The book is referred to as *Torat Hacohanim, The Laws of the Cohanim,* the priests. At first glance, it would appear that much of the book has no connection to *Am Yisrael* as a whole. The book opens with a description of the service in the *Beit Hamikdash,* the Temple. It deals with ritual purity and impurity and how the *cohen* was to treat this condition. Within it we find a description of sanctity, *kedusha,* that seems to be the domain of the *cohanim.*

How does all of this material relate to the task of *Am Yisrael?* God implores us to be "a kingdom of priests and a holy nation" (*Shemot* 19:6). The entire nation were to be priests; we are all *cohanim*. Whatever task was assigned to the *cohanim* within the framework of the Jewish people was relevant to the whole nation in the world arena. In the same way that the *cohanim* were to elevate the Jewish people, so we, as a nation, were to advance the world.

If we ascertain the role and task of the *cohanim*, we will find our task as *Am Yisrael*. Such is the book of *Vayikra*, *The Laws of the Cohanim*, a guide to the entire nation.

The first role that was assigned to the *cohanim* was to enhance world peace. This was a different type of peace than we might assume. Indeed, *shalom* is not a state of abstention from conflict but a matter of improving the lot of every individual and being. Aharon, the *Cohen Gadol*, or high priest, knew how to synthesize seemingly conflicting ideas. He was able to demonstrate that everything had a designated place and purpose. In this manner, he achieved true peace throughout the camp of Israel, and his descendants continued to act in a similar way. This method of achieving *shalom* was to be adopted by the entire nation. The *Book of Vayikra* strives to educate us to follow the example set down by Aharon. We too have to develop the will and capacity to set everything into its correct place.

Another role of the *cohanim* was to be the experts in *tumah* and *taharah*, impurity and purity. This required that they discern how to fuse each individual with his Maker. After all, impurity is not a physical affliction but a symptom of a problem in the connection between man and God. The *cohanim* were both "our messengers and the messengers of God" (*Nedarim* 35b). They were chosen to intermediate between the Almighty and *Am Yisrael* and to ensure that the two stayed in close contact. When they encountered examples of a weakened connection, it was their jurisdiction to mend the breach. So it is with the entire nation; our task is to connect the world with the Creator and achieve a state of world purity.

We also have to find our place in the Divine world order, God's great plan for humanity. It may seem like a simple task, yet there are many obstacles in our way. Death and other crises tend to suggest a lack of Providence and logical order. Aharon successfully drew order out of the chaos of his sons' untimely demise. In so doing, he achieved the level of *kedusha*, of holiness and sanctity. In Judaism, *kedusha* is not reserved for the rabbis and priests but is the property of the entire nation.

In order to succeed in our task, we must be capable of revealing our true nature, as individuals and as a nation. This is the intention of the *Shabbat* and the *Sh'mittah* (the seventh year) that are discussed at the end of the *Book of Vayikra*.

The *Book of Vayikra* is very much part of our national autobiography and not the sole possession of the *cohanim*. Priesthood is not personal but a national aptitude of the Jewish people. We are a kingdom of priests and a holy nation. To be priestly is our task. We are now in a position to discover the intricacies of this task.

Vayikra
Aharon, the Pursuer of Shalom

*Separate entities organize themselves and the beauty of the collective
starts to appear. Fusion and unity come from combining distinct
elements, and this brings* shalom *in every complete idea. Perfection
comes from fusing the separate parts and fitting them into a cohesive
unit.*

(Rosh Milin, "Vav")

*I am a man of peace and I pursue peace even in places where most
people would assume that it was absent. Such is my character,
especially as I come from the lineage of Aharon, who had a covenant of
peace.*

(Igrot HaRiyah, Volume I, Letter 136)

*Great souls are unable to distance themselves from the entire collective;
they desire the collective good. However, the collective is assembled of
infinite individuals, and the collective is only complete when all of the
component parts are complete, and they all compliment each other.*

(Orot Hakodesh, Volume II, p. 442)

The *parsha* of *Vayikra* deals with the major subject of the whole *Book of
Vayikra*. It discusses the laws surrounding the *cohanim*, priests, in general, and Aharon, the high priest, in particular.

The obvious task of the *cohanim* was to reside in the Temple and serve God.
Yet we find that, in addition to the daily sacrifices, the *cohanim* performed a

more mundane task. "When you have a query concerning a specific case—
be it between (pure) blood or (impure) blood, (guilty) judgment or (innocent)
judgment, or a (pure) leprous mark and an (impure) mark—you should go
up to the place that God has chosen. There you should approach the *cohanim*,
the *Leviim*, or supreme court of the time, and you should present your question. They will tell you the judgment. You must act as you are instructed in
the place that God has chosen. Keep all of his sound advice. Do according to
the Torah, as he instructs you and the judgment that he will tell you. Do not
deviate in any way" (*Devarim* 17:8–11).

The *cohanim*, therefore, had the task of settling disputes that arose amongst
the people. These were in the area of civil law and in the complicated laws
relating to purity and impurity.

Why were the *cohanim* chosen for this arbitratory task? Surely it was more
relevant to the role of the judge. It is true that the judge is mentioned together
with the *cohen* and the levi in the above verse, but there are areas of law that
are the sole responsibility of the *cohanim*.

The answer is that the *cohanim* were the lovers and pursuers of peace.
They were the ideal people, therefore, to make peace within *Am Yisrael*, the
Jewish people. This devotion to peace they acquired from the first priest,
Aharon.

Aharon was Moshe's brother. It was Aharon who was Moshe's mouthpiece
during the discussions and arguments with Paro in Egypt. After leaving
Egypt, Moshe became the leader of the new nation, and Aharon became the
high priest in the *Mishkan*, the Sanctuary.

Aharon is described as being "one who loved peace and pursued peace.
Who loved people and brought them closer to the Torah" (*Avot* 1:12). An
example is given as to how he pursued peace that will serve to shed light on
the true meaning of *shalom*, peace.

"If he heard of two people who were involved in an argument, he went to
each one separately. He said to each of them 'You know that your friend is
truly sorry and regrets what he did. He is also very embarrassed and seeks a
way to apologize. He therefore sent me to you to beg forgiveness.' Thus, when
they subsequently met, they would hug each other" (*Avot DeRabbi Natan* 12).

Aharon employed a rather novel way of ensuring that there would be fewer
arguments amongst the people. He would convince each one separately that
the other regretted the argument and his part in it. In this roundabout way,
the argument was forgotten and they reaffirmed their former friendship.
Indeed, Aharon stressed the point that the sparring partners had initially been
comrades. He refers to the other as "your friend."

Surely it would have been much simpler for Aharon to have gone to one of the disputants and said. "Look, why do you not simply forget your petty argument? Just give him the money and call the whole thing off." He would have achieved the same result, peace in the camp of Israel, and surely, everyone would have been happy. But here we come to the crux of the matter: what is peace?

The word *peace* could be explained as meaning a state of freedom from war. A lack of conflict, a lack of strife—that is peace. On the other hand, the word *shalom* is derived from the root *shalem*, meaning complete. *Shalom* is not a lack of anything at all. The converse is true: in a state of true *shalom* everything exists but appears in the right proportion. In order to achieve *shalom*, all must be present in the correct quantities and in the right place.

We assume that if everyone could be the same, and if we could successfully remove all barriers and borders, then we would reach a state of peace. The Torah has another view of peace. The way to attain it is to set very clear boundaries and define the appropriate place for all. This develops the individual skills and distinct qualities of each person. Together, they make up the whole, the complete picture. This is the Torah's method of achieving peace, *shalom*.

Aharon was an advocate and lover of *shalom*. He did not solve disputes by forcing a compromise. Instead, he encouraged each side to recognize his own position and importance. This was not exclusive to understanding the position of the other side. On the contrary, one could only define his own view in relation to others. By showing each side the relevance of both sides, the argument disappeared and the two became friends.

Indeed, the *Gemara* contrasts Aharon, the lover of *shalom*, with Moshe and even God Himself, who judged. In a court of law, the final decision must be clear cut: one of the sides is guilty; the other, innocent. The one must pay the other. This was Moshe's role; he dealt in justice and punishments. This is also the task of God—"justice is up to the Lord" (*Devarim* 1:17). Aharon, however, found a way to bring all the sides of an argument together. No one came out guilty and neither compromised. In the *cohen*'s system, there is a place for everything to exist together in harmony (*Sanhedrin* 6b).

This also explains why we are commanded to take our queries and questions to "the place that God has chosen." When one encounters a discrepancy in the world between two different types of blood or leprous marks, he takes them to the *cohen* in the *Beit Hamikdash*. That is the place that God has chosen.

The world is full of seemingly incompatible notions. There is purity as opposed to impurity. Some marks require an individual to undergo treatment in the form of isolation. There are others that do not require such therapy. What is one to do? How can man live his life in this divided, crisis-filled world?

The Torah supplies the answer. "You should approach the *cohen*" with your questions. The *cohen* will then show you how it all fits together and makes sense. The *cohen* has the ability to make true peace in the world. He will show you the relevance and place of both purity and impurity. He will prove that it can and must all fit together and fuse to form a grand system that is God's universe.

Such is the peace of the *cohen* and of the Torah. This is also our task as *Am Yisrael*—to fit everything into its rightful place. We are extolled to emulate Aharon: "Hillel would say, 'Be amongst the students of Aharon, love *shalom* and pursue *shalom*. Love people and bring them closer to the Torah'" (*Avot* 1:12). We, too, must develop the ability to fit the pieces of the human jigsaw puzzle together and achieve peace. In so doing, we will develop a love of each individual and his personal expertise. Each is an important and irreplaceable part of the greater whole. If we love each individual, they, in turn, will come closer to the Torah. Yet we must be careful not to fall into the trap of loving each person in order to bring them closer to the Torah. One must unconditionally love his fellows without constantly worrying about their spiritual accomplishments. They will come close to Torah if we can show them their place within its comprehensive order.

We are soon to celebrate the festival of Pesach. On the seder night, we talk of four sons—one wise, one wicked, one simple, and one mute who does not know how to ask. The amazing thing is that they all appear in the Torah. The Torah finds a place not only for the clever and the obedient but also for the wicked and the disinterested. Each is incorporated into the Torah and an answer is given to each. They all take a seat together at the seder table and ask their respective questions. What greater vision of *shalom* could we wish for?

Let us be like Aharon. Love and pursue *shalom*.

Tzav
The Complete Mishkan

*Faith only illuminates Israel in its healthy state, when she is complete
in defense, monarchy, the Temple, her land and all her possessions, both
physical and spiritual. The Temple and all that is connected with it is
only complete when the nation stands as a whole.*

(*Orot*, p. 163)

The Beit Hamikdash *is called the beauty of the world, and beauty is
due to the perfection of the picture. When the Temple exists in the
world, a great completeness descends on the world, and all of the facets
are rectified and fused.*

(*Ein Iyah, Berachot*, Chapter 5, Note 96)

The most significant feature of the shlamim *was all-encompassing*
shalom, *completeness, upon which rests social life and any societal
aggregation. They come to emphasize* shalom *and to influence life
with the blessing of* shalom. *Therefore, they assign strength to each
element—to the altar, to the* cohanim, *and to the bringer of the
sacrifice.*

(*Olat Riyah*, Volume I, p. 177)

In this week's *parsha*, we encounter for the second time the story of the dedication of the *Mishkan*, the Sanctuary. As previously mentioned, after the *Mishkan* was constructed, it needed to be dedicated for service. This was essential in order for the *Mishkan* to start normal, routine functioning. Aharon and his sons were inducted into Divine service with the *Mishkan*.

We have already seen that the account of the dedication is related three separate times in the Torah. We saw one at the end of the *Book of Shemot* (See the Chapter on *P'Kudei*, "Moshe's Sanctuary"). Each time the story is told, it comes to teach a specific message relevant to the place that it appears. Therefore, in the *Book of Shemot* the *Mishkan* symbolized the eternal meeting between *Am Yisrael* and God. We shall discuss its appearance in the *Book of Bemidbar* when we come to it.

What is the particular message of the account of the dedication in the *Book of Vayikra*?

The obvious answer is that the dedication of the *cohanim* and their place of work was most relevant to the *Book of Vayikra*. *Vayikra* is the book of the Cohanim and is concerned with them, mainly.

But what of our understanding of the *cohanim* as the makers of *shalom*? What is the relationship between peace and the Temple?

This account of the *Mishkan*'s dedication comes to show another side of the *Mishkan* and of the Divine service therein. The *Mishkan*, and later the *Beit Hamikdash*, came to bring *shalom* to the world. This was acheived through sacrifices and through the building itself.

One of the sacrifices mentioned in the Torah is the *shlamim*, the peace offering. The sages ask why was it given that name? Two possible answers were offered. "It caused peace in the world. Or it brought *shalom* to the altar, to the *cohanim*, and to he who brought the sacrifice" (Rashi on *Vayikra* 3:1, based on *Midrash Torat Cohanim*. See also *Tosefta, Zevachim* 11:1).

The sacrifices both brought peace to the world and *shalom* to all those involved. The intention behind the sacrifices was to create peace between *Am Yisrael* and the Almighty. For example, if one were to sin, he could in some way rectify his misdemeanor by bringing a sacrifice to the Temple. This showed his willingness to come closer to God and do His bidding. This brought peace to the world. The sacrifices are described as being a "pleasing smell to the Lord" (See, for example, *Vayikra* 1:9, et al.). This does not mean that God enjoyed the sacrifice and in some way needed them. Rather, He got pleasure from witnessing the enthusiasm with which the Jewish people acquiesced to and performed His commandments. This was the way of peace.

Am Yisrael was in its rightful place, the place that God had chosen for the nation. They were worthy as a result of having built the House of God. They knew their correct place as His servants and they fulfilled His wishes. The sacrifices served to bring peace to the world, peace being a state of completion, where everything has a place and a purpose. Peace is attained when all of the elements exist in their proper place; none tries to enter a place that is unsuitable for him, and each develops his own skill in the correct spot. All of these together comprise the entirety. That is *shalom*, true peace. The *shlamim* bring peace to the world. The word *shlamim* is derived from the root *shalem*, complete (as is the word *shalom*).

The *shlamim* brought *shalom* to the altar, the *cohanim*, and to the bringer of the sacrifice. In this particular sacrifice, blood was offered on the altar. Part of the meat was given to the *cohen*. The skin and the rest of the meat were the property of the person who brought the sacrifice.

All those involved had a part in this sacrifice. The *cohen* received part, as did the bearer of the sacrifice. Even the altar received a portion. All had a place and a share in the sacrifice.

This was *shalom*. All were present; all were important; and the sacrifice would be unfit if even one element were missing. The *shlamim* certainly were worthy of their name. They taught a great lesson in *shalom*. Even inanimate objects had an irreplaceable task.

The sacrificial worship was an expression of *shalom* and peace. It has a great relevance in the *Book of Vayikra* and shows this aspect of the Temple worship.

The *Beit Hamikdash* itself also caused peace. The Mishnah relates that there were ten constant miracles in the Temple. One of them was that, during the festivals, the Temple was full of people coming to worship. "They would stand packed together, and there was no room. Yet, when they all bowed down, there was room for everyone." Another miracle was that "no one ever had to say that he had nowhere to sleep in Jerusalem" (*Avot* 5:5).

Even though bowing requires more room than standing, by a miracle, when the Temple was overflowing with people, they all found room to bow. Also, despite the huge number of people flocking to Jerusalem for the festivals, there was room for them all to sleep.

The Mishnah also alludes to the peaceful nature of the Temple. When all *Am Yisrael* stood, each felt his own importance and there was no room. Yet they all bowed to God. When they were bound together in the service of the Almighty, then they all had a place (See *Ruach HaChayim*, ad loc.). When we are focused on the ultimate aim of *Am Yisrael*, that of serving God, we find that each has a special space and task. Such was the *shalom* of the *Beit Hamikdash*; it had the ability to develop each individual character for the greater whole.

This was not only in the Temple itself, but spread throughout Yerushalayim. The *Gemara* tells us that Jerusalem was not divided up into the tribes as was the rest of the land (*Babba Kamma* 82b). No one tribe had exclusive claim on Yerushalayim. Instead, it belonged to the entire people. Even when the whole of the Jewish people ascended to the holy city, everyone found space. No one ever had to say that they had nowhere to sleep in Jerusalem. Each had their place there, and the festivals required the presence of the whole nation.

The *Book of Vayikra* repeats the description of the dedication of the *Mishkan* in order to express this aspect of the Temple and the Temple service. Here was a utopian structure. Each individual was an integral part of the Temple and its service. Together, they forged a cosmic and Divine design that was pleasing in the eyes of the Lord.

The *Beit Hamikdash* and the sacrifices brought peace to the world and gave each a part. When the individual knows his place, a nation can be formed.

This is our task: to bring true peace to the world and to give each his deserved and rightful place.

Shemini
Nadav and Avihu,
Incomplete Service

The basic problem with making halachic decisions before one's rabbi is due to two factors governing one's perfection: intellectual perfection and ethical perfection. Even if the law decided is a correct one, it should go through the rabbi because of his moral and intellectual perfection. Therefore, one who decides halacha before his rabbi and frees his intellect from the bounds of morality is liable to the death penalty.

(*Ein Iyah, Berachot,* Chapter 5, Note 35)

When one allows the intellect to proceed and illuminate the emotions, then he will be successful, and even during times of great elation, he will be anchored to life. The emotions tend to emphasize the end product and ignore the means, whereas the intellect shows how the means lead to the end product.

(*ibid.,* Chapter 4, Note 32)

"[The cohanim] *will wash their hands and feet and they will not die." This is due to the relationship between practical action and Divine inspiration. There is a connection between the intellect, symbolized by the hands, and impulsive, emotional acts, symbolized by the feet. Through the fusion of these two, they work together in purity to remove death.*

(*Olat Riyah,* Volume I, p. 120)

This week's *parsha* relates the events of the eighth and final day of the dedication of the *Mishkan*. The festivities in the camp of the children of Israel were at a climax. After eight glorious days of preparation the *Mishkan* was ready to function. Aharon was to take over the task of *Cohen Gadol*, high priest. This had been performed, temporarily, by his brother Moshe. The atmosphere around the *Mishkan* must have been electrifying. The whole nation eagerly awaited the sacrifices that were to officially open the *Mishkan*.

In light of this, the account is horrifying. In the middle of this excitement, two of Aharon's four sons, Nadav and Avihu, entered the *Mishkan*. They were carrying fire pans, vessels used to offer *ketoret*, a type of incense. They took the fire and *ketoret* and offered it before God. However, this was "strange fire" (*Vayikra* 10:1), it was unauthorized; "God had not commanded such worship" (*ibid.*). For this, they were punishable by death, and indeed, we learn that such was their fate. "Fire came out from God and consumed them, and they died before God" (*ibid.*, 2). The expression "before God" refers to the interior of the *Mishkan* (that is, they died on the spot inside the Holy Sanctuary).

We can imagine what effect this had on the assembled masses. Nadav and Avihu were the sons of their beloved Aharon, and they were in line to take his place as *Cohen Gadol*. For this reason, "the whole house of Israel will mourn for those that were burnt" (*ibid.*, 6).

The scene is compounded by the fact that this occurred at the height of the dedication and in the holy *Mishkan*. What could have been so terrible that Nadav and Avihu had to die on the spot? What was their crime?

The sages offered two possible explanations. Either the sons of Aharon had entered the *Mishkan* in a state of inebriation (See Rashi based on *Vayikra Rabba* 12:1) or they had made a halachic decision before their teacher, Moshe (*Eruvin* 63a).

The rationale behind the first explanation is that, subsequent to this event, Aharon and his sons received the mitzvah to refrain from drinking wine before partaking in the Temple service (*Vayikra* 10:9). As this edict was given immediately after the death of Nadav and Avihu, we can assume that there is a connection. The first opinion, therefore, deduced that this was their crime.

The law concerning the second explanation is that it is forbidden to decide halacha before one's rabbi. If one's rabbi is present and has not expressly given his permission, the student must not set halacha. This is the task of the rabbi and not of the student. "It is forbidden to determine halacha in front of one's teacher. If one were to do such a thing, he would be liable to capital punishment" (*Rambam, Mishneh Torah, Hilchot Talmud Torah* 5:2).

The *Gemara* expounds the course of events leading up to the demise of Aharon's sons. The *Gemara* is of the opinion that their crime was that of setting down halacha without consulting Moshe. "What halacha did they decide? The verse states 'The sons of Aharon must place fire on the altar' (*Vayikra*, 1:7). They ascertained that even though fire descended from the heavens, they were required to light the fire themselves, in addition to the heavenly fire" (*Eruvin* 63a).

This is extraordinary in light of the fact that their decision was perfectly correct. The Rambam writes "even though fire descended from heaven, it was a mitzvah to add human fire" (*Temidim u'Musaphim* 2:1). Was it really possible that they were liable to such severe punishment? One who decides halacha before his rabbi is liable, yet their judicious reasoning produced a correct halacha. They were commanded to bring such fire. Why was their offering called "strange fire" and found unworthy?

In order to understand their actions and punishment, we must return to the task of the *cohen*. We have already discussed the role of the *cohen* as one who blended and united seemingly conflicting concepts. The *cohen* pursued *shalom* as an ideal. He showed the populace how all the components of God's world fitted together. He formed a complete, harmonious system.

In order to do so, the *cohen* had to know the proper place and proportion of all the elements in the world. He had to be aware of the correct position of all the separate parts. He was then able to arrange the components together.

The *cohen*, therefore, had to be fully conscious of the complete world order. If not, then he was incapable of fulfilling his task as *cohen*. Only a *cohen* who knew, intrinsically, the correct state of things would be able to convey this to the rest of the nation.

Now let us return to Nadav and Avihu. We have seen two opinions as to the nature of their crime. They were accused either of drinking wine prior to their Temple service or of establishing halacha without consulting Moshe.

Wine has a strange affect on a person. "Wine gladdens the heart" (*Tehillim*, 104:15). It tends to change the internal natural order of man: (that, in action, the emotions follow the intellect). "Action is a culmination of the thought process" (*Lecha Dodi*, prayers for *Shabbat* evening). After drinking wine, the heart is glad—the emotions rule. "If wine goes in, secrets come out" (*Eruvin* 65a). The ability for self control is impaired. The intellect comes after the emotions. This is not the proper state of affairs. One who becomes inebriated cannot function as a *cohen*. He proves that he is not fully aware of the correct order of things.

When Nadav and Avihu entered the *Mishkan* in a state of inebriation, they proved just that. They forfeited their rights to the priesthood and were liable to severe punishment.

The prohibition against deliberating in halachic matters without rabbinic consent is also connected to order. The sages forbade a student to decide halacha, but not because they worried that he would make a mistake. After all, Nadav and Avihu were correct in their exegesis and yet were still liable. The law was enacted in order to preserve the succession of the halacha.

"Moshe received the Torah on Sinai. He passed it on to Yehoshua, and Yehoshua to the Elders. The Elders passed it on to the Prophets, the Prophets passed it to the members of the Great Assembly" (*Avot* 1:1). This unbroken chain reaches from Moshe up to the present day. This is the order of halacha, and it cannot be changed. The rabbi is higher up in the hierarchy than the student. The rabbi usually takes precedence in halachic matters. The student must recognize his position in the transmission of halacha. The student is also an irreplaceable link in the long chain, but his teacher is before him. A student must not change the order and try to elevate himself above the rabbi in the hierarchy of halacha.

Nadav and Avihu reversed the order. They disregarded Moshe's role as receiver of the Torah. They did not seek his guidance before deciding the halacha. Even though the halacha that they arrived at was correct, they proved that they were not in touch with the world order. A *cohen* had to know Divine order. Ahavon's sons were incapable of acting as *cohanim*. Because they lacked comprehension of their place, even their sacrifice was worthless. It was considered "strange" by God as it was out of place and inappropriate.

All this occurred in the most public and graphic way in order to teach the entire nation a lesson in priesthood and order. The obligation to preserve order was not confined to the *cohanim* or the *Mishkan*. Each individual has to know the order of intellect before emotion. Each must cherish his place in the lineage of the Jewish people and the law. However, one must be fully aware of the limitations and responsibility of his position.

Order is peace. Disarray causes anarchy and potentially life-threatening chaos.

Let us seek to find the correct balance in all things to achieve peace and Divine harmony.

Tazria
Purity and the Divine Connection

Divine tahara *(purity) illuminates and purifies the soul. The person's soul becomes lit, holy, and strong with the Divine light that shines its powerful rays on him.*

(*Orot*, p. 63)

Tumah *(impurity) occurs to the individual as a function and an indication of how far he is from the Divine light, or how mixed up it is within him. When the Divine presence leaves him he remains weakened and* tamei.

(*ibid.*)

The Jewish people have been promised that they will never become totally impure. They will become impure, and will be adversely affected by this, but it will be unable to totally remove them from the source of Divine life.

(*ibid.*)

This week's *parsha* deals with the intricate laws of purity and impurity. We learn that a woman becomes impure on giving birth. A menstruating woman also has the same status as a *Nidda*, a state of impurity. Before arriving at the conclusion that this is a chauvinistic law, consider that a man becomes impure after ejaculation, entering a state called a *Ba'al Keri*. Anyone who comes in contact with a dead body also becomes impure.

Impurity is not connected with cleanliness. A postpartum woman, a woman immediately after birth, is not necessarily unclean, but she is impure. Someone who did not touch a dead body but merely entered the house where the corpse was lying is not unclean, but is impure. The way to remove impurity is not through regular washing but through a ritual of spiritual cleansing. It may involve a sacrifice or another religious ceremony. It always includes immersion in the *mikvah*.

A *mikvah* is a natural body of water of determined minimum size. The impure person must enter naked and ensure that nothing keeps the water from coming in contact with the entire body. Thus, the person is totally immersed in water and emerges pure.

It would be better to use the Hebrew terms *tumah* and *taharah*, than impure and pure. The English words have a certain connotation that is not relevant to the Jewish view of purity, *taharah*.

Why did the Torah single out certain events as bringing on a state of *tumah*?

Taharah is an expression of our close proximity to God. The more attached we are to the Lord, the greater the state of *taharah* we achieve. The prophet Yechezkel provides an allusion to this in the verse relating to the eventual redemption. When that moment arrives, God promises that He will purify us. "I will throw onto you pure waters and I will purify you from all your *tumah*" (*Yechezkel* 36:25). We will reach a period in which we will be close to God, and He Himself will purify us. *Taharah* exists when we are near to God.

The converse is also true. *Tumah* represents a condition where we are in some way detached from God. As Yechezkel prophesied: "In order that the children of Israel will no longer turn away from Me and will not become defiled (*tumah*) through their sins, they will be My people and I will be their God" (*ibid.*, 14:11). When we are in a state of *tumah*, we are distanced from God and are considered not to be His people.

The situation that is closest to God in this world is life itself. "You who cling to God, your Lord, are alive today" (*Devarim* 4:4). When we are in close proximity to God, we are alive, and whoever is alive is near to God. Therefore, it follows that wherever we find life, we should find *taharah*. In the absence of life, one discovers *tumah*.

The highest form of *tumah* is a deceased living entity. A corpse is called the father of the father of *tumah*. This means that anything that comes into contact with the corpse becomes *av hatumah*, the father of *tumah*. *Av hatumah* can subsequently pass on this *tumah* to utensils, food, and so forth. (See *Rambam, Hilchot Tumat Met* for a complete discussion of this principle.)

Death is the highest form of *tumah* since it expresses the distance between man and God. Man is commanded to live. "Today I have set before you life and death, a blessing and a curse. You must choose life in order that you and your children shall live" (*Devarim* 30:19). Life in this world is a function of the fusion of body and soul. Only in this world can man perform the will of the Creator and His commandments. It is imperative to fulfill His command, and this promises life.

Ideally, man would live until he had fulfilled his task and would then pass from the world. Indeed, we witness such cases of individuals, be they old or young, who died after completing their purpose in the world. But what of the many who pass on feeling that they still have much to do and accomplish?

The *Gemara* states that what kills a person is nothing other than "sin" (*Berachot* 33a). The *Gemara* does not mean that everyone who has died must have been wicked and sinful. Rather, that the human condition and the existence of sin is what brings death to the world. Were man to stop sinning, he would live eternally, yet this is an impossibility. "There is no such thing as a righteous person who only does good and never sins" (*Kohelet* 7:20).

Death is a result of the distance between the ideal aim of man and the reality of man's life. Life is the objective of this world. We find that a pregnant woman holds new life in her womb. This is a very holy condition. The woman is a partner with God in the creation of this new human being. During the pregnancy, the woman does not menstruate and remains in a state of *taharah*. She is so close to God that she remains pure throughout the pregnancy. However, when this period comes to an end, the state terminates. The child leaves the womb and with it the condition of *taharah* ends. What follows is similar to a mini-death. The placenta leaves the body, and the womb breaks down. Initially, the woman is incapable of bearing new life until the womb reforms and strengthens itself. This situation renders the woman impure, in a state of *tumah*. It comes not from sin but from the death that follows the duration of the pregnancy.

The appearance of menstrual blood also signifies death. It shows that the woman was unsuited, in the last month, to produce new life. Again the womb 'dies' before it rejuvenates and prepares for the next month. The menstruating woman is also in a state of *tumah*. She did not produce life, but was in contact with a type of death. Again, this is not necessarily due to sin, but to the condition of the lack of life and the appearance of signs of death.

The male who has ejaculated has also touched death. The millions of sperm that were emitted could not possibly have all been utilized to form new life. Even if one (or more) did create a new human entity, many did not achieve this. Each ejaculation brings with it a form of death and *tumah*.

In order to return to a state of *taharah*, one must rectify that which led to the *tumah*. If *tumah* is an expression of distance from God, then, to achieve *taharah*, one must draw closer to God. The ideal is to reach the state that exists before death and is above the possibility of *tumah*. Such is the *mikvah*.

The Kabbalists liken the *mikvah* to a return to the womb. (*Reishit Chochma Sha'ar HaAhava* 11:29. See also Rabbi Aryeh Kaplan, *The Waters of Eden*, NCSY Publications, p.13.) In the womb, there is no concept of death because the womb is concerned with life. It follows that the womb cannot be impure. *Tumah* and *taharah* have no relevance in the womb. When the person dips themselves into the *mikvah*, they are returning to that ideal state. Even the stance adopted during immersion is similar to the fetal position. We emerge from the *mikvah* reborn and ready for a fresh start.

"Whoever immerses themselves in the *mikvah* clings to God in order to purify themselves" (*Reishit Chochma ibid.*, 25). The *mikvah* returns us to God and, therefore, removes our *tumah*. We cling to God and trust in Him. We are completely immersed in the water and nothing comes between our spiritual desires and our physical being.

In the Messianic era, "the earth will be full of the knowledge of God" (*Yeshiyahu* 11:9). The whole world will be on such a high spiritual level that we will all cleave to God. When that happens, "I will remove *tumah* from the world" (*Zechariya* 13:2). We will no longer experience periods of proximity and periods of distance. There will be no more *tumah* and *taharah*. In that time, "death will be eliminated entirely and God will wipe tears off all faces" (*Yeshiyahu* 25:8). Man will be so close to God and know Him so intimately that there will be no death and no *tumah*.

"I will remove your stone heart and give you a heart of flesh. I will place My Spirit amongst you. You will be My people and I will be your God" (*Yechezkel* 36:26–28).

Metzorah
Purity and a Strange Skin Condition

The illumination of the holy spirit shows one the immense power of speech. It becomes clear how each word, from its conception until it actually emerges as speech, is drawn; how it works afterwards in space and is unified with all of existence. Securing such an idea in the subconscious, realizing the value of each word, will make one more responsible for every utterance that leaves his mouth. The words, full of value and sanctity, will be elevated to their true place, and one will be seized by an ethical sense that no word should be wasted, and that one should not be involved in idle chatter.

(*Orot Haḳodesh*, Volume III, p. 276)

Senseless words gain their strength from a weak and ineffectual spirit. When one speaks them, they give rise to an ugly force that defiles the soul, and the air of the world is clouded.

(*ibid.*, p. 279)

When a person elevates their soul, they feel the tremendous power of speech, and they recognize the great value of all their words, the value of their prayers and blessings, the value of their Torah and their conversations. They feel the influence that words have in the world.

(*ibid.*, p. 285)

This week's *parsha* deals with another type of *tumah* or impurity, that of *tzara'at*. This is usually translated as leprosy. However, the Torah's account of this condition is very different from what we know of the disease. It is true that both conditions affect the skin. *Tzara'at* was a skin condition that could appear anywhere on the skin or the scalp. In addition, we learn that it also could affect clothing (*Vayikra* 13:47). Even the walls of houses could get *tzara'at* (*ibid.*, 14:34). This was unlike any sort of known medical condition. The diagnosis was not made by a medical expert but by a *cohen*.

No one was qualified to evaluate the status of *tzara'at* but the *cohen*. Even a specialist in the laws of *tzara'at* was not in a position to pass judgment on the condition. This was the sole jurisdiction of the *cohen*. "Even though all are capable of looking at *tzara'at*, the status depends on a *cohen*. If the *cohen* is not fully versed in the laws, the expert gives his opinion; but the *cohen* has to verbally declare the final judgment" (*Rambam, Hilchot Tumat Tzara'at* 9:2).

A further difference between *tzara'at* and leprosy lies in the method of treatment. The remedy for *tzara'at* entails a period of isolation and a sacrifice. All this was supervised by the *cohen*.

Another very significant point is that someone who has *tzara'at* is *tamei*. He is ritually impure. Someone with leprosy may be ill, but he is not necessarily tamei.

In order to make some sense of the laws of *tzara'at*, let us see what the sages said about the cause of the condition.

The *Gemara* brings an elucidation: "Anyone who speaks evil speech is affected by *tzara'at*" (*Erchin* 15b). This is a play on the word "*tzara'at*." The *Gemara* explains that the word can be read to mean one who makes up stories about another. This is called *Motzi Shem Ra*—to create a bad name for someone, and sounds similar to the name of the *parsha*, *Metzorah*.

The condition of *tzara'at* is a result of evil and unnecessary talk. The Torah provides an example of this involving Moshe's sister, Miriam. She spoke against Moshe and accused him of pride. For this, she was punished with *tzara'at* (See *Bemidbar* 12:10). As a sign of respect for her, the entire camp tarried until she had completed the purification process.

What is the connection between the affliction and the crime? The Torah prohibits *lashon hara*, evil or unnecessary speech. This does not include lying about another, which is clearly forbidden. *Lashon hara* is idle chatter, speech that is true but has no purpose. People like to speak about others. This is a human pastime, but most of it is irrelevant and is just a way to pass the time. Some of it is damaging and involves character assassination. Much of it is not directly harmful, but unless it has a permitted purpose, it is forbidden by the

Torah. Rabbi Yisrael Meir Kagan authored an entire work on the subject. It is called *Chafetz Chayim* and he became known by the same name, The Chafetz Chayim.

The Chafetz Chayim found that someone who indulges in *lashon hara* can, in the course of conversation, transgress a great number of laws. He found seventeen negative commandments, fourteen positive commandments, and three curses connected with *lashon hara*. Thirty-four sins in one mouthful!

Why did the Torah see this activity in such a negative light? It is natural to speak about others and causes no direct harm. What is the problem?

The Torah commands us: "Do not go as a merchant amongst your people" (*Vayikra* 19:16). This is explained to mean that one should not trade in gossip. We are forbidden to say: "Did you hear what happened to so and so, and so forth" (See *Rambam*, *Hilchot Deyot* 7:2). The verse does not simply say "do not be a merchant," but stresses "amongst your people." This is the basis of *lashon hara*. It afflicts society.

A healthy society is built on good will between individuals and on trust. If these elements are absent, the particular society is doomed to failure. Where there is no good will, each is to his own. The mishnah launches a scathing attack on such people. "Whoever says 'mine is mine and yours is yours' is neutral (neither good nor bad). There are those who hold that this is considered the trait of S'dom" (*Avot* 5:10). It will be remembered that society was so corrupt in S'dom that God destroyed the area. This emanated from the attitude, mine is mine and yours is yours.

Another essential ingredient is trust. All trade is built on trust between individuals, and trade is the basis of society. In a place that lacks normal trust among its inhabitants, life cannot expand and develop. Such a society is stagnant and will eventually collapse.

The way we build good will and trust is through a state of mind and speech. The power of words is what differentiates man from the animals. This power enables us to advance and evolve as a society. However, we can misuse this strength and use words to destroy. When we indulge in chatter and gossip, we are shaking the very foundations of society. The Torah forbids us to talk *lashon hara*. We are commanded not to trade in gossip "amongst your people." *Lashon hara* destroys more than individuals; it destroys society and it destroys *Am Yisrael*.

What is the method by which we rectify the sin of *lashon hara*? The Torah tells us that the individual who speaks *lashon hara* will be afflicted by *tzara'at*. The *tzara'at* has the affect of removing the sin of *lashon hara*. The therapy that the afflicted one undergoes involves seclusion and isolation. This, initially, removes the possibility of speaking gossip that requires the company of others. But beyond that, by dealing in *lashon hara*, one has proved that he is unworthy to be part of *Am Yisrael*, so he is forced to leave society temporarily. He sits outside the camp and has ample opportunity to consider his actions and resolve to change. Only when *tzara'at* disappears is he allowed to return to his former house and neighborhood. When God sees that he has repented and is ready to be restored into society, He removes the *tzara'at*.

The end of seclusion proves that part of the *teshuvah*, the return, is complete. The individual has learned that his actions cut him off from *Am Yisrael*. He understands that, in order to be part of the nation, he must strengthen his connection with his fellows and not weaken it. But he is still not finished with the process of *taharah*. The next stage demands a sacrifice.

The sacrifice does not serve to bring the person closer to society. It has a different purpose. The sacrifice brings him closer to God. When one indulges in *lashon hara*, he not only sins against society, but he also sins against God. Anyone who draws away from *Am Yisrael* draws further from God. We are His people and nation; to insult us is to insult Him. It is not enough just to return to society; one has to return to God as well. Only after the sacrifice does the individual reach the level of *taharah*.

The whole remedy is administered by the *cohen*. It is the job of the *cohen* to bring *shalom* to the world. *Shalom* is made up of two elements. An individual must know his place in relation to other people. But *shalom* can only be achieved when one also knows his place in relation to the Almighty. The *cohen* teaches the person afflicted with *tzara'at* to make peace with *Am Yisrael* and with God. Then, and only then, can he reach the elusive stage of *taharah*.

Acharei Mot
The Scream of Silence

There are times of silence and times of speech. When it is a time of preparation to receive Divine influence, all is silent and listens. When the time comes that each entity can influence the next, then speech begins. One needs to prepare himself for the attribute of silence, in order to hear the heavenly voice, and God's word will be upon him.

(*Orot Hakodesh*, Volume I, p. 116)

Silence comes from the depths of the soul and from emotions that lie beyond human speech. When the deep person remains silent, worlds are being formed; songs are composed in the heights of sanctity, and a great strength elevates one's whole being.

(*ibid.*, Volume III, p. 274)

It would be disastrous for one to be unable to remain silent and have to speak at a time when the inner light deemed it a time for silence. This rebellion against the kingdom of silence destroys worlds. Afterwards, one would have to rebuild them from scratch, and so the wise remain silent at such times.

(*ibid.*, p. 275)

This week's *parsha* deals with certain injunctions that God commanded the *cohanim* and the nation. All of them were commanded after the death of Aharon's sons. Some of these injunctions were enacted as a direct result of their actions and came to ensure that such an event would never repeat itself. They were guidelines and strict boundaries for the priestly worship. "Do not enter the Temple at the unappointed time, in order that you should not die" (*Vayikra* 16:2).

The *parsha* is called *Acharei Mot*, After the Death. The *parsha* opens with the words: "God spoke to Moshe after the death of Aharon's two sons, who had drawn close to God and died" (*ibid.*, 1).

It is enlightening to note Aharon's reaction to what happened. If it was difficult for the whole camp of Israel and all who mourned the calamity, how much more so for Aharon himself. His own sons were killed in a most tragic fashion. We would assume that he would feel devastated and shattered. It is conceivable that he would feel anger toward God for taking his sons from him. However, Aharon did not react in such a fashion at all.

"Moshe said to Aharon 'This is what God inferred to me when He said that I will be sanctified through those that are close to Me. I will be honored in front of the entire nation'" (*ibid.*, 10:3). The midrash records the conversation between the two brothers, Moshe and Aharon.

"My brother, on Sinai I learned that God will dedicate the *Mishkan* through the death of a great man. I assumed that this meant that either you or I would die. Now, I see that your two sons were greater than both of us" (*Vayikra Rabba* 12:2).

The *Mishkan* was to be sanctified through the death of someone very close to God. As Nadav and Avihu were selected, Moshe deduced that they had a particularly close relationship with God, one that was stronger than that of Aharon or even Moshe. This was the method by which Moshe chose to comfort Aharon. Aharon had a unique reaction to Moshe's words. "*Vayidom Aharon*" (*Vayikra* 10:3), "And Aharon was silent."

But there is silence and there is silence.

There are times when, even though the mouth opens to speak and react, no sound emerges—the silence of despair that comes from a lack of ability to respond. However, there is another type of silence.

During the *Yamim Noraim*, Rosh Hashanah and Yom Kippur, the crux of the prayers centers around the prayer *U'Netaneh Tokef*. This moving prayer relates the awe of the day. "On Rosh Hashanah it is written, and sealed on Yom Kippur, how many will pass away and how many will be born. Who will live and who will die. Who will reach a timely death and who will be taken before his time."

One of the passages deals with the aura of sanctity and reverence surrounding the sealing of the world's fate. "You remember all the forgotten acts and open the Book of Remembrance. A great shofar is sounded and a subtle voice of silence is heard. The angels are hurried and exclaim 'Behold it is the Day of Judgment.'" Again, the prayer uses the word *demama* for silence. This is the same word used to describe Aharon's silence, *"vayidom Aharon."* The voice of silence is heard and it is heard throughout the heavens. It heralds the Day of Judgment. Indeed, it is not a voice of silence at all. In order to tear through the walls of indifference and apathy, it must be a scream, a huge cry. Yet it is called a voice of *demama*, of silence.

This is the other form of silence. It is not born out of despair, but out of a deep understanding. The mouth does not refuse to answer, but accepts the greatness of the Almighty and is in awe.

The heavenly voice is in admiration of the holiness of Rosh Hashanah and Yom Kippur. It respects the hallowed nature of the Days of Return. The angels realize that the Almighty is about to sit and set the fate of the world for the coming year. In bewilderment, they cry out and declare "Holy, holy, holy is the All-powerful God. His glory fills the earth" (*Yeshiyahu* 6:3).

This silence is earth shattering and appears as a roar. It is the scream of silence.

Such was the silence of Aharon. It was not the result of despair, but a realization of the infinite plan of God. On hearing Moshe's explanation of the demise of his two sons, he readily accepted the concept that this was a part of the Divine scheme. He knew that not only did he not have to weep and lament, but that every response was extraneous. He needed no reply and therefore, *vayidom Aharon*, he was silent. Not a silence of despair, but of acceptance and assent. Aharon had the ability to overlook his personal loss and pain and accept the decree. There is a judge and perfect justice reigns. "All that God does is for the best" (*Berachot* 60b). We may be incapable of comprehending the reason behind God's actions, but we must believe that all is revealed before the Creator. There is no chance and no accident. *"Vayidom Aharon"*— Aharon accepted God's decision.

There are numerous events in this world that we find incomprehensible. Possibly none more so than the Holocaust, which we commemorate on *Yom HaShoah*, Holocaust Day, the 27th day of Nissan.

A common question is one concerning reactions to the Holocaust. What should our response be, and what is our relation to the State of Israel that rose as a direct result?

From Aharon's silence, we learn that the most relevant response is one of silence. Not the feeble silence of despair, but the silence of acceptance, the silence of Aharon.

Even if we cannot understand, we must believe that all is part of the huge plan of Providence. We cannot respond, not because the words refuse to come, but because they are irrelevant and irreverent.

This is also connected with Aharon's role as the pursuer and creator of *shalom*. We have seen that Nadav and Avihu's untimely demise was due to their lack of *shalom*. They changed and confused world order. Man is a part of the huge master plan of the Creator. His choice is to try and fight against it, or to passively ignore it. Alternatively, the individual can choose to accept the responsibility of his God-given role and to contribute as much as possible. Such was the task of the *cohen*. He was to fit together the parts of the world and reveal the correct place for every individual. Aharon accepted his role and that of his family. As such, he was in a position to guide others in their own tasks and enable them to fulfill their potential.

Once Aharon knew that such was God's decree, he knew he must accept. Let us try to emulate Aharon in this trait as well as in many others that we have seen.

Kedoshim
Sex, Shechita and Sanctity

The basis upon which man should operate is that the body should also strive toward the elevation of the song of the soul. This is achieved through all of the actions and feelings of the body. If the soul alone is Divine and the body remains animalistic, it is empty. The concept of the Torah is to elevate the entire person.

(*Ein Iyah, Berachot*, Chapter 6, Note 2)

When one eats just to satisfy physical desire, it brings a certain sadness. But eating in a sanctified manner increases joy and pleasure. Through the sparks of sanctity in the food that are elevated, this illuminates the soul, and Divine joy is felt.

(*Orot Hakodesh*, Volume III, p. 292)

One should sanctify and enlighten the will until the strongest natural physical will that is planted in holiness is very strong due to the life that it contains (that is, the sex drive). The holy light shines on it until the holy side of it is strengthened and continues. The darker side, the profane and the impure, vanishes in the face of the sanctity.

(*ibid.*, p. 298)

This week's *parsha*, coupled with *Acharei Mot* and the *parsha* of *Shemini*, has a very similar structure. Both start off with a reference to the death of Nadav and Avihu, Aharon's sons, and later progress to different *mitzvot*. Both of the first *mitzvot* that God instructed were concerned, almost exclusively, with the *cohanim* and the service in the *Mishkan* and the *Beit*

Hamikdash. The *parsha* of *Shemini* deals with the prohibition on the *cohanim* to serve in the Temple in a state of inebriation. Our present *parsha* deals with the service in the Temple on Yom Kippur. This was the most important day of the year in the *Beit Hamikdash*. On this day alone, did the *Cohen Gadol* enter the *Kodesh Kodashim*, the Holy of Holies. This required suitable preparation and this is the subject of the *parsha*, together with the specific details of the service. The *Cohen Gadol* was involved in the many sacrifices of the day as well as reading the Torah to the assembly. In order for the service to be well-administered, the instructions as to its execution had to be exact.

In both *Acharei Mot-Kedoshim* and in *Shemini*, we subsequently find injunctions concerning the whole nation. This second group of laws both contain a select number of laws that relate to *kedusha*, holiness. We thus arrive at the name of the *parsha*, *Kedoshim*. Indeed, the *parsha* opens with the command to be holy. "You must be holy as I am holy, the Lord your God" (*Vayikra* 19:2). This seems to be a very difficult commandment; it is not easy to achieve holiness. If this is the case for an individual, how much more so for an entire nation.

We assume that holiness involves esoteric behavior. Maybe one needs to be sequestered in a monastery to become holy. The common understanding of the term *holy* is that someone completely removed from society and human endeavors is the most holy of all. If one were to fast and not speak, to remain celibate and live alone, some would claim that he was very *holy*.

Yet we find that the Torah brings a very different concept of *kedusha*. The *parsha* of *Shemini* deals with the animals one can and cannot eat. Also, with the appropriate way to kill them, causing the least damage and physical discomfort (that is, the laws of *Shechita*). The *parshiot* of *Acharei Mot* and *Kedoshim* deal with permitted and forbidden sexual relationships. Indeed, the Rambam, on writing his major halachic work, the *Mishneh Torah*, divided it into fourteen sections. Each dealt with a different topic and received an appropriate name. The section dealing with the laws of the festivals is called "*Zemanim*," "Times." The section dealing with Jewish philosophy was named "*Madah*," "Knowledge," and so forth. One of the sections is called "*Kedusha*," "Holiness." Within it we find an explanation of three areas of halacha: the laws of *shechita*—the correct slaughter of meat, permitted animals, and a discussion of sexual relations. The Rambam chose to name the section that deals with these laws "*Kedusha*."

This is very indicative of the nature of *kedusha* as opposed to holiness. *Kedusha* does not require detachment from the world; in fact, nothing could be further from the truth. *Kedusha* demands that one knows how to be completely involved with life and society. We have a religious obligation to marry and bear children. We also must look after our bodies. Judaism does not preach asceticism. We have a concern for the physical being and its welfare.

Kedusha is the ability to sanctify the world. Specifically, we are commanded to inject Divinity into every area of our existence, even into practices that were previously incorrectly considered somewhat "dirty" or "lewd." Judaism is not repulsed by the physical world. Indeed, all are commanded to marry, from the greatest rabbi and priest to the simplest member of the community. God "did not create the world in order for it to be worthless, but for habitation" (*Yeshiyahu* 45:18). We must not let the world go to waste but inhabit and develop it. However, the mitzvah to procreate exists side by side with the injunction to be holy. *Kedusha* demands from us that we sanctify our relationships. The Torah lists the permitted and forbidden sexual combinations in order to develop a system of sanctified relationships.

The same is true of the natural process of eating and satisfying hunger. The Torah directs us to make this conduct one imbued with *kedusha*. Instead of being simply a mechanical fulfillment of animalistic desire, eating, in the Torah, is part of the method of attaining *kedusha*. Which animals we may and may not eat, and how we are to prepare them finds a place in the Torah's account of *kedusha*.

The rationale behind all of these injunctions is contained in the first verses of the *parsha*. "You must be holy as I am holy, the Lord your God." We have a command to emulate God. The *Gemara* asks whether such a thing is truly possible. "'You must walk after God' (*Devarim* 13:5). This seems impossible in light of the verse 'God is like an all-consuming fire' (*ibid.*, 4:24). [It is impossible to cleave to such a Deity.] Rather that you should follow His example. In the same way that He clothes the naked, so should you provide clothing for the needy. As He visits the sick, you should also visit the sick. God comforts the mourners and buries the dead, so must you" (*Sotah* 14a). The *Gemara* implores us to try and emulate God's deeds and traits. The Torah commands us to imitate His *kedusha*.

God not only controls the great historic events, but also has dominion over the most mundane human events. "How great are Your works" (*Tehillim* 92:6) is coupled with how minute and intricate are Your works. In the words of the *Gemara*: "Wherever one discovers His greatness, there lies also His humility" (*Megilla* 31a).

In order to emulate God, we must also leave our mark of *kedusha* on the most mundane affairs—the way we sanctify sexual relationships, the way we eat and prepare our food. We elevate our lives to a level of holiness and inject sanctity into everything that we do. In fact, our whole lives become a service to God and a process of Divine revelation. This is the test of *kedusha*; the entire nation must live lives full of *kedusha*. Indeed, the mitzvah to be like God and "be holy" is not reserved for a particular class or subgroup within *Am Yisrael*. Instead, it is directed toward every single individual.

Kedusha requires one more factor and facet of our behavior. *Kedusha* is part of our harmonizing with God's plan for the world. In order to find our place in the Divine scheme, we must first recognize that such a system exists and be willing to be a part of it. We saw in last week's *parsha* that this was achieved by a scream of silent acceptance, that we must be able to acknowledge the existence of tragedy with a deep faith that all "that God does is for the best" (*Berachot* 60b).

Kedoshim (and *kedusha*) comes after *Acharei Mot* and the silent assent. In fact, it is quite common for the two *parshiot* to be joined and read together as one. There is a natural flow from the acquiescence of *Acharei Mot* to the *kedusha* in *Kedoshim*. When we become capable of recognizing the Divine world order, we are ready to fuse with the Divinity in the world.

The same is true on the personal level. After the death of a close relative, we are required to say kaddish. The word *kaddish* also means holiness. An interesting point about the kaddish prayer is that, although it is the "mourner's prayer," it contains no mention of death. "May His great name be exalted and sanctified in the world that He created. May His kingdom be established during your lifetime and the lifetime of all of Israel, and so forth." It is an exaltation of God and life, not death. When Aharon and the rest of the Jewish people successfully overcame their personal grief and accepted God's plan, they achieved *kedusha*. *Kedusha* is the ability to reveal God, not only in the huge events but also in the most tiny and mundane of places. Such is *kedusha*. The command to be holy was directed not only to the *cohanim* or to a specific generation. It is the lot of *Am Yisrael* from her conception until the present.

Emor
Beauty and Complete Purity

"Aharon and his sons washed their hands and feet." This holy washing engraves the eternal purity that is a suitable preparation for total devotion. It must be deepset in the foundation of the priesthood and their lineage. All tahara *that appears in each generation is due to this original purity.*

(*Olat Riyah*, Volume I, p. 119)

Everything that is all-inclusive requires a special level of tahara. *The Temple service contains within it the heights of intelligence with a combination of emotion and imagination. It, therefore, needs specific and exacting levels of* tahara.

(*Orot*, p. 81)

Hasidism turned more toward emotion and imagination than toward intellectual pursuits, and they, therefore, pushed for a higher level of observance with regard to tahara.

(*ibid.*)

In this week's *parsha*, we find a number of commandments specifically for the *cohanim*, the priests. The priest was required to maintain a higher level of *taharah*, ritual purity, than the rest of *Am Yisrael*. He was forbidden to be *tamei*, impure, forbidden to come in contact, even indirectly, with a corpse. Only in specific cases could this prohibition be waived. If the deceased was a close member of his family, he was allowed to deal with the burial. "He will not became *tamei* through contact with a corpse. With the exception of his wife, parents, children, or brother. Also his unmarried sister, for these people, he can become *tamei*" (*Vayikra* 21:1–3).

Even more strict were the laws concerning the *Cohen Gadol*. He was forbidden to become *tamei* even for these relatives. "He will not come in contact with any dead person. Not even his own parents" (*ibid.*, 11). Why did the *cohanim* receive such an injunction? The Torah supplies the answer in the following verses: "They will be holy to their God. Because they sacrifice God's fire, they must be holy" (*ibid.*, 6).

This seems to contradict what we stated last week. We asserted that *kedusha* is relevant and binding for every single Jew. We are all required to be holy and sanctify our lives, yet we are not required to refrain from coming into contact with a dead person. A non-*cohen* can become *tamei* and must purify himself before he is allowed to partake of sacrifices and the like. He is not forbidden to do so. He is permitted to become *tamei* and then *tahor*, pure, as often as he wishes. What was so special about the *cohanim* that God commanded them to totally remove themselves from any such process of impurity and purification? They had to remain in a state of *taharah* throughout their lives. They knew not *tumah* and then *taharah*, only constant *taharah*.

This command is directly linked to their role in the *Beit Hamikdash*, and this is shown in the verse that we quoted, as in other verses. The *cohen* had to remain pure "because he offers the food sacrifice of God." There must have been something special in the Temple service that necessitated constant *taharah*.

A system containing only a small number of elements has less possibility of contamination. A simple experiment needs less supervision than a more complex one. The same is true in spiritual matters. That which is a purely intellectual pursuit is less vulnerable than that which consists of both intellect and emotion.

The *Beit Hamikdash* and the service therein is formed from the union of a large number of separate elements. The sacrifices must be perfect on both physical and spiritual levels. It was not enough just to bring a sacrifice in order to atone for one's sins; prior to this, one had to undergo spiritual cleansing. This took the form of acknowledging the sin, repentance, and immersion in the *mikvah*. A sacrifice could become unfit because it was physically maimed. Alternatively, it could be disqualified due to unsuitable thoughts on the part of the *cohen* during the offering. "Whoever intended to offer the blood outside of the Temple, or to eat meat outside of the Temple, the sacrifice is *pasul*, disqualified. If the *cohen* intended to offer the blood on the next day, or to eat the meat of the sacrifice on the next day, the sacrifice is disqualified and the *cohen* is liable to the punishment of *karet*, death, and to die childless" (*Zevachim*, Chapter 2: *Mishnah* 2).

The service had to fuse the physical and mental agility of the *cohen*. In order to do so, the *cohen* had to be in a fit state to serve. Prior to taking up his position as an active member of the priesthood, the *cohen* had to "learn the ropes" for five years. "Twenty-five years old to study, thirty to serve" (*Chullin* 24a; and see Rashi on *Bemidbar* 8:24). He also had to enter the *Beit Hamikdash* to worship in a totally conscious state. "Do not drink either wine or liquor before entering the *Mishkan*, lest you be liable to capital punishment" (*Vayikra* 10:9).

The *Beit Hamikdash* itself was also a fusion of many constituents. It was a center of Divine service, but also contained elements apart from the sacrifices. The Leviim learned the art of song for several years, and also sang their songs of Divine worship. The building itself was full of aesthetic beauty. "One who has not witnessed the glory of the *Beit Hamikdash* has never seen a beautiful building" (*Succah* 51b). The walls were fashioned from the finest blue marble that gave the effect of standing in the sea. In such an environment, one had to be particularly careful not to be distracted by the physical beauty. For this reason, the *cohanim* had to maintain a high level of *taharah*.

The study of Torah is a source of nourishment for the intellect. This Divine intellect is pure and will always lead to the true path. The Torah cannot become *tamei*. In the words of the *Gemara*: "In the same way that fire cannot become defiled, so the words of Torah do not become *tamei*" (*Berachot* 22a). The intellect does not lead one astray and is pure, like fire. However, when we mix the intellect with emotions, we are creating a more vulnerable system. The emotions tend to effect a person's reasoning, sometimes even changing his power of judgement. In such a place, one needs to take extra special care.

The *cohanim*, who were to fuse intellect, emotion, art, and culture, needed protection from the possibility of failure. They received special laws of purity and *taharah* aimed at preventing them from being led astray. The misguided acts of Nadav and Avihu, the unfortunate sons of Aharon who were killed during inappropriate service, show how crucial this was. The *cohanim* had to remain physically pure, and this was to influence their inner purity as well.

If this was the case with every single *cohen*, how much more so with the *Cohen Gadol*. He entered the Holy of Holies that contained the *Aron*, Ark, adorned with the *ceruvim*. This was the most graphic example of art and sculpture in the *Beit Hamikdash*. He needed to preserve the highest possible state of *taharah*. He, therefore, was required to uphold the strictest code of purity.

Even were his own parents to pass away, he was forbidden to come into contact with the corpse and continued his holy service in the *Beit Hamikdash*.

The same is true of the entire Jewish nation. In the times of the Temple, all of *Am Yisrael* were aware of the laws of *tumah* and *taharah*. There were non-*cohanim* who would immerse themselves in the *mikvah* before eating. In the time of King Chizkiyahu, throughout the land of Israel "there was no child that was not knowledgeable in the laws of *tumah* and *taharah*" (*Sanhedrin* 94b). Yet after leaving the land, this widespread erudition was lost. In the *Galut*, exile, all that remains is the study of Torah. "Since the destruction of the Temple, all that remains is four cubits of halacha" (*Berachot* 8a). "Nothing remains for us except the Torah" (*Selichot*). As the Torah cannot receive *tumah*, the study of these areas became less urgent and, with time, were neglected.

The early Hasidim changed this perspective. They taught that Judaism is not confined to the study of Torah, but spreads through a much richer tradition. They started to fuse study with religious fervor, to unite the intellect with the emotion. In so doing, they opened themselves to the possibility of error. Therefore, as well as teaching the importance of emotion, they also preached a return to the study and practice of *tumah* and *taharah*. They reestablished the custom of men frequenting the *mikvah* and lived lives of exceptional purity. It is not a coincidence that they also revived the desire to return to the land of Israel. Indeed, many of the students of the Ba'al Shem Tov, the founder of Hasidism, attempted to settle in the land of Israel. Only in the Holy Land could these diverse elements be fused into a comprehensive unit.

The *cohanim* needed extra *taharah* in order to successfully bond the many different parts of the Temple service, particularly those that involve both intellect and emotion. *Taharah*, though, is not the exclusive province of the *cohanim*. Anyone who wants to fuse intellect and emotion, who realizes that Judaism is not composed purely of intellectual pursuits, must be wary. Our generation must also re-immerse ourselves in the *mikvah* and achieve the ultimate *taharah*. This will enable us to fuse the elements, to create a complete Judaism and a totality within *Am Yisrael*.

Behar
The Return to Nature

The individual is released from the strains of everyday life quite often. Every Shabbat *the soul begins to be freed from its harness and seeks for herself higher ideals, spirituality. It is a day when the true nature of the nation, a life directed toward spiritual pursuits, is revealed in its individuals.*

(*Shabbat Ha'aretz*, Introduction, p. 8)

The same affect that the Shabbat *has over the individual, the* Sh'mittah *has over the entire nation. It is essential that this nation that is founded on a Divine ideal should have regular opportunities and set times to reveal the Divine light in all its glory.*

(*ibid.*)

There comes, after the Sh'mittah, *a longer and more important period that succeeds in elevating not only the individuals of* Am Yisrael, *not just a single generation, but all generations—the* Yovel *comes at the time of the birth of the world and is arranged in accordance with the higher Divine freedom.*

(*ibid.*, p. 9)

This week's *parsha* deals with the laws of the seventh year of produce, the *Sh'mittah*. "When you come to the Land that I am giving you, the land will rest—a *Shabbat* to God. Six years you should plant and gather your produce. But the seventh year will be a *Shabbat* for the land, *Shabbat* to God. Do not sow your field nor prune your vineyard. It will be year of *Shabbat* for the land. That which grows during the *Shabbat* of the land is yours and your servants' and employees'. The produce will be for your beasts and for the wild animals that are in the land" (*Vayikra* 25:2–7).

The most immediate question is the relevance of these agricultural laws to the *Book of Vayikra*. The question is augmented by the first words of the *parsha*. "God spoke to Moshe on *Har Sinai*" (*ibid.*, 1). Rashi immediately asks: "What is the connection between *Sh'mittah* and *Har Sinai*?" (Rashi, ad loc.). Why does the *parsha* stress the fact that this set of instructions was related on *Har Sinai* specifically?

We find later in the *parsha* a super-*Sh'mittah*, the *Yovel*, or Jubilee Year. "You will count seven sets of *Sh'mittah*, making a total of forty-nine years. Blast the shofar on Yom Kippur throughout your land. Sanctify the fiftieth year, proclaim *Dror* (freedom) to all inhabitants of the land. It is a *Yovel*, a Jubilee. Each person will return to his family and inheritance. On that year, you must not sow nor reap the produce of the field"(*Vayikra* 25:8–11).

The *Yovel* bears similar features to the *Sh'mittah* year. During both there is a prohibition against actively working the land. All of the produce that grew of its own accord is *hefker*, ownerless, and can be consumed by any passerby. During *Sh'mittah*, all outstanding debts are revoked. If one owes another person money during the *Sh'mittah* year, at the end of the year the debt is wiped out. It is interesting to note that Hillel, a scholar during the period of the Mishnah, observed that this law had an adverse affect, and people stopped lending money in the year leading up to the *Sh'mittah*. In order to counter this, he created a halachic loophole called a *prusbol*, whereby one could sell the debt to the *Beit Din*, the law court. In this way, the *Beit Din* would continue to require repayment for the debt, and it would not be lost (*Shevi'it* 10:3).

The *Yovel* was on a much grander scale. All servants were released from service; even a servant who enjoyed his master's employment had to return to civilian freedom. Land that had been sold over the past fifty years reverted back to its original owners. A situation was achieved whereby the plots that had been divided amongst the tribes on entering the land were regained by the descendants of the tribe.

What is the relevance of all this to the *Book of Vayikra*, the book of our worldly task? Why did God dedicate almost an entire *parsha* to relate mostly agricultural laws? The midrash adds a further dimension that needs investigation. "In the same way that *Shabbat* is referred to as '*Shabbat* to God' so is the *Sh'mittah* called '*Shabbat* to God'" (*Sifra, Behar* 1). The fact that both

Shabbat and *Sh'mittah* are linked by the name "*Shabbat* to God" is not coincidental but points to an inner connection.

We have a hierarchy of these three *mitzvot*, *Shabbat*, *Sh'mittah*, and finally, *Yovel*. What is the connection and the meaning of each and of all of them together? In order to answer these questions, we have to understand the meaning of *Shabbat*, even though this is not part of our *parsha*.

Judaism is a way of life that dictates the importance of action. "Six days you shall do your work, and on the seventh day you must rest" (*Shemot* 23:12, et al.). Work is not a means to an ends but is, itself, service to God. However, God knew that this intense involvement with everyday work is potentially dangerous. One may become too tied up in financial and business matters. God, therefore, gave us the most wonderful present, *Shabbat*. On *Shabbat*, we are commanded to rest completely from any form of work. Not only is physical work prohibited, but "your speech on *Shabbat* should not be similar to your everyday conversation" (*Shabbat* 113a). We are commanded to differentiate completely between *chol*, the weekday, and *kodesh*, the holy *Shabbat*. On *Shabbat*, we must not talk about business; it is a day reserved entirely for spiritual pursuits.

Am Yisrael is a nation with a task, to develop *kedusha*, holiness, in the world. But, like all other nations, it also is involved with the physical. We work the land, do business, and wage wars. What is to be the world's *kedusha*? The answer: We also have the *Shabbat*—the "sanctuary in time" that enables us to return to our God-given task, to delve into *kedusha*. Such is the task of *Shabbat*; it reminds us of our roots and natural inclination. The innate *kedusha* that we possess can all too easily be forgotten in the daily rat race. *Shabbat* is a weekly opportunity to cultivate *kedusha* and promote it. In fact, *Shabbat* is not a break from the rest of the week. It is the pinnacle of our pursuits, and it affords credence and meaning to the rest of our existence. Throughout the week, we savor the taste of *Shabbat*, both as a memory of the joys of last week's celebration and in anticipation of the *Shabbat* that is yet to come next week. *Shabbat* gives our individual lives purpose and significance.

Yet *Shabbat* is an individual experience, "no one must leave their own abode on the seventh day" (*Shemot* 16:29). *Shabbat* is the ultimate time for the family and one's immediate environment. In the same way that *Shabbat* provides the individual with an opportunity to return to his intrinsic nature, so the *Sh'mittah* returns us to our original nature. This time, however, not as individuals, but as a nation. *Sh'mittah* has the same affect on the *Am* as *Shabbat* has on the individual.

During the *Sh'mittah* year, we are forbidden to actively work the land. The land must rest and the *Sh'mittah* is "a *Shabbat* for the land." Only what naturally develops is to be consumed; the land returns to its natural state. Together with the land, the entire nation returns to a more natural state. During the year, agricultural work ceases; debts are canceled; the land lies fallow. This affords an opportunity for the whole nation to refocus its efforts on developing its innate *kedusha*—not as individuals, but as a people united. We are at one with the resting land and the readily available free time allows us to redirect our national conscience toward the spirit. We rediscover our raison d'être as a nation. We inject *kedusha* into our lives and this, in turn, affects all that we are to do until the next *Sh'mittah* comes around again.

The highest rung on our scale is the *Yovel*. *Shabbat* returns us to the *kedusha* of the individual, *Sh'mittah* to the *kedusha* of the nation. The *Yovel* affects a much greater arena. The *Yovel* is the opportunity to restore the *kedusha* of an entire generation. During the *Yovel*, all returns to its original state. The land converts back to its original owners, even if they themselves have forgotten their inheritance. It is possible that the grandfather of the family sold out his inheritance nearly fifty years previously. Even so, the grandchildren recover what once was theirs. Servants who have been in service for decades return to their families and initial environments. All rediscover their roots and are given a fresh start. The past fifty years may have contained pain and strife, poverty or success. The *Yovel* affords a new chance.

It may be for this reason that the *Yovel* started on Yom Kippur, the Day of Atonement. Yom Kippur is the day when all our past misdemeanors are judged and evaluated. At the end of the day, we are presented with a clean slate and an opportunity to start the year on a fresh footing. We pray that whatever the old year held, the coming year will be definitely better. "May the past year end with her curses. Let the new year begin together with her blessings" (prayers of the High Holy Days).

Yom Kippur affords us a time to heal any scars that we may have inflicted on our own souls. It is a chance to start afresh, but it is also much more. On Yom Kippur we refrain from food, both as a "day of affliction" and in order to resemble the angels. We try to reveal the *kedusha* that rests within us yet is usually denied expression.

The same is true with the *Yovel*. We are presented with an opportunity to reveal our innate *kedusha*, not as individuals nor only as a nation, but linked with all past and future generations. We are taught to view ourselves as an integral part of the flow of the generations. Indeed, one of the classical commentators on the Torah explains the use of the word *dror*, freedom. In Hebrew, there are a number of words conveying a sense of freedom. The word *dror* is used very rarely; in fact, in this context, the word *dror* appears only once in the Torah, in the verse in our *parsha*. The prophet Yechezkel calls the *Yovel* "*Shnat Dror*," a year of freedom. (*Yechezkel* 46:17). This seems to suggest that it is not a coincidence that the Torah uses the word *dror* here, as opposed to the more common *chofesh*. The Ramban explains that the word *dror* is linked to the word *dor*, meaning generation. "In truth, *dror* is from the word *dor*, and so it is with the *Yovel* that each returns to his roots" (Ramban on the *Torah Vayikra* 25:10). The *Yovel* returns us to our roots and family, to the previous and future generations.

No matter what occurred during the past fifty years, the *Yovel* links us to our past. We reunite with past generations and this imbues us with hope and *kedusha* that will carry us into the future. Faith is only as far away as the next *Shabbat*, the coming *Sh'mittah* year, or, at the most, a future *Yovel*.

We have the task to reveal *kedusha* as individuals, as a nation, and ultimately, as a generation within the passage of history. The tools that we have been given to achieve this are *Shabbat*, *Sh'mittah*, and the *Yovel*. It is totally logical that the idea of *Sh'mittah* and the *Yovel* should find their way into the *Book of Vayikra*. They are part of the method by which we are to accomplish our God-given task. The *Sh'mittah* and *Yovel*, like *Shabbat*, give us periodic opportunities to reveal our innate *kedusha*. We have our task laid out for us, and they are to help us achieve it.

Bechukotai
It All Depends On Me

The obstinacy to remain with the same outlook and to use it as an excuse for sins that have become entrenched in one's nature, be they actions or thoughts, is a sickness that derives from slavery. It does not allow the light of freedom to illuminate us. Teshuvah *strives for creative and true freedom, that is Divine freedom, which contains no slavery.*

(*Orot Hateshuva*, Chapter 5:5)

We find natural, physical teshuvah *that encompasses all of the sins against one's own nature. Every bad action brings sickness and suffering. As a person becomes aware that he himself has caused this pain and lack of life, he attempts to rectify this situation, to return to the laws of nature in order that he may live life to the fullest.*

(*ibid.*, Chapter 1)

Through teshuvah, *all returns to Divinity; through the existence of* teshuvah, *all becomes connected to the complete Divine entity; through the concept of* teshuvah, *the ideas and feelings, thoughts and opinions, will and emotions, everything turns and returns to Divine sanctity.*

(*ibid.*, Chapter 4:2)

We certainly have our work cut out for us. This is the last *parsha* of the Book of *Vayikra* and, as we look back on the book of our task in the word, it is a daunting prospect. We are to bring *shalom*, completeness to the world, and emulate the *cohanim*. We are to revive the world through *kedusha* and fit into God's great world order. How are we to succeed in such an arduous task?

The first thing to remember is that if we were chosen by the Almighty for such a role, then He knows that we are capable of fulfilling it. Another crucial point to bear in mind is the words of the Mishnah: "You are not required to finish the task, yet you are not free to neglect it" (*Avot* 2:16). We have to be realistic in understanding that we are part of the plan. We are a crucial part, but only a segment, nevertheless. This is important, as one tends to desire to witness the completion of any given task. When man sees that his efforts will not bring about a complete world revolution, he tends to become despondent. He then assumes that it would have been better not to have started working at all. The Mishnah urges us to be realistic, but forbids us to become desperate.

Were we to consider our situation for a moment, we might claim that, from the outset, the possibility of success is bleak. After all, we were not responsible for the conditions that we find ourselves in. We did not choose our family nor where we were to be born. In many cases, we did not even choose the path our lives were to take, but found ourselves on a particular track. We are victims of circumstance and products of our surroundings. How can we be held responsible for anything that we did, do, or may do in the future?

The Torah does not believe in such determinism. One is always in control; our whole lives swing on the balance of one word: *If.*

In the words of our *parsha*, "If you follow My laws, I will give you rain in its season, and the land will produce fruit, and so forth. But if you reject My commandments, then I will deal with you accordingly" (*Vayikra* 26:3, 4, 14, 16). The whole *parsha* is full of promised rewards for correct behavior and punishment for laxity in keeping the words of the Torah. It all depends on *if* you keep My laws or *if* not.

The *Gemara* brings a rather graphic example of this rejection of determinism:

> There was a man named Eliezer Ben Dordia, who was renowned for having slept with every prostitute throughout the world. He once heard of a whore in a distant land and took sufficient money to pay her and traveled the great distance to sleep with her. As they were about to make love, she broke wind. She said to him: "In the same way as that will not return to the place that it just left, so too Eliezer Ben Dordia is incapable of returning to God."
>
> He left and sat between two great mountains. "Mountains and valleys, seek mercy for me." They refused, saying that they also were unworthy. "Heaven

and earth have mercy on me," he implored. They also refused. "Sun and moon, show my innocence." But they also rejected him. "Stars and the constellation, forgive me." Again, they refused.

Eventually, he declared, "It depends on me and me alone." He placed his head between his knees and cried uncontrollably until his soul left his body.

A heavenly voice was heard that pronounced, "Rabbi Eliezer Ben Dordia is accepted into the next world."

Rebbe cried and proclaimed, "There are those that achieve the rewards of the next world only after several years of serving God, and yet there are some that achieve it in one hour. Not only that, they are referred to with the title rabbi" (*Avodah Zarra*, 17a).

This is a most unusual story that needs careful analysis and explanation. Eliezer Ben Dordia had an interesting claim to fame and notoriety. He had sunk to one of the lowest possible levels of human existence. He was so driven by sexual impulse that, when he heard of a new prostitute, he endangered his life and spared no expense in order to satisfy his evil inclination. Yet this time, a strange event occurred. Regularly, the harlot would take care not to break wind during intercourse. However, despite her cautions, when they went to bed, this harlot did break wind. She saw this as a supernatural sign that was directed toward her client (See *Ben Yehoyada*, ad loc.). Her response was that Eliezer Ben Dordia was being told to return, and here was his last chance.

Her words so shocked Eliezer Ben Dordia that he immediately left her and started on the long road to *teshuvah*, return. Yet his method of doing *teshuvah* is extraordinary. Instead of facing up to his own failings, weaknesses, and sins, he approached the mountains, the sun, the moon, and the stars, hoping that they would beg forgiveness for him and be his *teshuvah*.

Eliezer Ben Dordia believed in determinism. The mountains were responsible for his plight. In this case, the mountains represent the geographical location of Eliezer Ben Dordia. He argued that he lived in a specific area and that this was the major cause of his behavior. However, this approach was rejected by the heavenly court. One cannot be excused simply because he resides in a particular place. He is still held responsible for his own actions.

Eliezer Ben Dordia tried another tactic. He turned to the heavens and to the earth to intercede on his behalf. He argued that he was only human, a product of heaven and earth. How could he be held accountable for his wrongdoings? Again, he was told that this was not a valid excuse. Even though he was human, he was expected to rise to the challenge to emulate his Creator and do His bidding.

The next counsel that he sought was with the sun and the moon, the keepers of time. He was a product of his age and had been influenced by the decadence that he witnessed all around him. He was blameless for his crimes because he lived in a corrupt era. Once again, his plea was rejected. No one can claim that he just flowed with the tide of history and that this was his downfall.

In a last attempt, Eliezer Ben Dordia turned to the stars and constellations to be his heavenly advocate. He was born in a particular star sign and had a specific temperament. This was the source of his problem, and he found himself unable to change his bad character. This argument received the same response as all of his previous claims. You are responsible, and you will not be reprieved by any external influences.

At this point, Eliezer Ben Dordia understood the whole foundation of *teshuvah*. One must take responsibility for one's actions. All of the outside influences may make a difference but are, in essence, irrelevant. "It all depends on me. I am the only person who can take my life in my hands." In the words of the sage Hillel: "If I am not for myself, who will be for me?" (*Avot* 1:14). Eliezer Ben Dordia realized that he could no longer blame his circumstances, his family background, his generation. "It all depends on me." He placed his head between his knees and returned to himself. This reminds us of the *Gemara* that describes the fetus in the womb as having its "head between [its] knees" (*Niddah* 30b). Eliezer Ben Dordia had returned to his initial state, even before coming into the world. Only by doing so again could he return to the real cause of his sins—himself.

At that moment, Eliezer Ben Dordia had fulfilled his purpose. He had arrived at the realization that he was responsible for his own destiny. He was ready to leave the world and enter the world to come. Entry into the next world is dependent on fulfilling one's God-given purpose. Therefore, Eliezer Ben Dordia was welcomed into heaven. He succeeded in doing so in one hour, an achievement that took others a lifetime.

The lesson that we learn from Eliezer Ben Dordia seems plain and obvious. Everyone knows that they are accountable for their own actions. Yet we live in a world rich in *ism's*. We are taught that outside forces control our decisions and our lifestyles. We are conditioned to believe that we are not fully in control of our destiny. Occasionally, we even excuse ourselves on the basis that we are not to blame, everyone does it, society made us do it.

If you walk in My ways, if you take your life in your hands and realize that it depends on Me, then the land will produce fruit both physically and spiritually.

Our task is to elevate the world through *shalom* and *kedusha*. It all depends on us.

IV

Bemidbar

Introduction

We have a life-giving drug connected to our nationality. It is accepted that each nation "dies" and passes from the world. All of the ancient nations have disappeared, and if one does remain, it has never faced dispersion and has not developed to influence the rest of the world. But to continue living and to remain strong and overcome many obstacles, this is unique to Am Yisrael. *It depends on the name of God that is attached to them and the elixir of life of the living Torah.*

(*Orot*, p. 157)

Miracles were performed to Am Yisrael *as they are extraordinary. The fact that the people are described as "My first-born son" is irreversible and nonchanging. This was not incidental but due to their enhanced sanctity and, therefore, it will not change. It is inconceivable that Israel's advantage should not be eternal.*

(*Ein Iyah, Berachot*, Chapter 5, Note 84)

The nature of the collective soul of Israel is Divinity. She was not chosen due to her individual choice or actions, nor due to her sense of justice and honesty. Rather it is due to lineage, both physical and spiritual.

(*Shabbat Ha'aretz*, Introduction, p. 7)

What forms a nation? On what basis does a people survive and flourish? These are not purely academic questions. Rather, they greatly influence the Jewish people. We are witness to the fact that many nations have entered the arena of world history, strutted on the stage for a few centuries,

and withered away. Despite this, one nation has weathered all the changes
that exist in the earth's climate. Our nation has beaten the generally accepted
rules of anthropology and survived.

Am Yisrael Chai—the Jewish people live forever. We have been successful
in defying logic and circumstance, and we are alive and kicking. No matter
what was hurled at us, by Divine command or human malice, we have stayed
alive and outlived them all.

The Egyptians, Babylonians, and Romans conquered us. They deported
and enslaved us. Logically, we should have assimilated into their cultures
and disappeared. However, the opposite is true. The very same Egyptian,
Babylonian, and Roman empires collapsed and disintegrated. Yet *Am Yisrael*
survived. The descendants of those slaves are today active in all walks of life
around the globe. We are still determining history as we did millennia ago.
Other nations are finite; we live forever.

This has lead some historians to an interesting conclusion. The Jews that
are around today have no connection with the Jews mentioned in the Torah
and the *Tanach*. We are not the descendants of Avraham, Yitzchak, and
Ya'akov, they say. After all, it defies all known laws and rules of nations.

They are wrong. We are *Bnei Yisrael*, the sons of Ya'akov and all of the
other characters mentioned in the *Tanach*. In our veins runs the blood of
Moshe, Yehoshua, and Yeshiyahu. *Am Yisrael Chai*.

Others are willing to accept that we are indeed the remnants of the chosen
people. They then rack their brains to explain the phenomena that is the Jewish
people. It is because we are wise and separatist, they claim. Others point to
exactly the opposite. We survive due to our stupid tenacity or our ability to,
chameleon-like, be absorbed into any foreign culture. They are also mistaken.
That is not the secret of our success.

So what is it? How do we survive?

The *Book of Bemidbar* is the fourth book of the Torah and deals with the
accomplishments of the Jewish people. One of our major accomplishments is
simply that we have survived for so long as a nation. Therefore, in order to
answer our question, it would be wise to see the blueprint for survival laid
down in *Bemidbar*.

"You shall be for Me a kingdom of priests and a holy nation" (*Shemot* 19:6).
We are to be a holy nation, a kingdom of *cohanim*. That is how we managed
to survive. The rules that govern other nations are not the same as they are
for us. We are God's chosen nation.

Yet, within this verse there is an inherent contradiction. We are to be a
kingdom of priests. But the king had a specific role and the *cohen* had a very

different one. The king was a political figure; he was in charge of national affairs. On the other hand, the *cohen* was a spiritual leader and his place was in the *Beit Hamikdash*, the Temple. We are to be a holy nation; but a nation, *Goy*, refers to all nations, yet we are to be holy, separate, different. How are we to be both kings and *cohanim*? Can we be like all the other nations and yet be strangely different?

That is our task—to combine many distinct concepts and ideals in one group, *Am Yisrael*. We are to be kings, politicians, warriors, economists *and* be priests—holy, Divine. We are to sanctify every walk of life and each part of our national existence. We are to be a national entity like the other nations, and we are to be holy. Indeed, we are to prove that even national affairs are holy and can be conducted in a manner befitting a holy nation.

Throughout the *Book of Bemidbar*, we shall see that the Torah implores us to elevate our national affairs. They are to be as much a revelation of God as the sacrifices and worship in the *Beit Hamikdash*. We are to combine the task of the king with that of the priest.

"You shall be for Me a kingdom of priests and a holy nation."

Bemidbar
Nationality and Divinity

The style of life and thought for humans encompasses all their essence, and is expressed through the concept of society and the concept of the spirit. They are the treasures of the national form and the religious form of human societies. They influence all strata of life, on an individual and on a national level, spiritually and practically, the national ideal and the Divine ideal.

(Orot, p. 102)

From the very beginning of Israel, who knew how to identify this great Divine ideal even whilst idolatry was rampant and dominant, Israel revealed an ambition to establish a nation that would keep God's path to do justice, to elevate the world through the Divine ideal.

(ibid., p. 104)

In the days of old, during the era of Israel's blooming and the start of her fame, her soul was filled with a national ideal that was founded in the depths of the clear Divine ideal. Israel did this with all the passion of her great love and all her glory. In the treasures of the national ideal was found the Divine ideal.

(ibid., p. 105)

In this week's *parsha*, Moshe and Aharon were commanded to count the Jewish people. "From the age of 20, all those that went to fight" (*Bemidbar*, 1:3). Moshe and Aharon were to appoint the heads of each of the twelve tribes to help them in this census. Together, they arrived at the number of men over the age of 20 in the camp. "The final number of those over the age of 20, those that went out to war, was 603,550 men." (*ibid.*, 45–46).

But the tribe of Levi was not included in this count. Indeed, the very next verse informs us "but the tribe of Levi were not counted amongst them" (*ibid.*, 47). That does not mean to say that they were not counted. "Count the tribe of Levi, each male from the age of one month and over" (*ibid.*, 3:15). The Leviim were counted, but the Torah stresses that they were not included in the census of the rest of *Am Yisrael*. The Torah mentions this several times: "The Leviim were not counted amongst the rest of the children of Israel according to God's instructions" (*ibid.*, 2:33). This, then, was obviously of great significance; that the Leviim and the rest of *Bnei Yisrael* were counted, but counted separately.

The most obvious difference between the two types of census is that the Leviim were to be numbered from the age of one month onwards, whereas the rest were counted from the age of 20. The Divine requirement that the Leviim were to be enumerated from such a young age necessitated a special method on the part of Moshe. In the words of the midrash: "Moshe said to God 'You asked me to count them from one month, what am I to do? Should I enter their houses to reckon each newborn infant?' God replied 'You do your job and I will do Mine.' Moshe stood at the entrance to the tents of the Leviim and a heavenly voice proclaimed the number of children in the tent" (*Bemidbar Rabba*, 3:9; and see Rashi on *Bemidbar* 3:16).

This was not the only difference between the two sets of figures. When the Torah describes the total number of Leviim, it does so according to "their families" (*Bemidbar* 3:15, et al.). However, when the account of the rest of the camp appears, they are numbered by "those that went out to war" (*ibid.*, 1:20, et al.). The Leviim held an importance, in terms of the census, in relation to their families. The importance of the rest of *Am Yisrael* seemed to emanate from their ability to fight.

In order to make sense of these verses, we must understand something crucial about the Jewish people.

Each nation exists and survives on the basis of the strength of two entities. A nation must have a national infrastructure. In order to develop, it must have an economic structure and political system, be it a monarchy or a democracy. To be able to defend itself, it must have an army and military might. Without these elements, a nation will eventually be swallowed up by its neighbors or other conquerors.

But this aspect of a nation alone is also not enough. Many nations, in the course of history, have possessed strong armies and political systems. Yet, somehow, they have disappeared, become extinct, and eventually left the world's stage. A strong infrastructure alone holds no guarantee that a nation will survive.

Apart from a political system, a nation has to develop a culture. A nation rises and falls on the strength of its culture and spirit. The ability to fight is meaningless if the morale of the troops is nonexistent. The will to fight is what enables weak peoples to defend themselves against great empires. Nations decline when their soul is spent and depressed. The will to fight often produces the way to fight and succeed.

On the other hand, a society cannot live on the success on its spirit alone. Just possessing a strong vitality and culture is not enough when one is being attacked on all fronts.

So a nation requires a national side and a spiritual side in order to survive and thrive. In the same way that the individual exists in both body and soul, so does a national collective possess body and soul. The body is the political side and the soul is the spirit.

This is true of any community and tribe, but how much more so is it relevant to *Am Yisrael*. The Jewish people are known to be giants of the spirit. This is seen through our huge contribution to general philosophy and ethics as much as through our religious endeavors in matters closer to the heart of *Am Yisrael*. Yet this, in itself, is not enough to form the Jewish nation. Judaism is not only a religion, but is the basis of a nation, *Am Yisrael*, the Jewish people. Therefore, it is imperative that the nation develop both aspects. We need giants of the spirit, but we also need champions of the physical.

Am Yisrael needs to fuse the idea of a national entity with a spiritual component. In the case of other nations, this may be connected with human wisdom and morality. In the case of *Am Yisrael*, this means that we are indivisibly linked with God. He is the source of our spiritual nature. This culture is to influence our national structure and, therefore, everything that we are to do as a nation.

Our national vitality is as much an expression of sanctity as is our spiritual culture. All that *Am Yisrael* does is imbued with the same *kedusha*, holiness, be it offering sacrifices or deciding foreign policy. However, it is clear that different branches of the nation were entrusted with specific tasks.

The Leviim were to serve in the *Beit Hamikdash* on a full time basis and to decide on matters dealing with ritual purity. They represented the Divine side of affairs; they were the spirit of *Am Yisrael*. The rest of the people were to be involved in more national affairs. They were to work the land and develop the economy. They were to become kings and ministers and to decide political matters. And they were to become soldiers and defend the nation against outside attack from all sides.

Both tasks were essential. A spiritual culture without a strong national base would be incapable of true expression. Conversely, a political infrastructure devoid of God would eventually collapse from the lack of the will to continue in the face of outside pressures. *Am Yisrael* is only complete when the physical and the spiritual are fused.

We needed both the tribe of Levi and the rest of the tribes. Each was to be counted, but in order to preserve the specific nature of each, they were to be counted separately. The Torah emphasizes that the people were counted from the age of 20, all "those that went out to war." Such was the task of the nation, to be involved in national affairs, including serving God in the defense of the nation and the land. The Leviim did not go to war; this was not their task. They represented the Divine side of affairs. They were not counted from the age of 20 "those that went to war." Rather, when we come to the account of the Leviim, they were numbered according to families. The Leviim fulfilled their task by belonging to a particular group, the tribe of Levi. Just by their physical existence, they injected *kedusha* into the camp of Israel. They were counted by families from one month of age. "From the time that they stopped being in imminent danger" (Rashi on *Bemidbar* 3:15), they were counted. (Within the first month after birth of the child, he is considered to be in danger and is only considered a "complete" individual after one month.) Each individual Levi contributed to the Divine side of *Am Yisrael*, and they were all counted, not only those that were capable of physical work.

Am Yisrael succeeded in finding a place for the body and for the soul. These were not separate tasks entirely; indeed, we will see in the coming weeks that they were to meld in the *Beit Hamikdash*. Our raison d'être as a nation is to continue to fuse them. This is the secret of our success.

Naso
The Princes and the Temple

*There is one spirit that vitalizes the State and the Temple in Israel.
This is not an artificial connection that links the national life together,
rather this is Divinely ordained. There are no halves, no fractions or
divisions within the elements of the national soul. A holy unity
pervades our life. Two sides emerge that emphasize the talents of the
nation: the State and the Temple.*

(*Ma'amrei HaRiyah*, p. 181)

*Torah and the monarchy are inextricably linked in the Jewish people.
The king was commanded to write a special* Sefer Torah, *in addition
to the commandment on every individual to write a* Sefer Torah. *We
learn from this that acceptance of the Torah is bifaceted. There is the
acceptance of the individual as an individual connected to the
collective. But also an acceptance of the nation as a nation and a
national entity.*

(*ibid.*, p. 173)

*Eternity; this refers to Jerusalem. And the Glory; that is the Temple.
Israel's stand is complete when it is filled with the strength of
sovereignty as a holy and great nation. The strength of the monarchy is
connected to Jerusalem [and the Temple] where they have a special
place for the throne of the kings of David.*

(*Olat Riyah*, Volume I, p. 233)

In this week's *parsha*, we find the third and final account of the erection of the *Mishkan*, the Sanctuary. It will be recalled that the Jewish people were instructed to construct a temporary Temple in the wilderness. This was to serve them until the entry into the land of Israel. There they would eventually build the *Beit Hamikdash*, the Temple.

The account appeared in the *Book of Shemot* and in the *Book of Vayikra*. There is no unnecessary repetition in the Torah, so we must attempt to understand the relevance of each account. The *Book of Shemot* spoke about the meeting between *Am Yisrael*, the Jewish people, and God. We can also understand the erection of the *Mishkan* in that context. Thus, the *Book of Shemot* concluded with the account of building the *Mishkan* as a way of continuing this auspicious association (See chapter on *Teruma*, "Make Me a Temple and I will Dwell Amongst You").

The *Book of Vayikra* is referred to as *Torat Cohanim, The Laws of the Cohanim*, the priests. As the *cohanim* were the people that worked in the *Mishkan*, and later in the *Beit Hamikdash*, it is logical that the account of building the *Mishkan* should appear somewhere in the *Book of Vayikra*. Over and above this, the *cohen* had the task of fusing together seemingly incompatible elements within the nation. The *Mishkan*, and later the *Beit Hamikdash*, had a similar task. It enabled every person to find his place and role (See chapter on *Tzav*, "The Complete *Mishkan*").

In this week's *parsha*, the account reappears. "On the day that Moshe completed building the *Mishkan*, he anointed and sanctified it and all the vessels therein" (*Bemidbar* 7:1). What is the point of repeating the story of the erection of the *Mishkan*? Why is it relevant to *Bemidbar*, the book that relates what *Am Yisrael* accomplished?

The answer lies in the continuation of the account given here. "The princes of Israel, the heads of the families, that had carried out the census, came to the *Mishkan*. They brought with them sacrifices" (*ibid.*, 2–3). "God said to Moshe: 'Each day, one of the princes will offer his sacrifice in order to dedicate the altar'" (*ibid.*, 11). The Torah then gives a long account of the sacrifice that each of the twelve princes brought. Even though each of them brought exactly the same sacrifice, the Torah repeats it twelve times. This forms the end of the *parsha*. Until "this was the dedication of the *Mishkan* on the day that it was anointed by the princes of Israel" (*ibid.*, 84).

It appears that the sacrifices that the princes brought were the final act of the dedication of the *Mishkan*. Although we have seen the account before, it seems that the *Mishkan* was only functional after these twelve sacrifices. What was the significance of the sacrifices of the princes?

The generally accepted view is that the *Beit Hamikdash* is the domain and the territory of the *cohanim*. They were the ones who brought the sacrifices and spent their days in Temple service. They did not receive a portion of the land as did the rest of the nation. This was so they might dedicate their efforts entirely to the purpose of serving God in the *Beit Hamikdash*. It was forbidden for anyone other than a *cohen* to enter certain parts of the *Beit Hamikdash*. All of these facts tend to indicate that the *Beit Hamikdash* was, indeed, the dominion of the *cohanim*.

However, this conception is mistaken. The *Beit Hamikdash* belongs to the whole nation. It is not the sole possession of the Cohanim, or indeed, of any other group within *Am Yisrael*.

The princes of the nation represented the political aspirations of *Am Yisrael*. They recognized that this inclination was as relevant to the *Beit Hamikdash* as was the Divine inclination of the *cohanim*. Not only was the *Beit Hamikdash* physically connected to the whole of *Am Yisrael*, but it was connected to both the spiritual and physical sides of the nation. Therefore, all of *Am Yisrael* had a part in the Temple and was connected to it.

In order to prove this, the princes of the nation brought sacrifices to the *Mishkan*. Indeed, the dedication of the *Mishkan* was only complete after the princes brought their sacrifices. Only when the two forces within the nation came together in this way was the *Mishkan* complete. The *Mishkan* was fused with both spiritual service and a political dimension.

This fusion manifests itself in several ways. The *Beit Hamikdash* functioned as the seat of the High Court, the *Sanhedrin*. "There were three courts there [in the *Beit Hamikdash*], one at the entrance of the Temple Mount, one at the entrance of the Temple itself, and one in the office of the *Gazit* [underneath the *Beit Hamikdash*]" (*Sanhedrin* 11:2). This was a body of judges whose task it was to decide the more complex and severe civil cases. They, definitively, represented the civil might of *Am Yisrael*. Even though the judges were called *Elohim*, God, the cases that they judged were civil cases and not directly connected with the Divine aspect of the *Beit Hamikdash*.

Another example was that the banks and the economic system were based in the *Beit Hamikdash*. "On the twentieth fifth day of the month of Adar, banks were established in the *Beit Hamikdash*" (*Shekalim* 1:3). This was initially to serve those who flooded into Jerusalem for the festivals and needed cash to buy sacrifices and redeem sanctified fruits that they had brought with them. But it is indicative that these banks were established on the grounds of the *Beit Hamikdash* and not in a convenient location nearby. The Temple was holy but it was also was the center of the nation. This encompassed all that was the nation, both the holy and the mundane. Sacrifices and economics fused in the *Beit Hamikdash* as they did in the daily life of *Am Yisrael*.

The king also had a special place in the *Beit Hamikdash*. He took an active role in certain ceremonies in the Temple. One such occasion was the *HaKhel*. At the conclusion of the *Sh'mittah* year, all of the nation would gather in the Temple on the final days of the festival of Succot. During the service, the king would read from the Torah. "Moshe ordered them 'At the close of the *Sh'mittah*, on the festival of Succot, when all of the nation are assembled in God's chosen place, read the Torah before them. Gather all of the men, women, and children so they may hear and learn to fear God'" (*Devarim* 31:10–12). The Mishnah describes the order of the service. "They would construct a wooden platform for the king in the courtyard of the *Beit Hamikdash*. The *Chazan* of the Temple took the *Sefer Torah* and handed it to the head of the *Knesset*, who, in turn, gave it to his deputy. He then passed it on to the *Cohen Gadol*, who handed the Torah to the king, who then read from the Torah" (*Sotah* 7:8). This was in contrast with Yom Kippur when it was the task of the *Cohen Gadol* to read from the Torah (See *ibid.*, 7).

The law from the Torah was designed to teach the assembled masses the word of the Lord. This would seem to be the task of the *cohen*. Indeed, it was he who read on Yom Kippur. Yet, this special ceremony of the *HaKhel* was significant in that it was the task of the king to read and teach the Torah.

There was no separation between the roles of the Divine leader and the politician. The *Cohen Gadol* and the king reversed roles on this occasion in order to prove that the king was also responsible for the spiritual welfare of his nation. In fact, the *Cohen Gadol* handed the Torah to the king. "This was to show respect to the king" (*Sotah* 41b). The *Cohen Gadol* recognized the role of the king, in the same way that the king respected the task and function of the *Cohen Gadol*.

All this took place in the *Beit Hamikdash* to demonstrate that the fusion between the spiritual and civil aspects of the nation occurred in the heart of *Am Yisrael*, in the *Beit Hamikdash*. The account of the dedication appears in the *Book of Bemidbar* to verify this fact.

There were those who could not understand and accept that the *Beit Hamikdash* was not a totally spiritual building. They argued that there was no place in the Temple for banks and government offices. In today's parlance, we could say that they tried to separate "church from state." One such person was Jesus. It is recorded that he attempted to throw the "money lenders" out of the *Beit Hamikdash* (See Mark 11:15). However, they are mistaken.

In *Am Yisrael*, everything is linked to the Divine source. Both the spiritual and political aspirations are holy. That is *Am Yisrael*. Not only do we succeed as individuals to bring *kedusha* and sanctity to our daily lives but we do so as a nation. The most graphic example of this was in the *Beit Hamikdash*. But it was not reserved only for the Temple; this is part of our national makeup. We fuse heaven and earth.

Beha'alotecha
The Remains of the Nation in Exile

Galut—*internal destruction and external dispersion—completely*
obliterated the national ideal, which had already been divided from the
Divine. When it became disconnected from the life-source, it became
defiled through idolatrous culture. The greatness of Israel and her glory
fell from heaven to earth.

(*Orot*, p. 108)

Because the Divine and the national ideals are so close to each other
and each contains a part of the other, the national ideal remained
through the divine ideal and the latter cannot relinquish its influence
over the nation. The Divine ideal was weakened due to the fall of the
national ideal but remained in a smaller state in the 'miniature
Temples' of the synagogue and the study halls, in the home and the
family, through an adherence to Torah.

(*ibid.*)

Israel in galut, *exile, neglected all her concerns for physical matters on*
a national level. Rather, her effort was concentrated only in the
heavens and in spiritual pursuits. The nation no longer had any
physical endeavors as a people, but the Divine spirit affected
individuals, and the spiritual side of the nation was enhanced.

(*Shabbat Ha'aretz*, Introduction, p. 12)

This week's *parsha* opens with a passage that seems to be out of place. "God told Moshe 'Tell Aharon that he shall light the candles of the menorah, the candelabra. The seven lights will give light'" (*Bemidbar* 8:1, 2). The following passage also appears out of context. "Take the Leviim out of the rest of the children of Israel in order to purify them" (*ibid.*, 6). In fact, the first chapter of the *parsha*, in all its twenty-six verses, deals with the candle lighting and the Leviim. These subjects seem to be more relevant to the *Book of Vayikra* than the *Book of Bemidbar*. After all, the *Book of Vayikra* is referred to as *Torat Hacohanim, The Laws of the Cohanim* (the priests). One would assume that all of the laws that were directly connected to the *cohanim* and their service would be contained therein. If that is the case, the laws that open this week's *parsha* should have been written there.

The lighting of the menorah was reserved for the *cohanim*, and the method of sanctifying and purifying the Leviim is not connected to the *Book of Bemidbar*. The *Book of Bemidbar* discusses the achievements of the Jewish people. What is the connection between this theme and the opening verses of the *parsha*?

The menorah was lit every evening in the *Beit Hamikdash*. It was placed in the south of the *Kodesh*, the inner chamber. In the morning, the *cohen* would clean the receptacles that held the candles. In the evening, he would fill them with a fixed measure of pure olive oil and light them. The oil would remain alight until the morning when the *cohen* would repeat this task.

The midrash also strives to explain the relevance of this passage in its context. "Why was this chapter placed next to the chapter dealing with the sacrifices of the princes? Aharon saw that all of the princes had brought sacrifices and that the tribe of Levi was left out. He assumed that this was due to some deficiency on his part. Therefore, God told Moshe to inform him that this was not the case; rather that he and his tribe had been reserved for a greater task. 'The sacrifices that they bring are only offered so long as the *Beit Hamikdash* is standing, but the candles in the menorah endure forever. The ability that I gave you to bless the children of Israel is eternal'" (*Tanchuma, Beha'alotecha* 5).

The midrash informs us that these verses *are* relevant to the *Book of Bemidbar*. They were placed here as a result of Aharon's initial response on witnessing the respect that the princes received when they brought their sacrifices to the *Beit Hamikdash*. This was in contrast to his own tribe, which was excluded from this particular sacrifice. Aharon feared that his own tribe was being left out and that this was a punishment for some misdemeanor that he might have committed. It was necessary that God ensure him that this was not the case. He and his tribe had the task of lighting the menorah in the *Beit Hamikdash*. This task was superior to that of the princes; God's reassurance was intended to put Aharon at ease.

The distinction of lighting the menorah was that it transcended time. Unlike the sacrifices that were only brought while the *Beit Hamikdash* stood, the lights were eternal.

The obvious question to be asked here relates to the everlasting nature of the menorah. Surely, the menorah was also only lit while the *Beit Hamikdash* was standing. If so, what was the advantage of Aharon and the tribe of Levi over the other tribes?

The midrash explains that the reference here is to the menorah that was to be lit by the descendants of Aharon in the second Temple period. The Maccabees were to rededicate the Temple after it had been overrun by the Greeks (See *Shabbat* 21b). They found one jug of oil that miraculously burned for eight days, until more oil could be prepared. This was the miracle that we celebrate on the festival of Hanukkah. During this eight day festival, we light candles. These, according to the midrash, are the eternal lights that God promised to Aharon and his tribe. They were established by the Maccabees, who were from the tribe of Levi, and burn throughout the centuries independent of the *Beit Hamikdash* (See Ramban ad loc. In the name of Rabbeinu Nissim, also *Torah Shleima*).

However, another question presents itself. Aharon worried about the glory that the princes achieved due to the sacrifices that they offered during the dedication of the *Beit Hamikdash*. Aharon's entire day was filled with offering sacrifices and worshipping God in the Temple. Why did the fact that the princes each brought one sacrifice cause him such anxiety?

Obviously, there was something special that the princes had that Aharon felt he and his tribe lacked. The princes had achieved a level he had yet to attain, and this caused him disquiet.

As seen, in last week's *parsha*, when the princes brought sacrifices to the *Beit Hamikdash*, it was clear that they had succeeded in fusing the elements of the Jewish people. The princes themselves represented the political, economic, and military aspirations of *Am Yisrael*. They were the heads of the army, the civil courts, and the administration for the families of the children of Israel. In bringing sacrifices to the *Beit Hamikdash*, they realized that their strength came from a fusion with the other force within the nation, the Divine. They came to God's "house" and brought offerings. In so doing, they linked the national ideal with the spiritual ideal. This was perfection in itself—the highest level that the Jewish people could reach.

Aharon and the tribe of Levi watched these princes bringing their offerings to the *Beit Hamikdash*. They saw that the princes had achieved a level that they themselves were incapable of reaching. The princes had both a political and a spiritual objective, which they succeeded in fusing.

The tribe of Levi represented the Divine side of Jewish affairs. They did not go out to war and were not counted within the rest of the nation for this reason. They did not own fields and, thus, were less connected with the economic side of national life. Instead, they were assigned work and worship in the *Beit Hamikdash* and taught Torah to the nation. The *Cohen Gadol* was the person responsible for the spiritual welfare of the nation (See *Makot* 11a; "he should have prayed for mercy for the nation." This refers to the *Cohen Gadol*). "Why did the Leviim not receive a portion of the land? Because they were set apart to serve God, to teach His laws and ways to the masses. They were, therefore, distanced from the ordinary ways of the world; they did not go to war with the rest of the nation nor did they inherit the land through their physical might" (Rambam, *Mishneh Torah, Hilchot Sh'mittah VeYovel* 13:12).

When the tribe of Levi saw the princes bringing their sacrifices, they knew that they would never achieve this fusion. They had been set apart for a special task. This task had its advantages, but it appeared that the lot of other tribes exceeded theirs. Was it not the ideal to fuse the spiritual with the physical? Weren't the *Leviim* missing out?

God Himself assured Aharon that he had a particular advantage over the rest of the tribes. True, they bonded politics with God, but their reign was limited. "Yours lasts forever." The princes hold dominion only in situations that offer an opportunity to express ourselves as a nation in political, economic, and military ways. When we have this opportunity, then the princes and kings rule. But when *Am Yisrael* is not in its land, when we are denied the opportunity to be a nation amongst nations, when we have no autonomy or army, what is to become of the Jewish people? Will we, like all the other nations, decline in the absence of the ability to defend ourselves?

God gives Aharon the answer. *Am Yisrael* will survive because what you have and represent is eternal. The spirit of the Jewish people lives forever; the Divine does not and cannot decline. What has enabled us to outlive all of our opponents and persecutors is the spiritual aspect of Jewish existence. Even when we were exiled from our land and dispersed amongst the nations of the world, we remained alive and were the messengers of God on earth. In exile, "nothing remains for us except the Torah" (*Selichot*). The Torah remains, gives us life, and supplies our life with meaning.

The menorah was a symbol of wisdom and Torah study. "Whoever wants to attain wisdom should go south; he who desires wealth should go north. As the menorah was in the south" (*Babba Batra* 25b). The menorah and the lighting of the lights, the jurisdiction of Aharon, suggests knowledge. Aharon and the tribe of Levi represented the spirit, the Divine, that is eternal. The Torah is not dependent on having a land, a government, an army, or the *Beit Hamikdash*.

If this is the case, then it would appear that we are not so bad off in *galut*, in exile. We survive and even thrive. The Torah developed in leaps and bounds. Most of the halachic literature that we have was written during the period when we had no land and were dispersed throughout the world. A quick look through any library of Jewish books reveals what a large volume of material was produced by the Jewish people in *galut*. The *Gemara*, the *Rambam*, the *Shulchan Aruch* were all written outside of the land of Israel.

However, the *Gemara* informs us that "since the destruction of the Temple, all that remains for God in the world is four cubits of halacha" (*Berachot* 8a). God resided in the *Beit Hamidrash*—in the houses of learning, and in the yeshivot.

What does the *Gemara* mean by the term "four cubits of halacha"? Four cubits is the area that a human being occupies. There are certain halachic implications that arise from this. It is forbidden to sit within four cubits in front of someone who is praying (*Berachot* 31b). The minimum requirement for a private domain is four square cubits (*Eruvin* 3b).

Four cubits refers to items and concepts that are human and are private. The *Gemara* is implying that in *galut*, God is relegated to having control over private, personal affairs; the synagogue and its surrounding community, the home, and the school. Halacha, and therefore God, no longer manifests itself in national affairs, in governmental decisions. God remains confined within the four cubits of personal halacha.

The Maccabees strove to reestablish Jewish autonomy in the land of Israel. But they rededicated the *Beit Hamikdash* as one of their first acts. They went part of the way toward fusing politics and Divinity. The lights of Hanukkah represent their struggle, and these lights are eternal.

So, even though Aharon's craft remains eternal, it is affected totally by the *galut*. True, we will survive, but as individuals—as a community here and a community there. We are no longer a national entity. That can occur only in specific circumstances, and it is essential that we strive to attain them. What happens when we reject these factors we will see next week.

Sh'lach
Spies, Politics and God

In the land of Israel, we can perceive how the physical body of Israel is as holy as the soul. It is unnecessary to belittle the body, but rather it should be elevated to taste the sanctity of true life that comes from the holiness of the Land, saturated with the special aura of Israel.

(*Orot*, p. 171)

There were a group of messengers—spies—that came to the land of Israel and did not sufficiently consider the spiritual nature of the Jewish people and their holy lives. They raised objections because of disbelief and a lack of confidence in the nation. This had a very adverse affect and stopped the realization of esteemed goals.

(*Igrot HaRiyah*, Volume III, Letter 878)

We are returning to Eretz Yisrael. *We are waiting for redemption, not only to leave* galut *and the suffering therein, but much more than that; to reveal the entire light, to pour the flow of life until the holy of holies, the source of Israel, the source of her elevated soul, that illuminate us in the special land, the Holy Land, the land of life and the land of light.*

(*Orot HaRiyah*, p. 63)

"The entire community began to raise their voices and the people cried on that night" (*Bemidbar* 14:1). "That night was the ninth of Av. God said to them 'Because tonight you cried unnecessarily, I will establish it as a night of mourning throughout the generations'" (*Ta'anit* 29a). The ninth of Av,

Tisha B'Av, is the saddest and most tragic day of the Jewish calendar. On that day, both Temples were destroyed, the city of Betar fell, and Yerushalayim was destroyed (*ibid.*, 26b). Throughout history, this date has been synonymous with tragedy. The Crusades, the Spanish Inquisition, and the Holocaust are all reported to have started on the ninth of Av. What could have been so terrible about the tears of the nation on that night? What sin was so grave that its memory clouded our national vision for so long?

The *parsha* opens with an account of how Moshe sent spies into the land of Israel to check it out. They were carefully chosen and were all princes of the nation. Twelve were sent, one from each tribe, to spy out the land and bring back a report to the Jewish people. They were fully briefed before embarking on the mission. "Note the quality of the land and whether the inhabitants are strong or weak, many or few. Whether the land itself is good or bad, and whether the cities are fortified or not, and whether there are trees" (*Bemidbar* 13:18–20). The final instruction was that they "bring back some fruit of the land" (*ibid.*).

The midrash explains that all of these directives were in order to accentuate the good of the land of Israel. "There are lands that cultivate strong people, and there are those that raise weak people. Some lands are conducive to supporting a large populace, whereas others tend to diminish the populace" (*Tanchuma, Sh'lach* 6). Therefore, Moshe instructed them to "note the quality of the land." If the people were strong and plentiful, this was an indication that the land was of the type that raised a strong and large population. "If the people reside in fortified cities, this is a sign that the residents are weak and afraid" (*ibid.*) and so may be easily defeated.

Unfortunately, the spies ignored, or misunderstood, Moshe's advice and instead, interpreted the signs that they saw for the worse and not for the better. "The people that dwell in the land are strong and the cities are greatly fortified. We also saw there giants" (*Bemidbar* 13:28). "We will be incapable of conquering the land, as the people that live there are very strong. It is a land that devours its inhabitants. All the people there are huge" (*ibid.*, 31–32). Their report totally contradicted Moshe's recommendations. They implied that the inhabitants of the land had strength as a result of the defense surrounding their cities. But Moshe had already told them that a greatly defended city indicated a weak and vulnerable populace.

The spies returned with horror stories of the land and the strange inhabitants that they saw there. They even brought strange oversized fruit to prove the unnatural qualities of *Eretz Yisrael*. Their intention was to dissuade the rest of the nation from wanting to enter the land.

If this was their intent, then they were extremely successful. "The entire community began to raise their voices, and the people cried on that night. They complained to Moshe and Aharon, 'It would have been preferable to die in Egypt or in the desert. Why did you bring us to this land to die by the sword and leave our women and children as captives? It is better to return to Egypt' They said amongst themselves 'Let us return to Egypt.'" (*Bemidbar* 14:1–4). As a result of the misleading report of ten of the twelve spies, the people turned against Moshe and Aharon. They ignored the appeals of Calev and Yehoshua, the other two spies, who told them: "The land that we passed through is wonderful" (*ibid.*, 7).

The reaction of the people to the report, and the report of the ten spies itself, was enough reason for God to choose that very night as the night of national tragedy. God intended for us to enter the land and dwell there. His plan was thwarted by the spies and their followers, who rejected the land and preferred to return to Egypt.

The immediate punishment was "Your corpses shall fall in the desert. As to your children, of whom you said that they will be captives, I will bring them into the land, that they should know the land you rejected. Your children will wander in the desert for forty years, corresponding to the number of days that you spied out the land—forty days. One year for each day for a total of forty years" (*ibid.*, 29–34). This was the punishment for the entire nation. Instead of entering the land of Israel, they were to wander in the desert until the older generation had all died off. Only then were their children to enter the land under the leadership of Yehoshua, one of the two spies who had brought back a favorable report. In addition, "the spies themselves, who had slandered the land, died in a plague. Except Yehoshua Bin Nun and Calev Ben Yefuneh" (*ibid.*, 36–38).

This was a fitting punishment. They had rejected the land and God punished them by denying them access to His land. The nation was devastated on hearing the news of their Divine punishment. "They were overcome with a terrible grief. They awoke early the next morning and ascended the mountain declaring: 'We have sinned, but we are now ready. Let us ascend to the place that God has chosen'" (*ibid.*, 39–40). This seems to be the ultimate repentance for their sin of renouncing *Eretz Yisrael*. We would assume that their behavior would please God and that He might even relent and allow them to enter the land. Nothing could be further from the truth. "Moshe admonished them: 'Why are you going against God's word? You cannot succeed. Do not continue, since God is not with you and you will be slaughtered by your enemies. Ahead of you are the tribes of Amalek and Cana'an.

You will fall by their swords. You have left God and He is not with you.'
However, the people were defiant and climbed to the top of the mountain.
But the Ark of the Covenant of God and Moshe was not amongst them. The
tribes of Amalek and Cana'an descended upon them and completely annihilated them" (*ibid.*, 41–45).

If God wanted them to enter the land, and this was most crucial, shouldn't
he have encouraged their efforts to enter the land at all costs? Why did God
not go "amongst them" when they tried to rectify their sin and gain entry to
the land?

Before we attempt to answer this question, we have to tackle another issue.
We know that the spies were carefully selected. They were the princes of *Am
Yisrael*, pious and learned men. How could they have rejected the word of
God? Why did they bring back such a negative report of *Eretz Yisrael*? They
certainly knew that God had chosen the land for His people, and that it was
Divinely ordained they enter when God decided. Why did they attempt to
discourage the nation from entering the land of Israel?

The *Zohar* relates the thoughts that lay in the innermost recesses of their
minds. "Here in the desert we eat bread from heaven and have no financial
worries; we have ample time to sit and learn Torah. However, if we are to
enter the land of Israel, we will have to work the land and this will disturb
our spiritual pursuits" (*Zohar* III:152a; and see *Em Habanim Semeicha*, p. 230).
A carefree life in the desert seemed preferable to a worrisome existence in the
land of Israel. This was the root cause of the spies' sin. They saw Torah study
as a distinct entity, disconnected from national life. It was better, they claimed,
to learn Torah and eat the bread of heaven than to combine the spiritual with
the physical. This misconception blinded them, so that the report they brought
back was not only false, it was illogical.

There is an opinion that the land of Israel is a mitzvah insofar as it enables
us to keep more of God's commandments. Only in Israel do we have the opportunity to observe the laws linked with the land. All of the agricultural
injunctions are dependent on living in the land.

However, the connection between the land and the people is much deeper
and more basic than that. *Eretz Yisrael* and *Am Yisrael* are intrinsically linked.
One does not come into fruition without the other. The nation only has a full
expression when we are in our land. The land only gives its fruit and rests its
Shabbat when we inhabit her. "The land will give her fruit, and there I will
settle the remnants of the nation" (*Zechariya* 8:12). They are two links in a
chain and two sides of the same coin. We are God's nation and we are to dwell
in His land.

The way to acquire the land in this manner is to fuse, therein, the physical with the spiritual. We must build the land and till the soil, but we must also realize that these are spiritual pursuits. Indeed, we are commanded to bring the first fruits to the *Beit Hamikdash*, to tithe our produce and give a portion to the tribe of Levi, the *Leviim*, and the *cohanim* (See *Devarim* 26:1–12; and, 18:4). In this manner, we will always have it in mind that our physical work is fused with the spiritual aspirations of *Am Yisrael*.

Only *Eretz Yisrael* affords us an opportunity to link politics with God. Here, in the land, we are the masters of our own affairs. Here, we have the possibility of proving to all that even mundane tasks can be sanctified and become part of Divine service. This can be achieved in Israel and only in Israel.

The spies tried to divorce Israel from Torah study and Torah study from Israel. Their punishment was that they were unable to enter the land. The punishment for the generations was that the Temple itself was to be destroyed. It will not be rebuilt until we realize the centrality of Israel and the *Beit Hamikdash* to our personal and national lives. From that night, we were destined to go into exile, as we demonstrated that we had yet to grasp the full implication of *Eretz Yisrael*.

Those that attempted to enter the land by force alone were also repelled. Were they to have gone in and been successful in capturing the land, it would have remained a political and military venture. They would have lost the essence of *Eretz Yisrael*. They could not succeed because "the Ark of the Covenant of God and Moshe were not amongst them." Moshe called after them "God is not with you."

The land of Israel cannot be conquered by might alone. Nor can it be captured by Torah alone. In order to enter *Eretz Yisrael*, we need both the spirit and the body. Then, Israel becomes part of *Am Yisrael* and we become part of the land.

Korach
Leadership, The Way to Success

The cry of "all of the people are holy" was, in fact, a call that
dismissed all sanctity and preparation that is essential in order to
establish holiness in life, so it may resist all outside influence.
Therefore, it was essential that he be swallowed into the earth, to be
lost to the congregation forever, to never be like Korach and his band.

(*Orot*, p. 32)

Priesthood, the intermediary between man and God through the
medium of chosen humans, is not really an intermediary but rather a
suitable arrangement. The individual and the nation with their
constricted strengths are incapable of cleaving to God; therefore, one
sets aside a portion of himself, the most Divine, to draw near to God.
The cohen *knows Divinity and, through his knowledge and feeling,*
elevates the entire nation.

(*ibid.*, p. 54)

The tribe of Levi, through their particular nature and distinct position,
improve and keep their status; they become sanctified until it is a
blessing for the whole nation. The cohanim *are elevated to a special*
holy state that brings Divine spirit for the elevation of the entire people,
the collective.

(*Orot Hakodesh*, Volume II, p. 440)

In this week's *parsha*, Moshe and Aharon were bombarded by an attack on their respective positions within the camp of Israel. The attack was launched by a cousin of theirs, a man named Korach, the son of Yitzhar. He was a great grandson of Levi, as were Moshe and Aharon, and they had a common grandfather, Kehot. Amram, Moshe and Aharon's father, was Yitzhar's brother. So Korach was a first cousin of Moshe and Aharon.

"He demonstrated against Moshe and Aharon and said: 'You have gone too far; all of the community is holy and God is with all of them. Why did you set yourselves up over the congregation of God?'" (*Bemidbar* 16:3). He objected to the fact that Aharon had received the high priesthood and that Moshe was the leader. He claimed that he should have been made the prince of the tribe.

"He disagreed that Elitzaphan should have been made prince over his family. Korach claimed: 'My father was one of four brothers. Amram was the first born, and he took for himself a double portion. His son Aharon became the *Cohen Gadol*, and his other son, Moshe, became the leader. The next in line of the four brothers should receive the next task. My father was the second brother, and, therefore, I should have been appointed the prince. Instead, Uziel's son was made prince [by Moshe], even though he was my father's younger brother. It is inconceivable that he should rule over me. I, therefore, reject all that he [Moshe] has done'" (*Tanchuma, Korach* 1).

Korach was not satisfied with a personal argument and tried to turn it into a national debate. He went around the camp, stirring up descent against Moshe and Aharon. "Korach took Datan and Aviram and On, the son of Pelet. They confronted Moshe, together with two-hundred-and-fifty heads of the community" (*Bemidbar* 16:1–2). He convinced them that Moshe and Aharon were wrong in appointing themselves leaders; after all: "All the community is holy; they all heard the voice of God on *Har Sinai*. Why have you raised yourselves up over them?" (*Tanchuma, Korach* 4). He tried to show the people that Moshe and Aharon did not have a monopoly over sanctity and *kedusha*. He then used this feeling of dissension to attack Moshe and Aharon.

Korach tried to make a mockery of the Torah that Moshe had brought from God to the Jewish people. The midrash relates that he approached Moshe with a halachic question. "'Moshe, a *tallit* that is made entirely of the blue dye *techelet*, is it exempt from the one thread of blue on the *tzitzit*, the tassels themselves?' Moshe replied that one was still obliged to tie the thread of *techelet* in the *tzitzit*. To which Korach exclaimed: 'A *tallit* that is completely blue is still obliged in one blue thread, yet the one thread exempts the rest of the *tallit*. How is it possible?'" (ibid.)

The Torah commands us to tie one blue thread to our *tallit*, a four-cornered garment. On each corner we tie *tzitzit*, made of four threads; one of the four must be of *techelet*, the blue dye (See *Bemidbar* 15:38). Korach claimed that if the garment itself was colored with the blue dye, this was sufficient. In such a case, he said, one would not need to tie the blue thread, as the whole garment was blue. Halachically, this is incorrect, and this was Moshe's answer. Even though the *tallit* is completely blue, you still need to tie the one blue thread on each of the corners.

Again he posed a question. "'A house that is full of holy books, is it exempt from the *mezuzah*?' 'No, it is still obligated in the mitzvah of *mezuzah*.' Korach replied: 'The Torah contains 275 passages, and yet it does not exempt the house, but the two passages in the *mezuzah* are enough for the whole room. These things were not Divinely ordained, but you made them up'" (*Tanchuma, Korach* 4).

We are commanded to affix a *mezuzah* onto our doorposts. It contains the first and second portion of the *Shema* prayer (See *Devarim* 6:9). Korach claimed that if a house is full of Jewish texts and the Torah itself, this should be enough. In such a case, one would not need to place the small *mezuzah* on the door. The answer was that this is a mistake and that the *mezuzah* is an obligation, whether the house is full of books or not.

The midrash then relates how Korach ordered his band of rebels to make clothes that were all blue. They wore them and they set a table and laid out a meal. "The sons of Aharon came to take the priestly portion, and they shouted at them: 'Who commanded you to take these?' 'Moshe.' 'We will give you nothing as God did not command such laws.'" According to halacha, the cohen has the right to certain parts of the slaughtered animal (See *Bemidhar*, 18:8–32; and *Rambam, Hilchot Bikkurim*). Korach and his band of men refused to give these portions of the meat to the *cohanim*. In addition, they taunted them and Moshe by dressing in their rebellious clothes and flaunting the halacha in a most public manner.

Moshe initially tried to reason with them. "Is it not enough for you, and the *Leviim*, that God set you apart from the rest of Israel? He brought you close to Him in order that you might work in His *Mishkan* and lead the people. This privilege was given to you and all of the tribe of Levi, yet you still demand priesthood?" (*ibid.*, 16:9–10). When this tactic was unsuccessful, Moshe stalled them. "Moshe then said to Korach 'You and your whole band will come toward God tomorrow, you, them, and Aharon'" (*ibid.*, 16). This delay would allow Korach and his men time to retract their objection and finish the argument (See *Tanchuma, Korach* 5).

Moshe also prayed to God that He should prove to the nation the legitimacy and veracity of all of his actions. So, the next morning, when Korach and his crew came to offer incense in the *Mishkan*, Moshe advised the rest of the people: "Move away from the tents of these wicked men and do not touch anything of theirs" (*Bemidbar* 16:26).

"When Moshe finished speaking, the ground underneath them opened. The ground opened its mouth and swallowed them and their houses, and all of Korach's men, and all their property. They fell into the depths and were swallowed alive; the ground covered them up, and they were lost" (*ibid.*, 31–33). "Fire went out from God and consumed the 250 men" (*ibid.*, 35).

Korach is the symbol of misplaced rebellion. We are even commanded: "Do not be like Korach and his band" (*ibid.*, 17:5). The Mishnah portrays him as the epitome of an unjust argument. "What is meant by 'an argument that is not for the sake of heaven'? Such as that between Korach and his band" (*Avot* 5:17).

However, Korach's argument and method of proving his point remain unintelligible. He may have had a just claim against Moshe and Aharon, and may have been deserving of the princehood. But why did he gather a large group from amongst the people? Why did he question Moshe regarding the *techelet* and the mezuzah?

Surely, Korach knew that it is a biblical commandment to tie the *techelet* to the *tzitzit*; it is clearly stated in the Torah: "You shall put on the *tzitzit* a thread of blue" (*Bemidbar* 15:38). This is a mitzvah that exists independently of the color of the garment. Why did Korach assume that a blue shirt would be exempt from the command of *techelet*? The same is true of the mitzvah to affix a mezuzah to the doorpost. The Torah says: "Write these words on your doorposts and on your gates" (*Devarim* 6:8). Whether one's house is filled with books or anything else, one is commanded to 'write these words' (that is, attach a mezuzah). How could Korach rationalize his claim that a house full of holy scriptures should not require a mezuzah?

These questions, in essence, reflect Korach's true intentions and his conception of *Am Yisrael*. He used his legitimate argument against Moshe and the appointment of Elitzaphan to voice a grievance against the whole hierarchy of the nation.

"All of the community is holy and God is with all of them. Why did you set yourselves up over the congregation of God?" Korach argued that Moshe had taken out a monopoly on *kedusha*, holiness, and this had an adverse affect on the rest of the nation. He objected to the fact that within the nation there were subgroups: *cohanim*, *Leviim*, kings, prophets, and so forth. He preferred that everyone be identical.

The idea of having an elite group within the nation may seem, initially, repulsive. Why are certain individuals singled out for specific tasks of *kedusha*? Surely everyone is close to God and is holy. However, among the Jewish people, no elite group exists for its own sake. If the *cohanim* were to take advantage of their lofty position, then they would very quickly lose their privilege. One example of such an instance occurred toward the end of the Shilo period. Immediately on entering the Land of Israel, the *Mishkan* was established in Shilo. The last *Cohen Gadol* of that era was a man named Eli. However, his sons did not inherit the priesthood. Rather, they forfeited it due to their actions. "Eli's sons did not acknowledge God" (*Shmuel* I, 2:12). They took meat that was brought to the Temple by force and caused the "people to despise bringing offerings to God" (*ibid.*, 17). Therefore, God sent a prophet to let Eli know that his sons' actions had disqualified them from the priesthood. "I will destroy your house" (*ibid.*, 31).

The priesthood is for the people, but it is also essential. A class was established that was relieved of other tasks in order that they might devote themselves to developing the spiritual side of the nation, for the sake of the entire nation. This was what enabled the nation to continue with mundane tasks and still be close to God. This was what gave *Am Yisrael* strength. Without spiritual leaders, the nation would have gone the way of many other groups. They would have become so involved with everyday life that they might readily have assimilated into the surrounding tribes. The leadership and the *cohanim* were the recipe for resistance and success.

Korach argued that *kedusha* was the possession of the whole nation, and in this, he was completely correct. However, he proposed that in order to effect this, the nation would do well to do away with the priesthood and all of the other groups. He wanted there to be complete equality within the nation. What he suggested would have had an adverse effect, instead of improving the nation, it would have caused the decline of the leaders. If there were no *cohanim*, there would be no leadership and, eventually, the whole of *Am Yisrael* would suffer.

Korach's argument attacked the basic idea of hierarchy within the nation; in doing so, he weakened the people and this, in turn, was an attack on God Himself. For this reason, Korach suffered a dramatic end. The earth swallowed him alive and left no trace of him; his claim was totally destroyed.

He asked Moshe whether blue clothing needed the *techelet*. The *techelet* is one thread, but it injects *kedusha* into the whole garment. Without the one blue thread, the whole garment is lacking that element of sanctity. The same is true of the *mezuzah*. The two portions of the Torah that it contains channel *kedusha* into the room and house. Without the *mezuzah* the entire house, even if it is full of holy tomes, is deficient in *kedusha*. Korach argued that the whole nation was holy and that, therefore, they did not need a leader or a channel for the *kedusha* that they were to receive. However, as with the room and the clothing, the small holy item elevates the larger whole, channeling *kedusha* to all else. The way to elevate the *kedusha* of the nation is to develop excellent leadership.

We are a nation that has always encouraged excellence in our ranks and produced outstanding leaders. Without this, we would have been swallowed into our bleak history. The leaders and their channeling of *kedusha* kept us alive. This is the secret of our success.

Chukat
Excellence and Red Cows

Appropriate leadership requires that the leader understand the plight of each individual and strive to improve the individual lot and, in this fashion, elevate the state of the whole nation. The generation is comprised of many individuals, and the leader needs to satisfy each and every one.

(*Ein Iyah, Berachot*, Chapter 4, Note 22)

The natural love of God and its practical application always appeared in Israel in special individuals, even in the worst times. These people were examples of the nature of the collective, and they allowed the nation to utilize their example and spirit.

(*Eder Hayakar*, p. 35)

Tahara *(purity) and holiness should elevate one to such a high level that they are incapable of any intentional sin. Even at a time of sin, one should sanctify oneself so that God may be always with him, to guard him from unintentional sin.*

(*Ein Iyah, Berachot*, Chapter 2, Note 58)

"I attempted to fathom it in my wisdom, yet it is beyond my comprehension" (*Kohelet* 7:23). King Shlomo was awarded the most elusive of Divine gifts: wisdom. "God gave Shlomo wisdom" (*Melachim* I. 5:9). He understood more than any man before him, and more than most after him. He was expert in the intricacies of the laws of the Torah and the rationale behind the

215

God-given precepts. He knew not only the *how*, but also the *why* of Judaism. Yet, even he admitted that there are certain *mitzvot* that were beyond his comprehension. The midrash tells us that this verse refers to the complicated laws of *parah adumah*, the red cow. "I investigated the laws of the *parah adumah* and they remain a mystery to me" (See *Bemidbar Rabba*, 19:3).

The laws of the *parah adumah* make up the first section of this week's *parsha*.

"God said to Moshe and to Aharon: 'This is a decree of the Torah. Take a totally red cow that has no imperfection and that has never worn a yoke'" (*Bemidbar* 19:1–2). The cow was to be burnt in its entirety by a *cohen*. The *cohen* was then to immerse his body and his clothing in the *mikvah*. Only then was he to reenter the camp and remain *tamei*, impure, until evening. He who burns the cow must immerse in the *mikvah* and remain *tamei* until the evening.

The laws are full of anomalies and seeming contradictions.

The ashes of the cow were used to purify people that had become *tamei* through contact with a dead body. In fact, there is no other way of become *tahor*, pure, from such a type of *tumah*, impurity, other than the *parah adumah*. So the ashes of the cow held great powers of purification. Yet, interestingly enough, all of the people who dealt with the *parah adumah*, themselves became *tamei* and needed to be purified. They required *tevillah*, immersion in the *mikvah*, the ritual bath, and only became *tahor* on the following evening (See *Mishnah, Parah* 4:4).

Indeed, the midrash tells us that these laws are part of an exclusive group that are so unfathomable, they seem ridiculous. For this reason, the *yetzer hara*, the evil inclination, chooses these laws to try and lead the people astray from God's service (See *Tanchuma, Bemidbar* 23). God refers to it as a statute, a decree that we are forbidden to explore since we will always be incapable of realizing the ultimate purpose of these laws (See Rashi on *Bemidbar* 19:2).

The cow had to be completely red. "If there were even two black hairs, even if the root of the hair was red, or black roots and red tips," the cow was disqualified. This was such a rare occurrence that there had only been a total of nine such cows throughout history. "The first was prepared by Moshe [this is the one that is discussed in this week's *parsha*], the second by Ezra [during the second Temple period], and five from the time of Ezra until the present, so said Rabbi Meir. The sages claimed that seven had been prepared since Ezra" (*Parah* 3:5).

It was not enough that the cow fulfilled the criteria with regard to color; it also had to never have worn a yoke. The Mishnah interprets this to include not only a yoke; even were one to spread his cloak over the cow in order that she carry it for him, the cow would be unfit to be a *parah adumah* (*ibid.*, 2:3).

All of these laws were so intricate, complex, and inexplicable that Shlomo was forced to admit that they were beyond his comprehension. The evil inclination uses them as ammunition to wear down our defenses, and try to get us to rebel against God.

But this was not all. The Torah informs us that "a pure man would gather the ashes of the *parah* and place it outside the camp in a pure place" (*Bemidbar* 19:9). This was to be performed by someone that had never become *tamei* and had always been "a pure man." The Mishnah relates the lengths to which the Jewish people went in order to find such a person. After all, it is relatively easy to become *tamei*. Anyone passing under a tree whose branches cover a grave becomes *tamei*, even if there was no direct contact with the grave. Anyone entering a building that contains a corpse, such as a hospital, is *tamei*. Again, no direct contact is required. So, in order to develop a "pure man," conditions had to be established whereby he had no possibility of even indirect contact with a corpse, or the like. These conditions had to prevail from his birth until he was ready to perform the task of gathering the ashes of the *parah adumah*.

"There were chambers in Jerusalem that were constructed on a huge rock set over a chasm, so there could be no possibility of a grave beneath the chamber. Pregnant women would come there, give birth to their sons, and raise them in these chambers" (*Parah* 3:2). They would remain there until the age of 7 or 8, but no longer, lest they become *tamei* through ejaculation (*Tosefta* ad loc.). "Oxen would then be brought, carrying boards on their backs, and the child would sit on the boards. The children would hold stone cups [as stone cannot become *tamei*] in their hands and, on arriving at the spring of the Shiloach, they would descend, fill the cups, and remount the oxen. Rabbi Yehudah said [that even this was not allowed, as we are concerned that they would become *tamei* if they alight from the animal, therefore] they would lower down the cups from their position on top of the boards" (*ibid.*).

The importance of the *parah adumah* was so great that women were willing to give birth to their children in such conditions. They would then raise the children in these protected enclosures. Someone was paid to guard the children, so they would not accidentally become *tamei*, or leave the chambers (See *Babba Metzia* 58a). All this in order to fulfill the Torah's requirements for a *parah adumah*.

All this was for one singular purpose, that the Jews be *tahor*, pure. The Torah went to great lengths to ensure that we would always have the opportunity to purify ourselves. Even if one were to come in contact with a corpse, there was hope. Throughout history, there have been the ashes of the *parah adumah* that could return him to the fold. Someone who is *tamei* cannot join the rest of his brothers and his people in the *Beit Hamikdash*, in the Temple. He remains cut off from the rest of the nation. The *parah adumah* returns him to the Temple, to *Am Yisrael*, and to God.

This is all part of being perfect and developing excellence. Distinction can only be achieved through *taharah* and connection with the Lord. Therefore, even though the laws of the *parah adumah* are incomprehensible to the human mind, even one as astute as Shlomo's, the rationale behind the concept is that we must preserve the ability to be *tahor*.

The Jewish people survived by encouraging excellence. This was seen last week in Korach's argument against Moshe and Aharon, and this week in the *parah adumah*.

Our *parsha* contains two more examples of the need for excellence within *Am Yisrael*. The *parsha* contains the deaths of two of the leaders of *Am Yisrael* in the desert—Miriyam and Aharon, Moshe's sister and brother. These two events are tragic within themselves, yet, interestingly, both are followed by national calamities.

In the case of the death of Miriyam, we read, immediately afterwards: "There was no water for the congregation and so they gathered around Moshe and Aharon, and argued with them. 'Were it that we had died with our brothers before God. Why did you bring God's nation to this desert, to die here? Why did you take us out of Egypt and bring us to this awful place? Nothing grows here, no figs, no grapes or pomegranates, not even any water to drink'" (*Bemidbar* 20:2–5). Immediately after the death of Miriyam, the nation was frightened that they would die a painful death from thirst. The *Gemara* finds a connection between these two events. "The well of water [that traveled with the nation] was due to the merit of Miriyam. When she died the well disappeared" (*Ta'anit* 9a). The whole time that Miriyam was alive, the entire camp survived on her merit; yet, when she died this credit left them. Suddenly, the nation was left with no water and faced imminent death. In their despair, they complained to Moshe and were even willing to return to slavery in Egypt.

Again, after the death of Aharon, the nation was faced with annihilation. "The whole nation saw that Aharon had died, and they mourned for him for thirty days. The Cana'anite king of Arad in the Negev heard that Israel was coming, and he fought them and captured hostages" (*Bemidbar* 20:29, 21:1). Again, a connection is noted between the two events. "What did he hear that he came to attack them? He heard that Aharon had died and that the protective clouds of glory that had enveloped the people were gone. He assumed that he would now be able to fight *Am Yisrael*" (*Rosh Hashanah* 3a). Throughout Aharon's life, he had protected the Jewish nation from attack by his presence and influence on the people. When he died, this defense disappeared and the nation was, suddenly, very vulnerable.

The Torah teaches us that, to survive, we need to rely on excellence within *Am Yisrael*. The Torah outlines the great lengths to which we must go in order to remain *tahor*, pure, and continue our dialogue with the Almighty. The perfectly red cow brings us close to God; a slight blemish is enough to disrupt this relationship. We need excellence.

The distinguished people within the nation provide sustenance and protection for the entire people. Without them, the whole nation is threatened with extinction. We can see just how wrong Korach was in attacking the hierarchy of *Am Yisrael*. If the leaders are to disappear, the result would be the demise and end of the whole nation.

Balak
A Separate Nation

There are times when one feels that he is totally gathered within
himself and concentrated on himself. The outside world has no effect
on him; he is concerned with internal solitude.It is the same with the
nation itself. When Israel is gathered inward, she feels a great
completeness, and she is quietly building the world. She recognizes her
strengths and effects the world.

(*Orat Haḳodesh*, Volume III, p. 269)

The special essence and nature of Am Yisrael *as a nation that dwells*
apart will not become evident only through external and collective acts,
nor only through concepts learnt by rote, but rather by the elevation of
all life in its inner uniqueness.

(*Orot*, p. 97)

The whole world is waiting for the light of Israel to appear, for the
higher light of clarity of God's glory, of this nation that was created by
God in order to relate His glory. This is unique to the nation that
dwells apart and is not reckoned among the other nations.

(*ibid.*, p. 22)

Until now we have seen the essential need for excellence and distinguished individuals within *Am Yisrael*. Without them, the entire nation would collapse. There is a school of thought that argues for a more inclusive style of education and national development. They claim that all should be equal and that this equality will improve everyone's lot. However, it has been seen that without strong leadership, the development of all is stunted. The result being that instead of improvement, we achieve the demise of the whole, where our initial concern was for its welfare.

The Torah instructs us to aim at improving a small, but elite group, and they will then, in turn, direct and elevate the entire corpus. It is essential, but it also means that the elite have a huge responsibility. They are obligated to devote their efforts to the welfare of others. They cease being private individuals and become public figures, whose aim and goal is to improve the lot of the entire nation.

The *Gemara* relates how Rabbi Gamliel wanted to appoint two of his students as rabbis. They refused the appointment as they thought that such a position commanded respect and honor. In their humility, they tried to run from honor and so replied to his offer in the negative. Rabbi Gamliel answered them: "Do you think that I am giving you glory? I am making you into servants of the congregation" (*Horaiyot* 10b). As the verse states, in reference to the king "they said to him: 'If you will be a servant to the nation today'" (*Melachim* I. 12:7).

The leader is, in a sense, the servant of the congregation and is at their beck and call at all times. Rabbi Kook signed his letters "the servant to God's people in the Holy Land." All this in order to elevate the nation and fulfill the task that has been placed on the leader.

Up until now we have seen how the Torah instructs us to develop excellence on an individual level. In this week's *parsha*, we start to notice an implication that this is not enough, that excellence has to be developed in a wider forum. We see this through the story of Balak and Bila'am.

Balak, the king of Moav, was frightened by the mass of *Am Yisrael* that he saw approaching his borders. He realized that the only way to beat them was to attack them with their own weapon. "Their strength is in their mouths. I will, therefore, attack them through speech" (*Tanchuma, Balak* 3). *Am Yisrael* survived because of their prayers and powers of prophecy. Balak attempted to fight us on our terms and outsmart us using prophecy. To do this, he invited Bila'am, a Midyanite prophet, to curse us. Even though Midyan and Moav were enemies, the common goal of annihilating *Am Yisrael* had fostered a pact of brotherhood.

Bila'am told God that he was about to go and curse the Jewish nation. God appeared to him and informed him: "You must not go with them, nor will you curse the nation since they are blessed" (*Bemidbar* 22:12). However, Bila'am was determined to fulfill his mission knowing that success would bring him riches and honor. Eventually, God allowed Bila'am to go with the messengers Balak had sent, on one condition: "Only do exactly as I will instruct you" (*ibid.*, 20).

So when Bila'am met with Balak and was prepared to curse *Am Yisrael*, God only allowed him to bless us. The curse was turned into an extra blessing and Bila'am was disgraced by Balak (See *ibid.*, 24:10–11).

For our purposes, we must investigate the blessings that God put into the mouth of Bila'am. "Who can count the dust of Ya'akov and enumerate the multitudes of Israel? I would like to die a righteous death and let my end be like theirs" (*ibid.*, 23:10). "There is no visible wrongdoing amongst (the children of) Ya'akov and no vice. God is their Lord" (*ibid.*, 21). The most famous blessing was "How good are your tents, Ya'akov, your dwelling places, Israel" (*ibid.*, 24:5) that has been incorporated into the morning prayers.

Yet one of the blessings leaves us perplexed. Bila'am blesses us: "They are a nation that dwells alone, and is not reckoned among the nations" (ibid., 23:9). How is this a blessing? Is it our lot to always live in solitude, even national loneliness—to always be separate, different, alien?

The truth is that this is also a blessing, and one linked to excellence on a national level. Separation is not necessarily a bad thing, as the midrash explains: "Yisrael is incapable of fusing with any other nation, but remains separate to itself. Even if one of the nations attempted to lead the people astray, decreeing that they transgress the *Shabbat*, or *mila* (circumcision), or practice idolatry, they would prefer to die rather than assimilate into the nations" (*Shemot Rabba* 15:8).

Bila'am noted that the Jewish people remained separate in order to preserve a way of life that was rooted entirely in the Torah. Were they to try to assimilate, they would lose their uniqueness. This would prove detrimental to their ability to carry out their God-given task. "They are separate in every sense: in their dress, their diet, and their ethical code" (*Midrash Y'lamdeinu* quoted in *Torah Shleima*). Israel was to remain separate throughout its history, from the exile in Egypt to the modern era. This allowed Israel to survive the influence of foreign nations and cultures and remain a nation apart. Bila'am prophesied this on a mountain in Moav several millennia ago.

All this isolation was not for its own sake but for a higher purpose. *Am Yisrael* has an all-important God-given task. We are to be an elite nation, God calls us "My first born" (*Shemot* 4:22). He sets our task "this nation that I formed, in order to relate My glory" (*Yeshiyahu* 43:21). We were chosen to publicize God's name and glory to the whole world. This job is to be performed not on an individual level but as a nation and a national entity. Only a people with a land, an economy, and a defense force can influence other nations. Only when a nation sanctifies such matters does this impress other nations and peoples. Only then are we in a position to inject Divinity into the world.

Again, the question could be asked: "Why did God need to choose a nation?" Surely, it would have been preferable to elevate the entire world, as opposed to doing so through the medium of *Am Yisrael*. The answer is the same as we gave to Korach. Only an elite is capable of elevating the entire world; only the chosen nation can inject spirituality into all the other nations.

But, to be able to do so, we must remain separate. This is not a contradiction in terms, rather it is a necessity. We are to be the light to the nations, but we can only do so on a national level. We must be a firmly established nation in order to fulfill this task. Indeed, the prophet Yeshiyahu relates that we are to be the light unto the nations, but this has to be examined in context. The verse says "and I formed you and I will make you into a nation, to be a light to the gentiles" (*Yeshiyahu* 42:6). The prophet says that we must influence the world, but he also explains how we are to do so. First and foremost, we must be a nation; then, and only then, will we be a light to the whole world.

Bila'am's blessing was a blessing indeed. We are to be a separate nation and this will afford us the ability to fulfill our task in the creation, namely that of relating God's glory to the world.

The *Netziv* explains that only when we are separate do we deserve, and receive, respect from the other nations. This is because only in such circumstances do we fulfill our purpose. However, when we attempt to mingle amongst the other nations and become indistinguishable from them, then we are "not reckoned among the nations." The people of the world lose their respect for us. This is because, when we try to be a nation like all other nations, we lose our unique assignment and responsibility (*HaEmek Davar* on *Bemidbar* 23:9; and see his article, "*She'er Yisrael*" on anti-Semitism).

This task is not only for our own benefit, but also for the improvement of the whole world. When we reject our special quality, we are rejecting God and His universe. In such a case we are, far from being the chosen people, less than any other nation. As each nation has a task and fulfills it, if we do not fulfill our task, then we are worthless.

Am Yisrael is unique, a chosen nation. This is a privilege that brings with it purpose and responsibility. "Do you think that I am giving you glory? I am making you into servants of the congregation." Servitude on a national level. Not servants in the sense of slaves and lower class citizens. On the contrary, the higher status brings a universal responsibility. We must fulfill our task, and we are to do so by remaining separate. Then we will truly be a light to the nations.

Pinchas
Joining the Elite

The love of God on the highest level turns into Divine zealousness in its purest form. It is expressed in the character of Eliyahu, and Pinchas is Eliyahu, the zealot who was the pinnacle of love of God.

(*Orot Haḳodesh*, Volume III, p. 364)

We have to purify zealousness that it should always remain only the love of God. Generally, it is impossible, and there must be a self-analysis to ensure that it does not become zealousness of a fellow human being, which is destructive, but only for God, which brings with it a covenant of peace.

(*ibid.*, p. 244)

Pinchas, the son of Elazar, the son of Aharon the Cohen; The only valid zealousness is that which is totally devoted to God. Therefore, God came and informed everybody that Pinchas' nature was identical to that of his grandfather, Aharon, who was good to all and pursued peace; and Pinchas was far from being a murderer since his intentions were all directed toward God.

(*Olat Riyah*, Volume I, p. 394)

After Bila'am saw that his plan to curse the people of Israel had been thwarted by God Himself, he tried a different tactic. He said to Balak, "Their God despises prostitution. I recommend that you entice them using Midyan prostitutes, dressing them as merchants of flax vessels. An older lady and a younger one. The older lady will set a price and the younger one will offer a lower price. When the Jews come to market, they will be enticed by the lower price and will strike up a conversation with the seller. She will invite them inside to check out the merchandise and then offer them some wine. In this manner, she will entice them to have relations with her. Before they start, she will trick them into worshipping the Midyanite idol, Ba'al Peor, and only agree to their requests to sleep with her after they have discarded Moshe's Torah" (*Sanhedrin* 106a).

This strategy was so successful that the camp of Israel was threatened with annihilation. Twenty-four thousand people were involved in this lecherous behavior, and they all died in the subsequent plague. "Those that died in the plague numbered twenty-four thousand" (*Bemidbar* 25:9). The midrash tells us that this advice was infinitely more damaging to *Am Yisrael* than any curse that Bila'am attempted to put on us. The verse states "and Bila'am returned to his place" (*ibid.*, 24:25). "However, when he heard that twenty-four thousand people had died as a result of his suggestion, he returned to Balak to claim his reward" (*Tanchuma, Balak* 14).

All echelons of society were affected; even the princes of the tribes. More demoralizing than the event itself was that the plague had completely overtaken the camp. Were it not for the drastic actions of one Jew, the entire nation may have been destroyed. In the midst of the degradation that fell on the camp, the prince of the tribe of Shimon, a man named Zimri Ben Salu, took a Midyanite prostitute in public. "He drew close to his brothers with the Midyanite, in full view of Moshe and the whole of the nation of Israel." (*Bemidbar* 25:6) To make matters worse, he also disgraced Moshe. "[Moshe] Ben Amram, what do you say? Is she forbidden or permitted? If you tell me she is forbidden, then who allowed you to marry the daughter of Yitro?" (*Sanhedrin* 82a). This claim was inaccurate. Moshe had converted Yitro and his whole family, including his wife Tzippora, to Judaism (See *Siftei Chachamim* on Rashi, ad loc.).

Not only was this an attempt to humiliate the leader of the Jewish people, but it was a *Chillul Hashem*, a desecration of the Divine Name, a most serious crime. The *Gemara* rates the misdeeds that a person can perform in the following way. "If he transgressed a positive commandment, he must return to God and will be forgiven on the spot. If it was a negative commandment, he must return and await the next Yom Kippur in order to be pardoned. If it was a sin punishable by *karet* (being cut off) or capital punishment, then repentance and Yom Kippur alone are not enough and only suffering will bring forgiveness. However, whoever is guilty of *chillul hashem, teshuvah,* Yom

Kippur, and even suffering are not sufficient, but atonement comes only at the point of death" (*Yoma* 86a). From this source, the severity of such a transgression is evident.

What is the definition of *chillul hashem*? This is a subjective concept, as the *Gemara* explains. "Rav said: 'Were I to purchase meat from the butcher and not pay immediately, that would be a *chillul hashem*. Rabbi Yochanan said: 'Were I to be seen when I was not learning Torah or wearing *tephillin*, even for a short time, that would be a *chillul hashem*" (*ibid.*). These great rabbis knew that their every action was observed and studied by their students and congregants. Were they to be involved in activities that were perfectly legitimate, yet inappropriate for someone in their position, such actions would constitute a desecration of God's Name.

The *Gemara* then arrives at a general definition. "You must love the Lord, your God" (*Devarim* 6:5). "This means that the Name of God should become loved through your actions. A person should learn and keep the company of Torah scholars, and deal fairly with others. About such a person, people say 'what fortune does this person's father and rabbi possess that they taught him Torah. What a shame that there are people who do not learn Torah, as it is obvious that those that learn Torah are pleasant and good people.' However, if one learns Torah and keeps the company of Torah scholars, yet deals unfairly with others and speaks in an unpleasant way, about him they say 'shame to the person that learns Torah, and to his father and rabbi that taught him Torah. See how his actions are unpleasant and disgusting'" (*ibid.*).

One in an exalted position has a responsibility to demonstrate the beauty of the Torah and the *mitzvot*. If he neglects to do so or, alternatively, repels others, then he is guilty of the grave sin of *chillul hashem*. His crime is so severe that he is prevented from doing *teshuvah* until his dying day.

If this is the case, then we can start to understand the gravity of Zimri's actions. He was a prince, and, in this capacity, was responsible for his tribe's physical and spiritual welfare. However, Zimri, instead of encouraging his congregation to adhere to the commandments and follow Moshe, led them away from the *mitzvot*. Worse than that, he disgraced and belittled Moshe in their presence to justify his own actions. This was more than regular *chillul hashem*. Not only was his crime punishable by death, but it had brought a plague that threatened to destroy the entire nation.

This extreme situation called for a radical solution. "Pinchas, the son of Elazar, the son of Aharon the Cohen, rose from the congregation and took a spear in his hand. He followed the Israelite into the chamber and impaled

both the Israelite and the [Midyanite] woman, and the plague ceased"
(*Bemidbar* 25:7–8). Pinchas' zealous actions saved the Jewish people.

For this he received a special reward. "God spoke to Moshe and said
'Pinchas the son of Elazar, the son of Aharon the Cohen, abated My anger
from *Am Yisrael* through his zealous actions. Thanks to him, I did not destroy the children of Israel. Therefore, tell him that I give him My covenant
of peace. He will have eternal priesthood for himself and his descendants as
a result of his zeal, which brought atonement for the children of Israel." (*ibid*.,
10–13).

Pinchas was not originally included in the children of Elazar who were
anointed as *cohanim* and, accordingly, was not in line to serve as a *cohen* in
the *Mishkan*, nor in the *Beit Hamikdash*.

Not all of the descendants of Aharon were anointed as priests, only those
that were old enough at the time of sanctification. Those who were dedicated
passed this merit on to their children. However, once this ceremony had taken
place, no more *cohanim* were added to the list of candidates. Pinchas, at that
time, was too young to be made a *cohen*, and had missed the opportunity (See
Gur Aryeh on Rashi *Bemidbar* 25:13). It had seemed he would never be a *cohen*.
Suddenly, all that changed. As the *Gemara* states: "Pinchas only became a *cohen*
on killing Zimri" (*Zevachim* 101b). This zealous action changed his life, and
through him, his descendants also achieved the elusive level of priesthood.

All this was unnatural and extraordinary. It was not priesthood achieved
through channels of lineage, but earned through personal action and example.

The Torah is sending us a very important message about the elite in *Am
Yisrael*. One should never assume that their selection is only based on lineage
and family connection. Anyone who has achieved this state deserved it. Moreover, if we think that the elite will always remain the elite, that no one can
join their ranks, we may drift into lethargy and apathy. One could claim that
it matters not what one does; you are born a priest or not, but you cannot
change your status. Pinchas comes to teach us that this is not the case. Someone who proves their worth through their actions can join the elite.

This is not only the case with priesthood. A simple person can change his
status through a sincere desire to do God's bidding. This is proven by a passage in the *Rambam*. The *Rambam* explains the laws surrounding the tribe of
Levi and concludes the chapter with the following remark:

> This applies not only to the tribe of Levi but to every person who desires this
> level and stands before God to serve Him and to know Him. If he is honest and
> rejects the regular business of life, he becomes sanctified. God becomes his lot

and he will receive what he needs in this world, in a similar fashion to the *cohanim* and the *Leviim* (*Mishneh Torah*, *Hilchot Sh'mittah VeYovel* 13:13).

If one sincerely desires it and is willing to sacrifice certain possessions, then, Pinchas teaches us, he can elevate himself and his whole lineage, joining the elite and the leaders of *Am Yisrael*.

Mattot
Eretz Yisrael—a Condition for Excellence

*It is impossible to identify the particular sanctity of the land of Israel,
to explain her cherished nature in a rational, human way. It derives
from the Divine spirit that rests on the entire nation, on the sanctified
nature of the Jewish collective soul.*

(*Orot*, p. 9)

*In the holy place, the young men of Israel will understand the central
force that affects* Knesset Yisrael *that dwells in the Holy Land. There
they will reveal the unifying light of "one people in the Land."*

(*Ma'amrei HaRiyah*, p. 63)

*The love of the land of Israel is the basis of the Torah as it brings the Jewish
people and the whole world to a state of excellence. Whoever has a
greater love of Israel and is closer to Israel takes precedence in the blessings.*

(*Ein Iyah, Berachot*, Chapter 6, Note 40)

In this week's *parsha*, we learn how several tribes came to Moshe with an
unusual request. "The tribes of Reuven and Gad had large herds of livestock and they noticed that the lands of Ya'azer and Gila'ad were excellent
for grazing. They came to Moshe, Elazar, and to the princes of the other tribes.
They said to them 'The land that God smote is good grazing land and we
have many flocks. If you grant us this favor and give us this land, we will not
cross the Jordan River'" (*Bemidbar* 32:1–5).

The Jewish people were about to cross the Jordan River and enter the land of Israel. They had fought a number of wars, and conquered a certain amount of land. This land was not originally part of *Eretz Yisrael* and was thus referred to as *Ever HaYarden*, the other side of the Jordan (See *Mishnah, Shevi'it* 9:2; *Ketubot* 13:10; *Babba Batra* 3:2). The tribes of Reuven and Gad were attracted to this particular region. They asked that Moshe allow them to remain there, graze their flocks, and establish residence in the area.

Initially, Moshe rejected their claim. "Is it fair that your brothers will go to fight [in the land of Israel] and you shall dwell here? Why are you attempting to dissuade the children of Israel from occupying the land that God gave them?" (*Bemidbar* 32:6–7). Moshe equates their actions with those of the spies who spoke evil against *Eretz Yisrael* and lengthened the exile in the desert. In fact, he only agreed after they swore that they would "go before God to fight. Every capable person shall cross the Jordan, until you successfully wrest the land from your enemies" (*ibid.*, 20–21). Only then were they allowed to return to their wives and families in *Ever HaYarden*.

This promise was so important that Moshe repeated it later when he recalled the events that had occurred to the Jewish people in the desert. "To Reuven and Gad I gave the land of Amon, but I commanded them, at that time, that God had given them the land on the condition that they fight together with their brothers until such time as they completely capture the land. Then they can return to their own inheritance" (*Devarim* 3:16–20).

Again, in the time of Yehoshua, the oath was brought to mind and they were reminded of their promise and duty. "Yehoshua said to the tribes of Reuven and Gad and to half of the tribe of Menashe: 'Remember that which Moshe made you promise, that you will lead your brothers in battle and assist them'" (*Yehoshua* 1:12–14).

Obviously, this was a sore point for the rest of the tribes, and explains their insistence that Reuven and Gad fulfill their oath. But what was their objection to Reuven and Gad's request? Why was it essential that all of *Am Yisrael* enter *Eretz Yisrael* together? Was it intrinsically wrong for a number of the tribes to settle in an area more advantageous to their situation?

The first concern was that, if they were to reside in another area, removed from the rest of the nation, they would be influenced by their surroundings. The *Gemara* explains this with an interesting example. One of the last tasks that Moshe Rabbeinu performed was to establish a number of *arei miklat*, cities of refuge. The idea of the *ir miklat*, such a city, was to protect someone who had unwittingly killed another. "The person that kills accidentally shall flee there and will be protected until he is given a fair trial" (*Bemidbar* 35:11–

12). Were one to fall off a ladder and, on his descent, kill a passerby, he could not be held responsible if he was not negligent. In order to protect him from vengeance from a close family member of the deceased, *arei miklat* were founded. "There shall be six such *arei miklat*, three of them will be in *Ever HaYarden* and three in Cana'an" (*ibid.*, 13–14). Three such cities were designated in Israel proper and three in the area that Reuven and Gad inhabited, *Ever HaYarden*. The *Gemara* relates: "Moshe established three such cities in *Ever HaYarden* and Yehoshua established three corresponding ones in Cana'an" (*Makot* 9b).

The *Gemara* then explains that the cities were equidistant from each other, but raises a question of mathematics. *Eretz Yisrael* is much larger than *Ever HaYarden*; proportionally, there are a great many more *arei miklat* in *Ever Ha-Yarden*, than there are in *Eretz Yisrael*. Either there should be less in *Ever HaYarden*, or more in *Eretz Yisrael*. "Three in *Ever HaYarden* and three in the land of Israel?! In Gila'ad [*Ever HaYarden*] there were many murderers" (*ibid.*). There was a greater need for *arei miklat* in *Ever HaYarden* than there was in *Eretz Yisrael*, as *Ever HaYarden* was full of murderers and needed these cities of refuge.

However, this answer is not so simple. The *arei miklat* were only for one who had unintentionally killed someone. The intentional murderer who tried to run to the *ir miklat* was not provided with the same protection. So the answer that the *Gemara* gives, that Gila'ad was replete with murderers, does not answer the question. We are still left wondering why there were so many *arei miklat* in *Ever HaYarden*, and the solution cannot be connected with murder, only with accidental death.

The *Gemara* is teaching us a lesson about the influence of society. True, the murderers were not helped by the *arei miklat* in *Ever HaYarden*. Yet, in a place were there are many murderers, the value of human life decreases in the eyes of the inhabitants. When that happens, not only do we find more murders and intentional crime, but we are witness to a corresponding increase in unintentional, accidental deaths. People are less careful with their belongings and accidents will just "happen."

The rest of the nation was concerned that, were the tribes of Reuven and Gad to settle in such a corrupt society, they, too, would be influenced and become lesser citizens.

Another reason was that those who left the land of Israel were liable to forget the centrality of the *Beit Hamikdash* in Jerusalem. This is clear from an episode that occurred in the time of Yehoshua.

After the tribes of Reuven and Gad had fulfilled their promise and remained in the Land Of Israel for the duration of the war to conquer *Eretz Yisrael*,

Yehoshua turned to them. "You have kept all that Moshe commanded you. Now you are free to return to your homes and the land that Moshe assigned to you" (*Yehoshua* 22:2–4). However, on their return to *Ever HaYarden*, they constructed "a sanctuary on the Jordan, a grand structure" (*ibid.*, 10). The rest of *Am Yisrael* were horrified when they heard of this. Pinchas immediately went to confront them, together with the princes of the remaining ten tribes.

"Why have you committed this crime against God, turning away from God to build an altar and rebel against him? Even if your land is *tamei*, come to the land of God that contains His sanctuary, and take possession amongst us. But do not rebel against God or against us by building your own altar in place of God's altar" (*ibid.*, 16–19).

There was a real fear that the tribes of Reuven and Gad would reject God and the rest of *Am Yisrael*. The fact that they had constructed their own sanctuary seemed to prove this. So, when news of this construction arrived in Israel, they felt an intense need to confront them. Only after Reuven and Gad assured them that they had other intentions did the tribes acquiesce.

"We only did so for fear that, in the future, our children would inquire 'what is our connection with God, the God of Israel?' We decided to construct an altar, not for the purpose of sacrifices, but rather as a witness between us and you that in the future, we may point to the sanctuary as a witness. God forbid that we should rebel against God" (*ibid.*, 24–29). Were it not for these assurances the rest of the tribes would have been forced to fight them on this point.

Yet there is a further problem. The verse asks: "Who is like your nation, Yisrael, one people in the land" (*Shmuel* II 7:23). The *Zohar* expounds on the verse: "In the Land, they are one people; they are only called one nation when they are in the Land" (*Emor* III 93b). *Am Yisrael* become bonded together as a nation in *Eretz Yisrael*. Only in our land and natural habitat are we called one people.

When Reuven and Gad decided to settle outside of *Eretz Yisrael* proper and apart from the rest of *Am Yisrael*, they weakened the entire nation. If *Am Yisrael* were not one people, they would be incapable of carrying out their God-given task of being the chosen nation, chosen by God as His first-born, chosen to set an example to the world and to elevate the world in the process.

Reuven and Gad were made to promise that they would join the rest of the nation in conquering the land. Later, they were invited to renew their links with the *Beit Hamikdash* and Yerushalayim. It was hoped that this would be enough to forge a deep emotional link with *Eretz Yisrael*, that this would suffice in the time that they were separate and away from the land.

We are one nation. Where? *Ba'aretz*—in the land of Israel.

Mase'ei
Journeys and Fusion

*The ideal was that both of these forces, the spiritual and the physical,
would be merged into one; not only would they not contradict each
other, but rather they would complement each other. Through this
synthesis, each of the forces would be enhanced. The physical would be
sensitized and sanctified through its association with the unique
holiness of Israel. The spiritual would be strengthened with a powerful
life force that would enable it to reveal its glory to all of Israel.*

(Ma'amrei HaRiyah, p. 95)

*But without an understanding of the supremacy of the spirit, that "God
is the people's portion, Ya'akov is His inheritance," then all Israel's
unique nature is lost, and they become the least powerful nation.*

(*ibid.*, p. 96)

*Israel, in her elevated state, in the old days, from the start and
beginning of her glory, her soul was illuminated with a great desire for
the source of the higher Divine light. The national ideal was firmly
planted in the Divine ideal with all the fire of this love.*

(*Orot*, p. 105)

This week's *parsha* contains a long list of the journeys of *Am Yisrael* in the
desert. Forty-two stops are recorded between the time that we left
Egypt and the time we entered the land of Israel, forty years later. What
interests us is not the places themselves, but rather the description of the
way that the camp travelled.

When *Bnei Yisrael* encamped in place, there was a most specific order and layout of the camp. "Each person shall camp, according to his family, surrounding the sanctuary. To the east was the flag of Yehudah. With them were the tribe of Yissachar and the tribe of Zevulun. The banner of Reuven was to be in the south. With them were the tribe of Shimon and that of Gad. When the camp travelled, the tribe of Levi proceeded in the middle of the camp. They travelled in the same manner that they camped, each person in his place according to his banner. The banner of Ephrayim was the west. With them were the tribe of Menashe and the tribe of Binyamin. The banner of Dan was in the north. With them were Asher and the tribe of Naphtali" (*Bemidbar* 2:2–29).

"The prince of each tribe had a flag and a specific color. The flag was of the same color as the tribal stone in the breastplate of Aharon. This was the source for kings designing a flag and choosing a specific color. Each tribe's color corresponded to the color of its stone. Reuven's stone was ruby and his flag was red, and so forth." (*Bemidbar Rabba* 2:7).

This arrangement of the camp was not an arbitrary one. Indeed, the midrash explains that there was an exact reason for the position of every tribe. "God wisely established the earth, and so forth" (*Mishlei* 3:19). "God created the four corners of the Earth. The East is the source of the light. The West is the seat of hot and cold weather. The South is the domain of the dew and the rain and the North is the place from which the darkness comes. Corresponding to the four corners, He arranged the flags. Yehudah will sit in the East, as he is the tribe of the kings. With him will be Yissachar, who are masters of Torah, and Zevulun, who are very rich. In every instance, Yehudah will be the first—the first to camp, the first to travel, the first to bring sacrifices, and the first to war. In the South will be Reuven who is a *Ba'al Teshuvah*, a penitent, and this is good for the world, as God is merciful when His subjects repent. With him is Gad, who are strong, and Shimon, who are to atone for them. They travel second, after Yehudah, as *teshuvah* comes directly after Torah. After these two groups, the *Leviim* will travel with the *Mishkan*. Ephrayim, Binyamin, and Menashe will be in the West to stand up to the harsh weather. They travel after the Torah and *teshuvah* because it is fitting that one should have strength in order to learn Torah and subdue his evil inclination. Dan darkened the world through idol worship in the time of Yerovam, who built two Golden Calves and was rejected by all the tribes, with the exception of Dan (See *Melachim* I 12:28–29). Therefore, they will dwell in the North, the seat of darkness. With them is the tribe of Asher, who lit the darkness, and Naphtali, who is imbued with blessings. They will travel last since anyone who practices idolatry regresses and goes last" (*Bemidbar Rabba* 2:10).

Without attempting to explain the significance of the allusions in the midrash, it is clear that the midrash is making a point. We would be wrong to assume that the Torah laid down a vague pattern for the camp of *Am Yisrael*. On the contrary, every single detail was carefully organized to achieve a camp that was, in itself, a reflection of God's world.

Indeed, the midrash continues and states "in the same way that God designed the four corners of the earth and the corresponding four banners, so did He surround His heavenly throne with four angels: Michael, Gavriel, Uriel, and Raphael. Michael was to His right, coinciding with Reuven; Uriel was to His left, corresponding to Dan; Gavriel was in front of Him, corresponding to Yehudah, and Raphael was behind, corresponding to Ephrayim" (*ibid.*). The camp was a counterpart to the heavenly court, not merely a convenient arrangement.

Interestingly, the camp centered around the *Mishkan*, and the tribe of Levi camped in the vicinity of the *Mishkan*. "The Leviim shall camp surrounding the *Mishkan*. That there should be no anger directed toward the rest of *Am Yisrael*, they will guard the *Mishkan*" (*Bemidbar* 1:53). But, the *Mishkan* was always the center and the focus of the entire nation.

This fact ties in with the concept developed in the first half of the *Book of Bemidbar*. *Am Yisrael* is composed of two halves: the tribe of Levi, both the *Leviim* and the *cohanim*, on the one side; and the rest of the tribes on the other. Each represented a different sphere of influence in the nation. The tribe of Levi was primarily concerned with matters of the spirit. They were the representatives of God in the world. The rest of the tribes had a more political, national, and financial task. It was their responsibility to reveal God through national affairs, just as He was revealed through Divine worship and liturgy.

The nation of Israel was formed through a merger of the two. The spirit gave life and meaning to the body. The body gave expression and realization to the spirit. Only when body and spirit merged did we become *Am Yisrael*.

Therefore, the camp was arranged in a specific fashion. We have seen that the midrash explained every detail of the camp layout. The camp was built in circles. The outer circle encompassed the rest of the tribes, while the tribe of Levi occupied the inner circle. The camp consisted of both inner and outer circles, and would be incomplete were it to consist of only *Leviim* or the rest of the tribes exclusively. If the camp was to endure, it required a combination of both the religious and the national ideal.

This arrangement was relevant for the periods during which *Am Yisrael* camped. But the Torah also states "they travelled in the same manner that they camped, each person in his place according to his banner." Not only did *Am Yisrael* manage to fuse the spiritual with the physical when they camped and all was well and in order, but also during times of strife and turmoil, when the camp was on the move. This was a real skill and merit, that they were able to combine Torah and politics in the most difficult circumstances.

As the relative positions of the tribes were Divinely inspired, it is relevant to notice them. The outer circle consisted of the rest of the tribes. As the Midrash explains, they were kings, princes of Torah, and controllers of wealth. It was logical that they would reside on the outside since their task was to defend the camp from attack. But there was an even greater significance. The Torah teaches us that the center of the nation was the *Mishkan*. The spirit gave life and meaning to the body. The *Leviim* were at the center since they were to breathe life into *Am Yisrael* by upholding the Divine ideal.

This was the case during the periods of travel as well. This week's *parsha* contains forty-two such journeys in the desert. The Torah stresses that the *Leviim* were at the center of the camp. The verse: "When the camp travelled, the tribe of Levi proceeded in the middle of the camp" appears in the middle of the description of the arrangement of the other tribes. Also, in the midrash "after these two groups travelled, the *Leviim* travelled with the *Mishkan*" is written amongst the other tribes. The *Leviim* were in the middle and center of *Am Yisrael*. All eyes were turned to them. They set the tone of the nation, in the camp and during their journey.

However, we should not assume that these two elements were two separate ideals. On the contrary, the midrash explains that the colors of the banners corresponded to the color of the tribes' stones. These stones were arranged on the breastplate of the *Cohen Gadol*, a breastplate that he wore constantly during the service in the *Beit Hamikdash*. The *Cohen Gadol* served God, wearing the stones and names of the tribes. His service was not only to promote the spiritual ideal, but also to advocate the ideal of the entire nation. Indeed, were the *Cohen Gadol* to serve without wearing the breastplate, his service would be disqualified (See *Zevachim* 2:1).

Am Yisrael survived due to their ability to fuse the spirit with the physical. In fact, the Torah shows that, far from being separate entities, these two are different sides of the same coin. God chooses to reveal Himself through the Torah and the Temple service, as well as through the national affairs of *Am Yisrael*. Both are essential and both ensure that *Am Yisrael Chai*, the Jewish people live forever.

V

Devarim

Introduction

Moshe, our teacher, was specifically connected with the Torah. His purpose was to advance the means to the ends and, by doing so, the ends were achieved.

(*Ein Iyah, Berachot*, Chapter 5, Note 32)

Redemption is forged in the nature of Israel. Moshe illuminates the light of Torah and Eliyahu, the light of the clean nature of the Jewish people, the sanctity of the brit. *Moshe and Eliyahu will be fused together in the nation and within each individual.*

(*Orot*, p. 44)

The congregation of Israel drew her strength from the center of knowledge and intelligence, through the glorious holiness of Moshe, our teacher.

(*Ma'amrei HaRiyah*, p. 464)

Moshe's life is drawing to an end. This, in itself, is a scene full of sad emotions. Moshe, the great leader of *Am Yisrael* is about to depart from the world and leave his people. Yet there is a happy twist to the tale. Moshe will die, but then the Jewish people will enter the land of Israel. Indeed, Moshe was refused entry to the land on numerous occasions, even though he prayed that this decree would be overturned. Moshe was not to enter *Eretz Yisrael*, but *Am Yisrael* were commanded to enter. Therefore, they would have to wait until Moshe passed away in order to enter the Land under the leadership of Moshe's most trusted servant, Yehoshua, Joshua.

So the event was filled with contrasting emotions. On the one hand, sadness and despair at the death of Moshe. After all, it was he who had saved them from Divine punishment and wrath on many occasions. Would they survive under the tutelage of Yehoshua, and was he really capable of leading them into the land of Israel? On the other hand, there was anticipation and hope in the air. They were returning to their long lost home. The land of Israel had remained a dream for 210 years of exile in Egypt and forty years in the desert. Now, they were about to recapture her. In *Eretz Yisrael*, they would have unheard of opportunities that they had been denied during their stay in Egypt and their desert journey. In Israel, they would have authentic expression as a nation and all that that implied. Only in Israel could we be a completely unified nation, *Am Yisrael*.

It was at this juncture that Moshe made his final speech to the nation. The *Book of Devarim* is Moshe's closing address, immediately before his death. Moshe knew that the nation was apprehensive and a little worried. He knew that he was about to die and they had to enter the land of Israel. And so he delivered a message that would help them to overcome their fears and successfully tackle the future. Such is the *Book of Devarim*.

Moshe related his story to the nation: How he had successfully led them out of Egypt and brought them to the borders of the land of Israel, where he had found the strength, and thus the ability, to succeed.

He revised the whole Torah. That was Moshe's strength, what made him special. He was imbued with the messages of the Torah. They were his guiding light and the source of his strength.

Moshe realized that if the Jewish people could absorb the deep messages of the entire Torah, they would be able to master any situation. If they could live by the Torah, they would be able to survive the death of Moshe and conquer the land of Israel. They would weather the storm of history and come out on top. Moshe repeated the Torah, from *BeReishit* to the *Book of Bemidbar*.

But Moshe did not necessarily repeat the story or relate the events that happened. That would not have been enough to arm *Am Yisrael* for the untold future. Rather, Moshe taught the essential lessons of the Torah, the messages and directives of the Torah. The Torah contains vital information that the Jewish people need to survive. It is our national autobiography and instruction manual. It is our Torah.

So Moshe took the message of fusion of Heaven and Earth from the *Book of BeReishit*. The idea of universal responsibility is from the same book. He reminded the nation that they were a people who met God on a regular basis as we learned in the *Book of Shemot*. He discussed the role of the tribe of Levi in inspiring order and preserving Divine harmony in the world. This was one of the messages of the *Book of Vayikra, Torat Hacohanim, The Laws of the*

Priests. Moshe completed his account with a lesson from the *Book of Bemidbar*. He spoke of the task of *Am Yisrael* as a nation of diverse ideals. Within the nation there are certain groups that have to deal entirely with spiritual matters. However, the majority are entrusted with working in the physical world. They are to embrace life and sanctify the world. Together, these two groups were to form *Am Yisrael*.

If the nation could absorb these messages, they would be perfectly prepared for their uncertain future. This was what they needed to outlive Moshe. Even if he died, *Am Yisrael* was sure to survive and thrive given this knowledge. If they learned the principles of the Torah, they would successfully conquer the land, both physically and spiritually.

This was Moshe's final lesson, and with this, he passed from the world. The *Book of Devarim* is a review of the entire Torah and her teachings; it is a message for the life of the Jewish people. It was to be her survival manual throughout history.

Far from being the end, the *Book of Devarim* is just the beginning. True, it is the end of Moshe's Torah, but it is the start of life for the Jewish people in the land of Israel. It is the prologue to the eternal story of Jewish history, of a nation who lived independently in their land, of a nation whose history was all part of a Divine plan and of a nation assigned the task of revealing God's Divine name in her actions and history. *Devarim*, and the whole Torah, is the first chapter of our history, but definitely not the last.

Devarim
Leaders, Nations, and Fusion

Israel clarifies within her the basic principle of Divine Providence over nations and kingdoms, and over the all of existence. Through this, we come to a spiritual demand to purify practical and intellectual life.

(*Orot*, p. 143)

In order to influence the generation, it is imperative that the leader of the generation is close to them in stature and, thus, suitable to influence them. Were he to be significantly elevated above the rest of the people, they would not want to accept his leadership, and he would be unable to persuade them in any area.

(*Ein Iyah, Berachot,* Chapter 5, Note 33)

To be capable of receiving and being nourished by this delicate Divine sustenance, a nation would need special preparation, on the genetic, ethical, and historical levels. This was accomplished by Israel alone.

(*Orot*, p. 154)

This week's *parsha* opens the *Book of Devarim* and Moshe's summation of the Torah. Moshe related the events that had occurred to the Jewish People before they were to enter into the Land of Israel. He did not mention any events prior to the exodus from Egypt, since they were not directly relevant to *Am Yisrael* at this juncture. The fact that God had created the world and led the family of Ya'akov into Egypt was not significant to them. What concerned them now was that God had taken them out of Egypt and was leading them into the Promised Land.

However, Moshe had another purpose for reviewing the Torah. He wanted to stress certain crucial moral messages that had been taught throughout the Torah. In this regard, he had a lot to say regarding the *Book of BeReishit*. Indeed, the first two *parshiot* of the book touch on subjects that were developed in the *Book of BeReishit*.

The first idea that appeared in *BeReishit* was that of a fusion between heaven and earth or, to be more precise, the lack of such fusion. Since the time of the sons of Adam, Cain and Hevel, there had been a serious rift between heaven and earth, a rift so serious that the way they proposed to deal with the "problem" was to split the "earthly" concepts from those that they perceived as being heavenly and divine. This lead to the very first crime between two individuals, the murder by Cain of his brother Hevel. All this due to ideological differences and greed based on the split between heaven and earth (See Chapter on *BeReishit*, "The Break Between Heaven and Earth").

This rift continued in the generation of the flood, and later during that of the Tower of Bavel. The generation of the flood corrupted one of God's gifts to humanity, that is, love and marriage. Not only is this a Divine gift, but it also affords an opportunity for the world to fuse the spiritual and the physical. The act of love is a physical act between man and woman, and yet it has the most sublime, Divine element. It is a spiritual pleasure that also has the ability to "create" new life. Thus, man becomes a partner with God. In the words of the *Gemara*: "There are three partners in the creation of a human being: God, the father, and the mother. The father contributes the white substance that forms the bones, the fingernails, and parts of the brain. The mother gives the red that goes to make the flesh and the hair. God gives the spirit, the soul, and the Divine element. The ability to see and hear, intelligence and sense" (*Niddah* 31a).

The generation of the flood corrupted this ability and degraded it. They used the act of love as a method to achieve physical pleasure and rejected the spiritual content (See Chapter on *Noach*, "The Continuing Rift").

The generation of the tower of Bavel tried to wage war on God. They constructed a tower in order to fight Him in heaven. Far from fusing the heavens and the earth, they continued the rift. True, they forced God to "descend" to earth for a fleeting second to see their tower and destroy it. This was not the type of fusion of heaven and earth that the Creator had intended (See *ibid.*).

The world had to wait twenty generations, from the creation until the appearance of Avraham Avinu in order to rectify the situation (See the Chapter on *Lech Lecha*, "Avraham—Mending the Rift").

Avraham was the father of many nations, thus his God-given name Avraham, the father of many nations. More specifically, he was the father of Judaism and *Am Yisrael*. In this capacity he set out to teach the world the essence of Divinity. He strove to teach the basic idea that God is the Ruler and Master over both the heaven and the earth. In so doing, he fused the two and mended the gap between the spiritual and the physical.

Not only did Avraham act in this manner but it was to be the lot of his children and their children throughout the generations. This was the essence of the family of Avraham and of the Jewish people. We were to fuse heaven and earth and to prove to the world that it was possible and plausible to do so.

This was the first message that Moshe spoke as a reminder to *Am Yisrael* during his great final speech that is the *Book of Devarim*.

The *parsha* opens with Moshe rebuking the nation for all of the times that they rebelled against God. The most severe of these was the request to send spies into the land of Israel. God had brought *Am Yisrael* to the borders of *Eretz Yisrael* in a very short time and was ready for them to enter the land immediately. However, the people were too cautious and asked Moshe, prior to entering, to send twelve spies to "check out" the land. The heads of the tribes were chosen for this task, and they secretly entered the land and spied it out for forty days.

At the end of their time in *Eretz Yisrael*, the spies returned and brought back their report. They told of giants who ruled the land and brought back strange oversized fruit to prove their point. The land seemed unconquerable. The people cried "God hates us and therefore took us out of Egypt in order that we should be annihilated by the Emori tribe" (*Devarim* 1:27). They could not be convinced of the truth, preferring to believe that they were destined to die in the desert rather than to believe that "God has led you up till now, He will fight for you, in the same way as He did in Egypt" (*ibid.*, 30).

God was incensed by their attitude and their lack of faith. "None of that bad generation will see the good land that I swore to your forefathers" (*ibid.*, 35). The exceptions were the two spies who had delivered a favorable report, Calev and Yehoshua.

The entire generation was to die in the desert and their children would enter and capture the Land. And so, the nation wandered in the desert for forty years until the generation that had left Egypt had all died. Only then were they ready to enter the land. In Moshe's words "when all of the people had died, and God spoke to me 'Today you are to cross the border of Moav'" (*ibid.*, 2:16–17). They were to take Moav. This was the beginning of the conquest of *Eretz Yisrael*.

The way that Moshe relates this passage is interesting and significant. When the entire generation had died off, then God spoke to him. He almost said that God spoke to him only after all those who had been involved in the affair with the spies had passed away. Indeed, the *Gemara* notes such a connection and learned from these verses: "God did not speak to Moshe the whole time that the generation of the desert lived" (*Ta'anit* 30b). God ceased speaking to Moshe at the time of the spies' betrayal and did not speak to Moshe again for a period of nearly forty years, until that entire generation had passed away.

This does not necessarily mean that God did not speak to Moshe at all. We do know that there were a number of laws that were commanded during this period. Rather that, instead of speaking to him directly—"face to face" (see *Bemidbar* 12:8), as was the norm with Moshe—He appeared in a dream, as he appeared to the other prophets (See *Ben Yehoyada*, ad loc.).

Whatever the explanation, we see that the relationship between Moshe and God was greatly affected by the state of the nation. The *Yerushalmi* states it thus: "What can the leader do if the nation is judged according to the deeds of the majority? We find that God did not speak to Moshe for thirty-eight years" (*Ta'anit* 3 4). The *Yerushalmi* points to an incredible concept. The leader is part of the nation and the nation is so much part of the leader. It is possible that the leader will be restrained by the majority of his flock. So it was with Moshe. God did not speak to him, not due to some misdemeanor on his part, but due to the sins of the generation. As Rashi puts it "to teach you that the Divine presence only resides on the prophets for the sake of *Am Yisrael*" (Rashi on *Devarim* 2:16).

Moshe chose to teach this message to the entire nation just before his demise. The word of God, prophecy, is one of the ways to fuse heaven and earth. We develop a point of interaction between the Divine and the human; we talk to God and He converses with us. This is a great Divine gift, the ability to communicate with the Creator. But Moshe taught the nation that it should not be taken for granted that we can speak to God. Indeed, not even the most righteous leader can divorce himself from the state of the nation.

Moshe was denied the special intimacy that he had previously experienced with God because of the peoples' actions, not his own. Heaven and earth can only be linked when the entire nation strives toward this ideal. Even though the gift of prophecy did not come to every member of *Am Yisrael*, all had an effect on the dialogue between Moshe and God prevailing. The whole nation had to allow the leader to communicate with God. Then, and only then, could the whole nation fuse heaven and earth.

Moshe implored the people to fuse, to enable the mundane to rise up and touch the Divine, the spiritual to vitalize the physical, not only as individuals but as an entire nation.

This was the first message that Moshe chose to teach the Jewish people as he was about to leave them. To fuse heaven and earth, the entire nation must be ready and fully conscious of their abilities and responsibilities. Only then will God speak to man and fuse the finite with the infinite.

Vaetchanan
Moshe in the Land Of Israel

Eretz Yisrael *is not an external entity, an addition to the nation or a*
means to attain physical or even spiritual achievements. Eretz Yisrael
is an integral part of the nation, inextricably bound to her inner
existence. It is impossible to explain in a rational way the particular
holiness of the Land.

(*Orot*, p. 9)

Thought in the land of Israel is clear, clean, and pure and liable to
bring with it Divine truth, to address the elevated desire for sanctified
idealism. It is conducive to prophecy, to Divine revelation.

(*ibid.*, p. 10–11)

The process of Divine spirit continuously appears in Eretz Yisrael.
Prophecy that emanated from the land of Israel continues even outside
the land if the overflowing holiness started in Israel. Anyone who
cannot stand the air outside of Israel, this is a sign of inner absorption
of the sanctity of Eretz Yisrael, *that never leaves one who merited to*
bask in the glory of the Land of the Living.

(*ibid.*, p. 11)

The *parsha* opens with Moshe's great plea to God: "God, You have begun
to show me Your greatness and infinite ability. Please, let me cross the
Jordan River and I will behold the good land, Jerusalem, and the holy Temple"
(*Devarim* 3:24–25). This was Moshe's last request, a plea from the heart, im-
ploring God to allow him to enter the land of Israel.

Yet the request was rejected. God replied to Moshe, "Enough! Do not speak to Me again concerning this matter" (*ibid.*, 26). Instead of being allowed to enter, Moshe was instructed to ascend a high mountain that bordered with *Eretz Yisrael* and from there "cast your eyes west, north, south, and east. See it with your eyes, but you will never cross the Jordan" (*ibid.*, 27).

The reason that Moshe was denied access to the land of Israel is recorded in the *Book of Bemidbar*. On one occasion, the people had complained to Moshe that they needed water to drink. God had commanded Moshe to supply them with some refreshment in a miraculous manner. "Take your staff and assemble the community together with Aharon your brother. Speak to the rock in their presence. The rock will give water, allowing the community and their animals to drink" (*Bemidbar* 20:8). Thus, the nation would realize their dependence on and subservience to God. In the words of Rashi: "The people would say 'This rock can neither speak nor hear and has no need for sustenance [from the Almighty], yet it fulfills God's word. How much more so must we fulfill His desire" (Rashi on *Bemidbar* 20:12).

However, Moshe slightly altered God's instructions. Instead of talking to the rock, he hit the rock with the staff. "Moshe raised the staff, hit the rock twice, and a tremendous amount of water came out, sufficient for the community and all their flocks to drink" (*Bemidbar* 20:11).

God immediately informed Moshe and Aharon, "Because you did not believe in Me and did not sanctify Me in the presence of Israel, you will not lead this assembly into the land that I have given them" (*ibid.*, 12).

This was a very severe punishment. Moshe tried on numerous occasions to annul this decree. One such example is in the opening verses of our *parsha*. On each occasion, God refused to reverse His decision. Moshe was to die before *Am Yisrael* entered *Eretz Yisrael*.

The midrash offers yet another conversation between Moshe and God regarding this judgement. "Moshe said to Him: 'Master of the World, at least modify the decree. I will not lead them into the land as a 'king'. At least let me enter, but not as the leader.' God replied that a king could not go back to being a normal subject. 'If I cannot enter as a king nor as a regular subject, then let me enter through the tunnels of Caesarion that are underground.' This was also rejected. 'At least let my bones be buried in the land of Israel.'" Even this was refused him (*Mechilta, B'shalach*).

Moshe wanted so desperately to enter *Eretz Yisrael* that he was prepared to surrender his role as leader. Barring this, even entering underneath the land was enough. At the very least, he wanted to be buried in the Holy Land. But God denied him entry under all circumstances. Moshe was to die in the desert and be buried there without entering *Eretz Yisrael*. Thus, his lifelong wish to enter the Land of Israel was to remain unfulfilled.

The question remains: Why was Moshe so intent on entering *Eretz Yisrael*? So much so that he chose to reveal his deepest longing for the land to the entire people in his farewell address. Obviously, there was an important message regarding *Eretz Yisrael* for the Jewish people and, perhaps, for the whole world.

All agree that God had endowed *Eretz Yisrael* with a particular *kedusha*, sanctity. Yet the question is: What makes the land so special? There is an opinion that the land of Israel is special as a result of the large number of mitzvot connected with the Land. These are known as the *mitzvot hateluyot ba'aretz*, commandments that are dependent on the land. There is a whole class of agricultural laws that are, in the main, only applicable in *Eretz Yisrael*. The laws of *terumot* and *ma'asrot*, tithing produce, the laws of *Sh'mittah* and *Yovel*, the seventh and fiftieth fallow year, are indigenous to the land and only apply there. In fact, one of the six volumes of the Mishnah is almost entirely concerned with laws that are dependent on the land. *Seder Zera'im*, *The Order of Seeds*—the first volume of the Mishnah—deals with these laws.

So we can see that the land is very important as it supplies us with the opportunity to fulfill many *mitzvot* that we are denied in the Diaspora. Indeed, the *Gemara* seems to point to this as the rationale behind Moshe's request. "Why did Moshe desire to enter the land? Did he want to eat the fruit or enjoy the good life?! Rather, Moshe said 'Israel has received many *mitzvot* and they are only relevant in the land of Israel. Therefore, I shall enter in order to keep them all'" (*Sotah* 14a). However, this cannot be the only reason.

Moshe pleaded with God that he should be allowed to enter even in tunnels underneath the Land where the *mitzvot* are inapplicable. More than that, he was willing to accept entry after his own demise. Just being buried in the land would have been some solace for Moshe. If the only reason that he wanted to live in *Eretz Yisrael* was to keep the *mitzvot hateluyot ba'aretz*, then a dead person is not obliged to keep *mitzvot*. What sort of annulment of the vow would that be?

Rather, Moshe realized that simply entering the land of Israel had special merit. The land of Israel held a special quality that was absent in the Diaspora, in *chutz la'aretz*. Indeed, what makes the land holy is not the *mitzvot*. The opposite is true. These agricultural laws are called *mitzvot hateluyot ba'aretz*, the laws that are dependent on the Land. The *mitzvot* are a result of the *kedusha* of the Land; it is they who are dependent on the Land and not the other way round. Rather, *Eretz Yisrael* is holy and sanctified and for that reason is con-

nected with many more commandments than other places. The more holy
the place, the more commandments are connected with it.

Moshe relates the unique qualities of the Land in another passage of the
Book of Devarim. "The land you are about to enter is not like Egypt, where
one plants seeds that are irrigated without labor. The land that you are to
inhabit is full of mountains and valleys that receive water from the rain alone.
It is a land that God always watches over; the eyes of God are on it from the
beginning until the end of the year. If you listen to My commandments and
love God with your whole heart and soul, then I will grant the rains in your
land at their appointed times. You will harvest grain, oil, and wine. I will give
plants in your fields for your animals, you will eat and be satisfied. Be careful
not to be tempted away and worship other gods, because God will become
angry and suppress the rain and the land will cease to yield produce. You will
vanish from the good land that God has given you" (*Devarim* 11:10–17; this
passage from "If you listen" is also the second paragraph of the *Shema* prayer).

Moshe marks a contrast between *Eretz Yisrael* and Egypt. Egypt is easily
irrigated; the Nile runs through it and regularly overflows its banks. This
afforded a wonderful system of irrigation. The Egyptians built channels from
the Nile to their fields. They had no worries and were certain that they would
always have enough water for their crops.

The land of Israel was very different. It was full of "mountains and valleys" and did not have the luxury of a huge river running through it. The water
was supplied directly by rain. This meant that the Israeli farmer is constantly
preoccupied with the rainfall. A dry winter meant that his crops would die
and there would not be enough for him and his family to eat.

Moshe was absolutely correct to state "the land that you are about to enter
is not like Egypt." They are completely different and it would seem, initially,
that Egypt is much better off. Surely it is preferable to reside in a country that
has no concern than in one that is constantly looking skyward to see when
the rains are to come.

However, the qualification of Moshe's statement is in the next verse. *Eretz
Yisrael* is "a land that God always watches over; the eyes of God are on it from
the beginning until the end of the year." God continually monitors the Land
of Israel. If the people are deserving of rain, they will receive it "in its appointed
time." If the rains do not come, that is a sign that all is not well in the land.

In *Eretz Yisrael* there is a continual interaction between heaven and earth.
God looks down on His people and deals with them according to their con-
duct. In *Eretz Yisrael*, heaven and earth meet in a way that is inconceivable in
Egypt or anywhere else in the world. "The land that you are about to enter is

not like Egypt." It is a special place. There you will succeed in fusing the spiritual with the physical.

For this reason the land has more *mitzvot* connected with it in order to control and enhance the union between heaven and earth. It is for this reason that Moshe strove to enter the land of Israel. He was willing to enter even though he knew that he would be incapable of fulfilling the commandments. It would have been enough just to enter the land where heaven and earth meet. Yet God denied Moshe access and he was to die in the desert.

Moshe taught *Am Yisrael* another crucial lesson. Our task is to merge the holy with that which appears profane and mundane. In order to fulfill this task, we have been given a number of tools and gifts. Maybe the most important of these is the land of Israel, a land that is constantly monitored by God. In *Eretz Yisrael*, we can elevate the physical to its holy roots and sanctify our national life. Such is the country that they were about to enter.

Ekev
The Torah and the World

---

*The change that occurred to Israel and to the whole world through
receiving the Torah in the wilderness, on* Har Sinai, *in a place that
was not specific to Israel—a place that was ownerless, a no-man's-
land—shows that the inner essence of the Torah is relevant to every
single person, to all nations on Earth.*

(*Ma'amrei HaRiyah*, p. 169)

*The Torah is not some lofty ideal that is removed from humanity.
Rather, it is totally suited to mankind, and without it man is just
another animal. Therefore,* Har Sinai *negated the special qualities of
Israel, that they can control nature, that they are illuminated by the
Divine light beyond nature, that is connected to the many miracles that
were performed for Israel. The giving of the Torah on* Har Sinai, *in
the desert, shows that the source of the Torah is the source of all life
and is a life-giving source for all the families of Earth.*

(*ibid.*)

*Moshe accepted the mixed multitude into the nation. Even though this
was not what he was commanded, it definitely was not totally negative.
Even though they may have caused us a lot of pain and anguish
throughout the generations, the eventual completion in the end of days
will be blessed by these forces that came from the mixed multitude.*

(*Ein Iyah, Shabbat,* Chapter 2, Note 79)

Moshe had completed teaching *Am Yisrael* their first lesson. He had conveyed the importance and necessity of fusing heaven and earth. This was to be done on a national level and the most conducive setting was to be *Eretz Yisrael*. This was the first concept that was discussed in the *Book of BeReishit*.

The second subject developed there was the idea of universal responsibility. Avraham was the father of many nations. He stressed the importance of teaching the lessons of Divinity throughout the world. Avraham's tent was open on all four sides, symbolizing his total devotion to transmitting spirituality to the world. He was an individual who was unconcerned with his own welfare, only with that of others. He was willing to teach others, even if this meant that he might suffer spiritually as a result (See the Chapter on *Vayera*, "Universal Responsibility").

Avraham passed this trait on to his son Yitzchak and, in turn, Yitzchak taught Ya'akov the importance of universal responsibility (See the Chapter on *Toldot*, "Yitzchak—Avraham's Successor"). However, Ya'akov was different from his father and grandfather in a very significant way. They had been individuals, he was the father of the Jewish people. He was to father twelve sons who would be the founders of the twelve tribes of Israel.

Consequently, not everything that is relevant to a person is directly translatable to a nation. A nation has the opportunity to expand horizons and influence a much greater arena. Yet a people is also more vulnerable, containing different types of individuals with specific skills and expertise. Not all people are successful at changing the world. Moreover so, this is not the task allotted to everyone.

Ya'akov fully understood this and assigned different duties to his sons. Some were to continue the job laid down by Avraham and Yitzchak; they were to teach Torah throughout the world. Others were to preserve the Torah inside and develop it for the Jewish people. Those who were descended from Rachel were ideally suited for the former assignment. They were connected to what is called the *alma d'itgalya*, the revealed external world. On the other hand, the children of Leah were more connected to the *alma d'itkasya*, the hidden, inner world. They were to fulfill the latter task of preserving the inner core of Torah for the Jewish people. They were in charge of education and the service in the *Beit Hamikdash*, the Temple (See the Chapter on *Vayeitzei*, "Leah and Rachel, Inside and Outside").

These distinct responsibilities were to continue throughout history. The "children" of Rachel always went out into non-Jewish society and imparted moral lessons to the world. At the same time, the "children" of Leah guarded the Torah from outside influence, ensuring that it would always be preserved for future Jewish generations. However, we find certain individuals who succeeded in crossing these very defined boundaries. There were descendants of Leah who went out successfully into secular society and had a resounding influence on those around them. An example of this type of behavior is to be found in Moshe.

Moshe was from the tribe of Levi, a descendant of Leah and, as such, was part of the *alma d'itkasya*. However, Moshe succeeded in growing up in the court of Paro, the ruler of Egypt, and retaining his Jewish values. He later changed Egyptian society and was so influential that, when he left, many Egyptians and non-Jews flocked to join him. They wanted to convert and join the Jewish people in their journey from Egypt to the Promised Land. This presented some problems and one such predicament is related by Moshe in this week's *parsha*.

Moshe recalled how the people had constantly tested his and God's patience. "Remember how you provoked God in the desert. From the day that you left Egypt until the present day you have rebelled against God. Even at *Horev* [another name for *Har Sinai*], you angered the Lord and He was ready to destroy you. When I went up the mountain to receive the two tablets of the Law and remained there for forty nights and days without sustenance, God gave me the tablets that were written in His hand and all of the words that He had spoken to you on the mountain out of the fire. At the end of this forty-day period God gave me the two tablets, but then He said: 'Get down fast from here. Your nation that you took out from Egypt has become corrupt. They have left the path that I commanded them and made a statue for themselves'" (*Devarim* 9:7–12).

This was the sin of the Golden Calf and it was almost the end of the nation. Yet we find an interesting remark. God refers to *Am Yisrael* as "your nation that you took out of Egypt" to Moshe. Surely they were God's nation and not just Moshe's people. Maybe the intention is that God disowned them due to their terrible behavior. But is that really possible? Would God so easily reject His people?

The midrash gives another explanation of this verse. The midrash relates a conversation between God and Moshe. "When we were in Egypt, I (God) said to take out My people, but I said not to take out all of those that came to convert and join the Jewish people. However, you (Moshe) were humble and said that one must always accept those that want to draw close. I knew what they were capable of doing (i.e., the Golden Calf) and told you not to accept them, but you went against My words and converted them" (*Shemot Rabba* 42:6).

They were indeed Moshe's people. Those that had made the Golden Calf were members of the *Erev Rav*, the mixed multitude that Moshe had converted and taken out of Egypt on his own volition. This is an example of Moshe's understanding of universal responsibility. It was so crucial that it was worth contravening God's command in order to spread His word throughout the world.

The question still remains why *did* Moshe decide to teach the nations God's Torah? Surely the nations have no intrinsic link with the Torah in the same way that *Am Yisrael* do. After all, only the Jewish nation received the Torah from God on *Har Sinai*.

The answer can be found in the explanation of a passage in the *Gemara*. The *Gemara* asks an interesting question: "Why was the mountain called *Har Sinai*? It means the mountain where *Nissim*, miracles, were performed for *Am Yisrael*. If that was the case, then it should be called *Nisai*. Maybe it means the mountain that was a *Siman Tov*, a good omen for Yisrael. If so, then it should have been called *Simai*. Rather, it was the mountain from which *Sinah*, aversion, came onto the other nations" (*Shabbat* 89a).

The *Gemara* is explaining to us an important message about the nature of the Torah and its connection to the world. The question as to the meaning of the name of the mountain is really a question about the essence of the place and of the Torah that was given there. It is as though the *Gemara* asked: "What is the nature of the Torah?"

The Torah is not exclusively pertinent to *Am Yisrael*. Indeed, the Torah was given in the desert in an area that was no-man's-land and not in *Eretz Yisrael*, the land of the Jewish people. In the words of the midrash: "The Torah was given in the desert in an ownerless land, as if, had it been given in *Eretz Yisrael*, the nations would claim that they had no part of it. Therefore, it was given in the desert and anyone who so desires can come and take part of it" (*Mechilta, Yitro* 1).

In essence, the Torah is relevant to the whole of humanity and its entire existence. The Torah was the blueprint of the world. As the *Zohar* remarks: "God looked in the Torah and created the world" (*Zohar* II, 161a). Therefore, every human being and every part of the universe is linked to the Torah.

The Torah was not given to Israel due to her supernatural, miraculous nature. Nor was it merely a result of some special quality that we hold. It was neither *Har Nisai*, the mountain of miracles, nor *Har Simai*, the mountain of the good omen.

The Torah is linked to the whole world and it is for this reason that *Har Sinai* was the start of the aversion against the nations. All humanity is connected to the inner depths of Torah, yet the nations rejected it. Instead of searching for their natural link to the spiritual, they found all sorts of reasons to abandon the spirit. For this reason, the Torah is a source of conflict for the nations. This causes them to further reject her.

Moshe attempted to rediscover the natural link between the nations and the Torah. He drew them near, took them out of Egypt, and brought them to *Har Sinai*. Yet they were incapable of absorbing the *kedusha* of this event. They rejected Moshe and built the Golden Calf.

At this point, Moshe changed his plan. Instead of giving the Torah to the whole world, he gave it to *Am Yisrael* alone. "Moshe gave the Torah solely to *Am Yisrael*" (*Mishneh Torah, Hilchot Melachim* 8:10). Yet the nations still have the ability to merge with *Am Yisrael* and thus reveal their own hidden potential. We, therefore, learn that in the glorious future. "Thus says God, in those days ten gentiles will grab the *tzitzit* of each Jew and say: 'We will come with you as we know that God is with you'" (*Zechariya* 8:23).

This was the next lesson that Moshe wanted to stress to *Am Yisrael*. They were to spread the Torah throughout the world, because it was naturally linked to the whole world and was the basis of all that existed. Yet they were also to recognize that they would be incapable of achieving total success in this endeavor; this total success would only come in the messianic future. Then, when *Am Yisrael* was on the correct level and the world was open to learn the word of God, the words of the prophet would be realized. The whole world would recognize the centrality of the Torah and the Jewish people.

Re'eh
Private Sacrifices
and National Meetings

We see that private altars were acceptable in the time of the forefathers and were eventually forbidden when the eternal House was established. When Avraham started to serve God, it was not in a set and determined fashion; rather he tried to turn all hearts to serve God. This was a preparation for the eventual service that was organized in God's spirit and was particular to the Jewish nation.

(Igrot HaRiyah, Volume III, Letter 746)

Private altars, bamot, *were of, themselves, a positive concept, but they were forbidden as they negate a higher ideal, the completeness that was constructed through the recognition of the Divine. The* bamot *were only acceptable until the establishment of a central collective site of worship.*

(Ein Iyah, Berachot, Chapter 2, Note 22)

In the Jewish people, the individual souls draw life-force from the collective soul, and the collective gives life to the individuals. Were one to want to break away from the nation, he would have to break his soul away from its life-force. Therefore, each individual needs the collective.

(Orot, p. 144)

The next lesson that Moshe taught the Jewish people was one straight out of the *Book of Shemot*. It will be recalled that *Shemot* is the book of the birth of the Jewish people. The birth was intrinsically linked with meeting God. *Am Yisrael* was born out of the earth-shattering meeting at *Har Sinai* (See Chapter on *Yitro*, "The Birth of the Nation"). However, the meeting and the *Book of Shemot* do not end there. Rather, *Am Yisrael* continued to meet God through a variety of media. The halacha and the law courts afforded a continuation of this encounter (See Chapter on *Mishpatim*, "Between Man and Man, and Man and God"). But no other platform acted as a better and more tangible meeting place between us and God than the *Beit Hamikdash*, the Temple (See Chapter on *Teruma*, "Make Me a Temple and I will Dwell Amongst You").

The *Beit Hamikdash* was a forum for the daily meeting between *Am Yisrael* and God. This was through the building, the *cohen's* clothing, and the sacrifices. The *Beit Hamikdash* was also the center of the nation, as it was the raison d'être of the nation. If there were no *Beit Hamikdash*, and the meeting between God and His people were to cease, this would have signified the end of the nation as it was then recognized.

In this week's *parsha*, Moshe goes to great lengths to stress the centrality of the *Beit Hamikdash*. We find many verses that point to the importance of Jerusalem and the Temple as the focus of the entire nation. "The place that God has chosen to establish His name, there you shall go to seek Him." One is to bring all sacrifices to the *Beit Hamikdash* and "you shall eat there before God and rejoice in all that God has blessed you" (*Devarim* 12:5,7). "Beware not to sacrifice in any way that you see fit, but only in the place that God has chosen. You are to ascend there to offer sacrifices and do as I have described" (*ibid.*, 13–14). One is only allowed to consume tithes "before God in the place that He has chosen, and you will rejoice in all that He has given you" (*ibid.*, 18). And so on and so forth.

This motif repeats itself again and again in the space of a few verses. We are constantly reminded that the holy Temple in Yerushalayim is the only place where we are allowed to offer sacrifices. We are to rejoice there and meet our Maker.

Within the verses, Moshe states: "Do not then do all that we do here today, where each does according to his whim. You have yet to reach the resting place and the final inheritance that God will give you. You are to cross over the Jordan and live in the land that God is giving you. When He grants you security and you dwell safely, then there will be a specific site that He will choose to dwell in. It is there that you are to bring your sacrifices" (*ibid.*, 8–12).

Moshe alluded to a specific form of service that was currently permitted but was to be forbidden sometime after entry into the land. What is it that they did according to the individuals' desire until the *Beit Hamikdash* was constructed? Why was it permitted before, yet not after, the establishment of the Temple?

The Mishnah explains that what was permitted before the building of the *Beit Hamikdash* was the offering of sacrifices on personal altars, called *bamot*. The *bamah* was a construction that was used for offering personal sacrifices. Were one to pledge an animal, he was allowed to offer it on a *bamah* and was not required to bring it to the central altar.

However, all public obligatory sacrifices were offered exclusively on the central altar. Even this halacha changed as the nation developed. In the words of the Mishnah: "Until the *Mishkan* was built, the *bamot* were permitted; when the *Mishkan* was constructed the *bamot* were prohibited. On entering the land of Israel, they came to Gilgal, and the *bamot* were again permitted. Yet later, the Temple was established in Shilo and the *bamot* were forbidden. Later, in Nov and Givon, the *bamot* were allowed. When the *Beit Hamikdash* was built in Yerushalayim, the *bamot* were forbidden, and they were never to be permitted again. This was the 'final inheritance'" (*Zevachim* 14:4–8).

The Mishnah describes in detail the journeys and development of the new nation in her land. Initially, the *bamot* were permitted, and every time there was a central altar they were temporarily forbidden, only to be permitted again in the absence of a central altar. During the time of the *Mishkan* in the desert, and later in Shilo, the *bamot* were forbidden, only to reappear during periods when the *Mishkan* was dysfunctional.

Yet when the *Beit Hamikdash* was built and the *Shechina*, the Divine presence, resided in Jerusalem, the *bamot* were forbidden permanently, never to return. Jerusalem was the "final inheritance" that Moshe cited as reason why the *bamot* were permitted in the desert. But he alluded to the fact that when they were to arrive at this "final inheritance," the *bamot* were to be eliminated for good.

Why the change? There were generations who lived through periods of the *bamot*, while there were those who knew only the *Mishkan* and, later, the *Beit Hamikdash*. What was the difference between these two. Also, what was so significant about the *Beit Hamikdash* that it had the power to negate the concept of *bamot* forever, up to the present day?

The Temple service and the sacrifices were two of the ways that *Am Yisrael* met God. They were not the only ways, but they were significantly special.

The Mishnah tells us that the *Beit Hamikdash* was so distinctive that there were ten miracles that existed there during the entire time of the first Temple (See *Avot* 5:5). And what is a miracle if not a direct link between Man and God? In that vein, the *bamot*, the *Mishkan*, and the *Beit Hamikdash* were all expressions of this link. The difference was that each was suited for its own time.

The relationship between God and *Am Yisrael* changed in its expression but not in essence. There were generations that communicated with God through the medium of prophecy and those that conversed through more earthly halachic channels. Both were legitimate pathways, each relevant to a particular generation.

The *bamot* were most significant during the time of the *Avot*, our forefathers. During this period, the service of God was a matter of individual practice. Avraham, Yitzchak, and Ya'akov were all individuals, fathers of the nation yet individuals, notwithstanding. The service of God was to take place through the medium of *bamot*, private altars. This was suitable to the period. But God had greater plans for their children. No longer were they to be individuals; they were to become a nation. In this capacity, they were to meet God as a nation, together. The time was ripe to stop the service on the *bamot* and to start worshipping in a central location. Therefore, after receiving the Torah and meeting God as a nation, the command was given by God to build the *Mishkan*. During the time that the *Mishkan* was standing, the *bamot* were forbidden. It was inappropriate for the previous private style of worship to continue in the new circumstances.

However, the *Mishkan* was not a permanent structure and did not hold the power to totally eliminate personal service. Therefore, during the entire period of the *Mishkan*, the *bamot* were forbidden only to reappear later. But, when the *Beit Hamikdash* was constructed, the *bamot* were prohibited forever. It was no longer conceivable to have private service in the face of the permanent Temple.

In order to understand this, we have to realize the significance of the entire nation worshipping God together. There is a verse that assures us that if we keep the Torah, we will successfully encounter our enemies. "Five of you will chase away one hundred of them; and one hundred of you, ten thousand of them" (*Vayikra* 26:8). Rashi immediately asks a simple mathematical question. "The calculation is incorrect. It should be that one hundred chase two thousand [On the basis of one to twenty.]. But there is no comparison between a few keeping the Torah to many keeping the Torah" (Rashi, ad loc., based on *Torat Cohanim* 2:4). A multitude have more power and ability due to the myriad strengths they possess.

Yet the strength of a nation is more than just the sum of the individuals therein. A nation is not just the sum of its component parts in the same way that a human being is not just a thinking animal, nor merely a collection of individual cells. Rather, a nation is a completely separate and new entity. It has its own pattern and life, a unique national soul and existence. When *Am Yisrael* entered *Eretz Yisrael* and established the *Beit Hamikdash*, the national soul took preference over the sum of the individuals. This is not to say that the people were not important. On the contrary, in Judaism the human is the center. Yet the individual had expression and meaning in relation to the collective, to the national soul.

For this reason, the *bamot* were outlawed permanently and are to remain so forever. The only legitimate sacrificial service is the one conducted by the whole nation in the *Beit Hamikdash*. "Who is like Your people Israel, one nation in the land?" (*Shmuel* II 7:23).

We are to meet God, both as individuals and, more significantly, as an entire nation. In order to facilitate this meeting, there must be a defined and controlled medium through which the encounter occurs. The *Beit Hamikdash* was built as a center for the whole nation to meet God and elevate the nature of the world. That is what it remains as, until the present day.

Shoftim
Divine Judgment
and the Human Element

The mitzvot *that enable us to reveal the Divine light in our souls, both of the individual and of the congregation, of the nation and of the world, in nature and in all of existence, they are the highest channels that draw life and connect all of the social commandments as the ways of God.*

(*Orot Hakodesh*, Volume III, p. 344)

"The wise man is preferable to the prophet" as the ambition of wisdom comes from the Torah which is the highest revelation, and already deals with all of the specific mitzvot *and their details, and the higher house is built on the firm base of the social construction.*

(*ibid.*, p. 345)

Therefore, the laws of damages are connected with righteousness of ethics and blessings, and whoever wants to be wise should deal with the monetary laws, as they are like a powerful river, and the basis of prophecy is elevated through them, together with the wisdom of the Torah.

(*ibid.*)

In this week's *parsha*, Moshe continues to talk about meeting God and the importance of preserving this connection. He develops the idea that we have already seen in the *Book of Shemot*. There, the meeting had an influence on everyday life, and it was noted that there is a seemingly mundane way to meet God. The law courts and the administration of justice gave evidence of God's existence and interaction with the world. It is He who set the laws of Israel in all walks of life, in the liturgical service as well as in the laws of monetary matters. Divinity permeates our entire existence as individuals and as a nation (See Chapter on *Mishpatim*, "Between Man and Man, and Man and God").

In the same way that, after receiving the Torah and meeting God on *Har Sinai*, the Torah dealt with civil justice, so this is one of the next subjects that Moshe mentions. Our *parsha* is called *Shoftim*, judges, who are also called *Elohim*, the representatives of God in this world. This is the next way to meet God on a daily basis, by establishing courts of law that function in accordance with God's will and command. "You must pursue justice in order that you should live and inherit the Land that God has given you" (*Devarim* 16:20).

The judges were to uphold justice and be exceedingly careful in its execution. "Do not pervert justice and do not give anyone special consideration. Do not take bribes, as they blind the wise and twist the words of the righteous" (*ibid.*, 19). This is very reminiscent of a similar command in the *parsha* of *Mishpatim*, in the *Book of Shemot*. "Do not take a bribe, as it blinds the clever and twists the words of the righteous" (*Shemot* 23:8). Almost the same wording is used in both places, the idea being that bribes are bad and forbidden as they blind the wise and twist justice. The bribe is the cause of the perversion of justice in most instances and therefore is forbidden.

Bribes are even more strongly condemned in the Talmud. The sages foresaw gloom for those who allowed themselves to take bribes. "If bribes blind the wise, how much more so for the unwise; and if they twist the words of the just, how much more so for the unjust. Even a great scholar who takes a bribe will go blind" (*Ketubot* 105a).

The rationale behind the prohibition against taking bribes is also mentioned in the *Gemara*. "What is the reason for bribes? If a person accepts a bribe, he draws near to the giver, and the giver becomes like his own person. And one is incapable of recognizing his own faults" (*ibid.*). The danger is that because of the bribe, one will be incapable of recognizing the truth. "They justify the wicked due to bribery" (*Yeshiyahu* 5:23) or "One takes a bribe from an evil person in order to pervert the course of justice" (*Mishlei* 17:23).

The administration of justice in the most perfect way is very important in the Torah and, therefore, bribery was prohibited. Yet this was not the only problem, in the words of the Rambam. "It is obvious that it is forbidden to accept a bribe with the intention of perverting the law. But this prohibition refers to accepting bribery in order to find the guilty culpable and the innocent blameless"(*Mishneh Torah, Hilchot Sanhedrin* 23:1).

Even in a case where justice would prevail, the prohibition of bribery remains in place. Obviously, the law against accepting bribes is not only in order to ensure the correct administration of justice. The *Gemara* also brings a number of cases that, at first glance, would seem to be permissible and within the borders of fair play and correct behavior. Yet, in each case, the *Gemara* implies that they were beyond Divine justice, even if they were acceptable to human justice.

"A person must not judge someone whom he likes or one whom he detests. He will be incapable of finding any misdeeds on the part of the one whom he likes and equally, he will find no favor for the one whom he dislikes" (*ibid.*).

"[Rabbi] Shmuel was once crossing a bridge when a man stretched out his hand to assist him. 'Where are you going?' asked Shmuel. 'I have a trial.' Came the reply. 'If so, then I am now incapable of judging you [due to your assistance.]'" The *Gemara* summarizes and states that "bribery not only takes the form of money and gifts, but even sometimes appears in the shape of help and words."

The *Gemara* then relates the following remarkable story:

Rabbi Yishmael ben Rabbi Yossi had a field that he loaned to a farmer. The man regularly brought the rabbi a basket of fruit on *Erev Shabbat*, Friday, as payment for the rent. On one occasion, he brought the fruit on Thursday. The rabbi asked him: "What is special this week that you brought the fruit earlier than usual?" "I on my way to a trial that I have and I said to myself that I will use this opportunity to bring you your fruit." The rabbi refused to accept the fruit. "I am disqualified from judging you due to your actions."

The farmer went on his way to the trial and was judged by other judges. Rabbi Yishmael ben Rabbi Yossi happened to pass by the courtroom during the trial of his farmer and overheard the proceedings. He said to himself "If he would make such and such a claim, then he could win the case." Suddenly, he caught himself and exclaimed: "Bribes are terrible and extremely powerful. As for me, I did not accept the bribe, and even if I had done so, it was my fruit to begin with. Yet I was influenced by the innocent gift that my farmer tried to give me. How much more is one who accepts a bribe incapable of arriving at the truth."

Rabbi Yishmael ben Rabbi Yossi taught us an important lesson regarding human nature. Man is naturally influenced by material wealth. It has such a powerful hold over him that, under its grasp, he is incapable of seeing the truth. In a court of law that is influenced by money, the Divine truth will never prevail. It may accidentally be the case that the verdict acquits the innocent and punishes the guilty, but this is an exceptional case and occurs despite the bribe.

The judges, the representatives of God's justice in the world, are commanded to be extraordinarily careful with regard to material pressure. We are to ensure that the judges have sufficient material wealth that they will not be tempted to accept bribes (See *Mishneh Torah*, *Hilchot Sanhedrin* 2:7).

Yet the problem of bribery is closely connected to the principle of Divine justice. Our court system is an opportunity to meet God in this world. The trial and the verdict are to be tuned to the Divine desire and will. When man interferes with the workings of this system, the Divine element is lost. When human weakness and inclination become part of the process, the judges cease to be the representatives of Divine justice. Instead, the law court becomes an extension of human will, far from the seat of Divine justice. Such a setting does not create an opportunity to meet God and is not a court of law.

The judge who accepts a bribe is punished in a unique way. The judge who accepts a bribe goes blind, and a blind man is disqualified from being a judge (See *Mishneh Torah*, *ibid.*, 2:9). The judge who attempts to inject his own failings into the courtroom is simply precluded from the process of Divine justice.

The judges are partners with God in the development and administration of justice. Yet they must be partners and strive to reveal God's will in the world. When the judge puts his own tendency in front of God's, then he will find himself outside the process.

We must meet God and continue to do so, yet it must be God that we meet and not our own worst self.

Ki Tezteh
Shalom Bayit—Domestic Peace

Simple education starts when the child begins to have a basic understanding, Scientific education starts when the child enters the world. Education regarding faith begins with conception: "You shall sanctify yourselves and be holy."

(Midot HaRiyah, Emunah 1)

The basis of domestic holy life that is capable of reaching the highest level, but can also sink to the deepest depths, depends on the outlook one develops. When all follows the regular pattern and order; when, from the outset, family life is purified from any perversion that could be attached to such life; when it is established on the order of purity that attracts light, then the house will be blessed with sanctity and God's blessing for a holy life of peace and joy.

(Ein Iyah, Shabbat, Chapter 2, Note 179)

God's spirit, the spirit of sanctity and purity only rests on a house when the individuals within it are bound together through elevated emotions; when the strength that directs them is to establish a house in His name, a life of justice and righteousness. Without this, what remains is a purely animalistic, physical attraction that becomes a consuming fire.

(ibid.)

This week's *parsha* opens with Moshe relating a very unusual halacha. "When you go out to war, and through God's help you are successful and take hostages, if you see a beautiful woman amongst the hostages, you may take her as your wife. Bring her to your house. She must shave her hair and let her fingernails grow long. She must remove the garment that she was taken captive in, and sit in your house and mourn her parents for a whole month. Only then can you take her as your wife" (*Devarim* 21:10–13).

This law needs some explanation as it seems to contradict the concept of marriage that Judaism proposes. Marriage is for the purpose of continuing the Jewish nation. In this capacity, we search for compatibility between the couple. They must develop a deep love built not just on physical attraction but on the basis of mutual aims and aspirations. They must be willing to give each other of themselves and sacrifice their personal wishes for the common good. Only in such a union of love and understanding can Jewish children be raised and nurtured.

Yet here Moshe offers another alternative, a love based not on understanding and harmony. The model discussed here is one of lust and immediate satisfaction. The soldier is allowed to take a woman from the captives, a non-Jewish spouse, just because he so desires. What is Moshe trying to convey here?

In order to begin to make sense of this passage and the following *parsha*, we have to remember that Moshe is relating to *Am Yisrael* a summary of moral messages that were developed throughout the books of the Torah. He has already discussed the principle of merging heaven and earth and the concept of universal responsibility. Both of these were seen in the *Book of BeReishit*. He then discussed the importance of continuing the meeting between God and *Am Yisrael*. He reminded his listeners of the place of the *Beit Hamikdash* and the law courts in this dialogue. These were ideas from the *Book of Shemot*. He then moved on to discussing the basic principles of the *Book of Vayikra*.

It will be recalled that the *Book of Vayikra* is termed *Torat Cohanim, The Laws of the Priests*. The most important role of the *cohanim*, in terms of the rest of the nation, was their task as pursuers of *shalom*, peace. *Shalom* means the ability to synthesize diverse concepts into one unified system. *Shalom* is the faculty to put everything in its proper place, to reveal the world order (See the Chapter on *Vayikra*, "Aharon, the Pursuer of *Shalom*").

Such was the task of the *cohanim*. They were the pursuers of *shalom* and it was their responsibility to show each his place in the Divine scheme.

This was the next lesson that Moshe taught *Am Yisrael*. Each individual has a God-given place and role. One has to strive to discover his own particular letter in the Torah and in the Divine plan. He must fall into place and perform his specific function. One must not blur the boundaries and differences between people, and thus assume that he will discover peace. The diversity between individuals is part of the Divine plan. Each is special and individual and has a unique role. Only through this variety of talents can the world be completed. There is a need for different tasks and people to fulfill them.

Yet, occasionally, there are external circumstances that force one to act in a manner that is contrary to this principle. Certain times compel us to break down the barriers and boundaries that bind Man.

War is such a time. The laws that govern man in times of peace are untranslatable to times of conflict. War has its own morality and course of action. This is the explanation of the halacha that forms the opening of this week's *parsha*.

"The Torah addressed the evil inclination of the person" (*Kiddushin* 21b). The Torah understands the psychology of the soldier and the incredible pressures that he is under. Therefore, God developed a way that the soldier would be able to quiet his natural desire in a permissible way. If the Torah were to treat the soldier as it would an individual in normal circumstances, the result would be disastrous. Some soldiers would be unable to fight their evil inclination and would succumb to the temptation. They would then realize that what they had done was forbidden and would be extremely remorseful. This would, in turn, undermine the morale of the entire army and they would lose the war.

Therefore, "the Torah addressed the evil inclination" and slightly relaxed the law, temporarily. All this for the greater good.

Yet even this relaxation had its limitations and was designed to create a perfect system. "The soldier must not come on her and leave her, but he must take her into his house. He cannot have intimate relations with her again, until he marries her" (*Mishneh Torah, Hilchot Melachim* 8:2). Once the pressures of war had subsided, the soldier returns to being a civilian. He cannot simply reject the female captive, but must take her into his house. Not only does he take her in, but she is to shave her head and remove her dress of captivity. The midrash explains that the Cana'anite women would dress up in times of war in order to seduce the enemy (*Sifrei, Devarim*). This was a tactic of psychological warfare. This dress had to be removed. She would sit in simple clothes and allow her fingernails to grow. She was commanded to cry, and to do so for a whole month.

All of this was to have a specific affect on the soldier. "In order that she will not be attractive in his eyes. She shall be in his house. He was to enter and see her, go out and see her. That he will despise her" (*Mishneh Torah, ibid.*, 5). True, the Torah had to allow the soldier this indulgence, but could not condone it. The halacha was such that the occasion arose only rarely and remained the exception to the rule.

This type of behavior was not to be the general order of events. The normal behavior expected and demanded from *Am Yisrael* was more closely aligned with marriage. We are to develop a strong basis for the continuation of the nation and our task. We are to teach the world the truth of the Divine world order. This temporary relapse was a necessity to save the nation at a critical point.

The *parsha* continues with two other laws that initially seem unconnected:

> When a person has two wives—one whom he loves and another whom he hates—he should not prefer the son of the beloved wife over the son of the hated wife with regard to birthrights" (*Devarim* 21:15–16).
>
> And when a person has a rebellious son who does not listen to his father and mother, and they have him punished by flogging and he still does not listen to them. His parents must seize him and take him to the elders of the city. They shall declare to the elders: "Our son is rebellious. He refuses to listen to us and is a glutton and a drunkard." The men of the city will stone him to death, to purge the evil from amongst you, and all of Israel will take note (*ibid.*, 18–21).

These two halachot describe rather depressing scenes. Men hating their wives and trying to deceive them. Sons rebelling against their parents and having such a detrimental affect on society that they must be killed. Interestingly, in both verses the Torah uses the expression "when" this occurs. It would appear to be more appropriate to use the term "if," or "lest." The Torah, however, says "when." And implies that this will definitely come about. It is a fait accompli; these will definitely happen.

This is what led the *Gemara* to comment: "These verses are next to those dealing with the female captive, in order to teach you that whoever marries such a woman will have a rebellious son" (*Sanhedrin* 107a).

The *Gemara* is trying to teach us that there is a world order. Anyone who attempts to fight this order and change his position to suit his own inclination and desire will ruin the whole basis of society. He who marries a female hostage has not committed a crime, but it is not something that is recommended. It is against the Divine order that preaches marriage as a building unit of the nation and not as a fulfillment of a fleeting desire. The man who listens to the voice of his evil inclination will also hate his wife. He tried to build a marriage on lust instead of deep love. "Love built on an outside factor is unstable. When the external influence is gone, love disappears" (*Avot* 5:16). Such a marriage cannot be a building unit of a nation.

Children born into this sorry union are also affected by what they see at home. The result: the wayward, rebellious son who steals and keeps bad company. He is considered a liability to society and, as such, has no place in *Am Yisrael*. The end of this episode is that the parents themselves have to admit to their own failings and hand their son over to the local courts.

It is such a tragedy as the end is so obvious, so inevitable. The result will always be the rebellious son or rebellious generation, and with them, the weakening of *Am Yisrael* and the whole Divine world order.

Moshe taught the Jewish people about the correct order of actions and events. This was the task of the tribe of Levi and the whole Jewish people, to make order out of the diverse elements of the world. To show that there is beauty in merging the different elements and revealing God's harmonious design. If we do not do so, then we weaken the tenets of the nation, and with it, the basis of the whole world.

Ki Tavo
First Fruits and Nationhood

The basis for all good and higher ethic, faith, is rooted in the depths of man's nature that is good and just. In the laws of God surrounding the process of planting, there is a connection with the basic force of faith.
(*Ein Iyah, Shabbat*, Chapter 2, Note 153)

Am Yisrael, *the one nation in the land, cannot bear division. She feels the separation of physicality and spirituality as a deep, strong pain, and she strives to find a way to return to unity.*
(*Ma'amrei HaRiyah*, p. 234)

I ask myself if it is possible that our national rebirth will be only a secular one, if holiness will remain in exile, lifeless, not renewed by the redemption? Is such a thing possible? Definitely not!! All of Israel will return. We all know that our life force is sanctity, and this sanctity will reveal its original power, and eventually all will realize this.
(*ibid.*, p. 336)

When you come to the Land that God is giving you as a heritage, and you occupy and settle her, take the first of every fruit produced by the land that God is giving you. Place them in a basket and go to the place that God has chosen to dwell in. Come to the *cohen* of the day and say: "Today I am declaring to God that I have indeed come to the Land that He swore to our forefathers that He would give us." The *cohen* will take the basket from you and place it before God's altar (*Devarim* 26:1–4).

277

These are the opening words of this week's *parsha*. The continuation is a description of the ceremony accompanying the bringing of first fruits to the *Beit Hamikdash* that is known as *bikkurim*, the first fruits.

The bringer was required to make a declaration that spanned most of Jewish history, and we shall soon see the significance of this statement.

First, we must answer a query on the opening sentence of the *parsha*. The Torah states: "When you come to the land." This seems to be an affirmation; we are being promised that we are indeed going to enter *Eretz Yisrael*. Is there a link between this assurance and the following law of *bikkurim*?

The midrash binds the two and states: "Perform this mitzvah in order that you shall enter the land as a reward" (*Sifrei, Ki Tavo*). The midrash implies that there is a special quality that the mitzvah of *bikkurim* possesses that is unique. As a reward for fulfilling this mitzvah one earns the right to enter the land of Israel.

What is so special about the mitzvah of *bikkurim*? What is the mitzvah and the idea behind it?

The Mishnah describes the events leading up to bringing the *bikkurim* to the *Beit Hamikdash*. "A person notices in his field the first fig to appear, or the first bunch of grapes or pomegranate. Immediately, he ties a thread around it and announces, 'This is the first fruit'" (*Mishnah, Bikkurim* 3:1).

In order to understand what is so significant about this practice, we have to understand the psychology of the farmer. He has toiled for the entire winter under difficult conditions, nurturing the trees and the fruit. He receives no guarantee whatsoever that his work will be successful. The elements are often against him and the odds are not necessarily in his favor. Yet he faithfully carries out his task of working the land.

It is not a coincidence that the *Gemara* remarks on the verse in *Yeshiyahu*: "It shall be the faith of your times, a store of salvation, wisdom and knowledge" (*Yeshiyahu* 33:6). "Faith" in this verse, says the *Gemara*, "refers to the order of *Zera'im*" (*Shabbat* 31a). *Zera'im* is the order of the Mishnah that deals with all of the laws governing agriculture. Anyone who deals with these laws and such matters must be full of *emunah*, faith, that his efforts will be rewarded.

The *Gemara* can be explained in another way, that all who see the miracle that is nature are bound to be strengthened in their own faith in the Providence of the Creator.

Eventually the big day arrives. The farmer enters his field and espies the first fruit. Here is the product of his toil, the first fruit on the tree. The farmer may have several reactions to such a happy event, yet the Mishnah gives him explicit instructions. He is to mark this fruit; it is not his and as such he cannot derive any direct benefit from it. Instead, he is to sanctify the fruit and take it to the *Beit Hamikdash*. There it is to become the property of the *cohen* of the time (see *Mishnah ibid.*, 2:1 and 3:12).

We may assume that the farmer would be upset and frustrated by this edict. He had to leave his home and take one of his most treasured possessions, the *bikkurim*, to the *Beit Hamikdash* and give it away to the *cohen*. However, this was not the case at all.

> The people of the area gathered in the capital of the district and slept in the street until the mayor announced: "Rise up and let us go to Zion to the house of God" (*Yermiyahu* 31:5).
>
> The procession set off. "A bull went before them with gold plated horns topped with a crown of olive branches. They were accompanied by a flute. When they approached Yerushalayim, they beautified the basket of fruit. They entered Yerushalayim in order of importance, and all of the city came to greet them declaring: "Our brothers from such and such a place, come in peace." They were still accompanied by the flute when they reached the Temple Mount. When they reached *Har Habayit*, the Temple Mount, even the king would descend and enter the *Beit Hamikdash*, carrying the basket on his shoulder. On entering the *Beit Hamikdash*, the Leviim would greet them with a special song: "I exalt You, God, for You have lifted me up and my enemies have been unable to rejoice over me" (*Tehillim* 30:2). With the basket still on his shoulder, he would announce: "Today I am declaring to God that I have indeed come to the land that He swore to our forefathers that He would give us" (*Mishnah, Bikkurim* 3:2–6).

This must have been a very impressive ceremony. En masse, the entire area brought their *bikkurim*. The decorated bull, the fruit, and the singing added to the festive atmosphere. This was not a sorry farmer fulfilling his dues and paying "Temple tax." Rather, it was a nation expressing its love for the *mitzvot* and the land.

Now we can start to understand the importance of the mitzvah of *bikkurim*. We learned in the *Book of Bemidbar* about the difference in emphasis that set the tribe of Levi apart from the rest of *Am Yisrael*. The tribe of Levi were to worship God "full-time" in the *Beit Hamikdash*, whereas the rest of the people were to work in the secular interests of the nation.

The unique quality of *Am Yisrael* was that both of these tasks were, in fact, in the service of God. He desired that we work the land in the same way that He desired liturgical service in the *Beit Hamikdash*. Only when both of these elements existed side by side did *Am Yisrael* have complete expression as a nation. Without the religious ideal, we would collapse ideologically; without the national ideal, we would expire physically (See the Chapter on *Bemidbar*, "Nationality and Divinity").

In *Eretz Yisrael*, we were to fuse nationality with spirituality; thus we would serve God. The Israeli farmer understood this completely. He knew that without the *cohanim* and the *Beit Hamikdash*, all that he strove to do was worthless. The first fruits represented the success not only of the farmer but of the entire nation. It was an occasion for public celebration. Therefore, the *bikkurim* belonged to the *Leviim*; they breathed life into the nation as much as the farmer did. Without both there was no *Am Yisrael*.

And so the entire district ascended as one to the *Beit Hamikdash*. Here was *Am Yisrael* affirming their link with the land and their national identity. They were overjoyed at the opportunity to come to the *Beit Hamikdash*, to renew their connection with the *Leviim* who served there.

The farmer entered the Temple with his fruits and declared: "I have indeed come to the land that He swore to our forefathers that He would give us." The fruits are a sign that I have entered the land and I make this affirmation in the *Beit Hamikdash*, the heart of *Am Yisrael*. When the two come together, then the individual can announce: "I have indeed come to the land." There he fuses the national, agricultural ideal, with the Divine, the Temple itself, and the tribe of Levi that serve there.

This also explains the relevance of the passage that the bringer of the *bikkurim* must recite: "An Aramean [Lavan] tried to destroy my father [Ya'akov], and he went down to Egypt with a small number of men and dwelt there. There, he became a huge and powerful nation. God brought us out of Egypt with a strong hand and brought us to this place and gave us a land flowing with milk and honey. Now, I am bringing the first fruits that You, God, have given me" (*Devarim* 26:5–10).

This passage suddenly makes a lot of sense in the context of the ceremony of the *bikkurim*. The farmer is affirming his claim to the land of Israel and his link with the aim of the Jewish people. Therefore, the bringer of the *bikkurim* recalls how the nation developed. Originally, it was just a handful of people. But, by the time God took us out of Egypt, we were already "a huge and powerful nation." A nation that had different talents and elements, all of which were dedicated to a common task. All of the tribes were to serve God; some through physical labor, others through spiritual endeavors. Together, we came to "a land flowing with milk and honey" and conquered her both physically and ideologically. God gave us the first fruits and the ability to survive as a nation, and we recognize that in bringing the *bikkurim* to the *Beit Hamikdash*.

Am Yisrael is a nation that is to combine the national ideal with that of a spiritual, Divine one. A classic example of this is the *bikkurim*, a ceremony that involves both the farmer and the *cohen*. This is the message that Moshe strove to teach the Jewish people on the eve of their entry into the Promised Land. In order to enter the land they needed to fuse spiritual and physical, then, and only then, could they be fruitful in the land of Israel.

Nitzavim
The National Covenant

The inheritance of God is truth. It gives strength and life to every single individual within Israel. Each individual soul contributes life and light, such that each individual is capable of adding holiness and sanctifying the days of the festival.

(*Olat Riyah*, Volume II, p. 254)

The Divine spirit comes through the aggregation of Israel to the heart of every single individual according to their deeds. Each individual becomes imbued with the nature of God, the ultimate good and pure ethics.

(*Orot*, p. 145)

The holiness of each Jew is hidden in humanity, in a deep hiding place, but it appears and flows slowly, until it becomes apparent in the soul of each Jew.

(*Orot Hakodesh*, Volume II, p. 303)

Moshe was about to end his final speech. All were gathered and hung on his every word. The entire nation strained to get a last glimpse of their great leader, Moshe. Moshe's life and the Torah were drawing to a close. Toward the end of his final address, Moshe assured the nation that God would forge a covenant with *Am Yisrael*.

In Moshe's words: "You are all standing, today, before God. Your leaders, elders, law enforcers, everyone of Israel. Your children, women, the converts, even the woodcutters and water carriers. You are being brought into God's covenant and His oath. In order that He should establish you as a nation, and

He will be your God, as He promised your forefathers, Avraham, Yitzchak, and Ya'akov" (*Devarim* 29:9–12).

Moshe stressed the fact that this covenant is relevant not only to a specific group within the nation. Everyone was present—men, women, and children, those who converted to Judaism, and those who joined the Jewish people as servants. All were there and therefore, at that time, Moshe decided to make the declaration concerning the *brit*, the covenant.

In the Torah there is no monopoly on *kedusha*, on holiness, and sanctity. No one individual or subgroup can claim that they have exclusive possession of the spirit. Every individual and tribe was linked to God and the Torah. All entered the covenant and took the oath.

One might assume that the *cohanim* are more holy then the rest of the nation. They received more laws concerning their conduct and spent their entire working lives in the service of God in the *Beit Hamikdash*. Surely this allots them an extra large dose of *kedusha*?

However, this is not the case. Both the *cohanim* and the nation entered the covenant and were part of God's nation.

Maybe men are more holy then women. They have the "upper hand" in the religious services in the *Beit Knesset*, the synagogue. Only they are allowed to lead the prayers and read from the Torah. Does this not lend them more spirituality?

Both men and women swore allegiance to God's Torah and met Him on *Har Sinai*. All the people, including both sexes, heard Moshe proclaim: "He will be your God, as He promised your forefathers, Avraham, Yitzchak, and Ya'akov" in this week's *parsha*.

The Torah is teaching us a very important lesson in *kedusha*. It belongs to everyone—leaders and the most simple individuals, men and women, *cohanim* and other tribes, adults and children, those born of a Jewish mother, and those that converted later on in life to Judaism, even the woodcutters and water carriers—all are part of the Torah and have a part of the Torah. Each has its own letter in the Torah and a novella to add to its richness.

Who were the water carriers and the woodcutters? Surely there is nothing special about these occupations that Moshe singled them out. Were not every woodcutter and water carrier included in the previous categories? How was it possible that they were not "everyone of Israel?"

Rashi brings the midrash that explains that they were neither Jewish nor were they regular converts. They were members of the tribe of Givon who came to convert (Rashi, ad loc., based on *Tanchuma, Nitzavim* 2). Their story is related in the *Book of Yehoshua*.

The tribe of Givon were settled in the land of Israel and, as such, had to either make peace with *Am Yisrael* or face them in war. Givon contrived a devious plan. They dressed in old clothes and took dry water bottles to give the impression that they had come from far away. They then approached Yehoshua and the rest of *Am Yisrael* to convince them that they had come on a long journey and were desirous of making a pact. So Yehoshua made a pact with them and did not discover the truth until three days later. He then discovered that they had been tricked.

This presented a serious dilemma for the Jewish people. They could not harm them since they had made a pact in the name of God, yet they were not true converts, since they had come under false pretenses. Yehoshua solved the problem by making them water carriers and woodcutters forever. They accepted this compromise since the alternative, that they face *Am Yisrael* in battle, was worse (See *Yehoshua* 9).

The midrash states that a similar occurrence took place in the time of Moshe. These were the woodcutters and water carriers that Moshe referred to in the opening verses of the *parsha*.

The *Ramban* is of the opinion that this refers to "the mixed multitude" of converts that joined the nation when they left Egypt (*Ramban*, ad loc.). In either case, Moshe is alluding to the fact that there are even members of the covenant whose link is dubious. They are "converts" who joined *Am Yisrael*, but not in order to "enter the covenant and crowd under the wings of the *Shechinah*, the Divine Presence" (*Rambam, Mishneh Torah, Hilchot Issurei Biyah* 13:4). Rather they converted under duress, due to panic and fear. Even these groups had a part in the covenant and were bound by its edicts. They also shared in its responsibility and enjoyed the glory of God's chosen nation.

But Moshe did not end with entry into the covenant. It was not sufficient to make a *brit* with God and take the oath. Moshe continued: "In order that He should establish you as a nation, and He will be your God, as He promised your forefathers, Avraham, Yitzchak, and Ya'akov."

God's intention in forging the covenant and making the people swear the oath was that we become His nation. In order to form the nation, the entire people had to be there. Only in the presence of the "leaders, elders, law enforcers, everyone of Israel. Your children, women, the converts, even the woodcutters and water carriers." Only thus was there to be a *brit*; only in such circumstances could there be a nation.

Am Yisrael was made up of spiritual leaders and lay leaders, workers and priests, men and women. Each of these had a specific task in the founding and continuation of the nation. Without any one group, the nation would be deficient, lacking, and in some way dysfunctional. All parts of society united to make the nation.

All of the tasks were the will of the Creator. No one group served God at the expense of any other. Rather, the entire nation served God together. The water carrier was as much fulfilling Divine will as the *cohen*. Men and women had true equality in serving the Creator. Each in their specific, Divinely-ordained way, yet each was essential and part of the *brit* of God.

Moshe forged the *brit* at the end of his life in the presence of the entire nation of Israel. Each was to be a small but significant part of the nation. Together, they were to enter *Eretz Yisrael* and form a nation that was to do God's will and sanctify His name. Such is *Am Yisrael*. Together we serve God, each in his or her own way, all toward the common goal.

Vayelech
War and Peace

The early generations that are spoken of in the Torah were involved in wars, and together with this, they were great and holy people. We understand that the spark of the soul is the most important thing. Those necessary wars caused the formation of those great souls. The wars of the establishment of the nation were Divine in an inner sense. They were strong in their spirit and knew, in the darkest hour, how to choose good from evil.

(*Orot*, p. 14)

Our national renaissance is developing before our eyes in the land of Israel. It needs to encompass all the values of life. It is not a true rebirth while it still only affects a small section of society and only certain values. It needs to deal with all strata and all our values. Our national life contains two values, the holy and the secular.

(*Ma'amrei HaRiyah*, p. 45)

[Even] eating in the land of Israel sanctifies at the center and only gives physical satisfaction as its external nature. This is why we mention Yerushalayim when we eat, during the blessings after food; the longing for Israel softens the food.

(*Orot Hakodesh*, Volume III, p. 295)

This is the last *parsha* in which Moshe describes events that occurred to the Jewish people. In next week's *parsha*, the final *Shira*, psalm, is recorded. The death of Moshe takes up the final *parsha*, including the farewell blessings to the tribes.

The *parsha* opens with Moshe relating again how he was prevented from entering the land of Israel. Here he speaks of the Divine opposition to his entry and offers a practical explanation. "I am 120 years old today, and I am no longer capable of coming and going so easily" (*Devarim* 31:2).

However, Moshe was not content just to inform the nation once again that he would not be leading them into *Eretz Yisrael*. In almost the same breath, he continued: "God is the One who will lead you. He will destroy the nations in your path that you should uproot them. Yehoshua is the one to lead you, as God has promised. God will do as He has already done to the kings of Emor, Sichon, and Og, and to their lands. He will give them into your hands, and you shall do as you have been commanded. Be strong and brave. Do not be afraid nor insecure before them, as God is with you. He will not fail you" (*ibid.*, 3–6).

Moshe seems to indicate that there is concern and fear in the Jewish camp. He felt the need to reassure them that all would be well as God was with them. The implication being that were God to forsake them, there would be ample reason for concern. The only way that they could hope to overcome the physical obstacle presented by the gentile nations that dwelt in the land was through Divine intervention and help.

Yet it was not going to be a purely miraculous acquisition. "God is the One who will lead you." God was not going to uproot the nations; he was going to lead the Jewish nation into battle. In the end, they were the ones who were going to fight. This they were to do in accordance with the Divine command.

Moshe chose this last opportunity to address the Jewish people and remind them of an important principle. In the *Book of Bemidbar*, we learnt about Jewish nationality and nationhood. There we saw that the nation is comprised of two distinct elements. On the one hand was the tribe of Levi, the priests. Their task was to serve God in the *Beit Hamikdash*, to learn and teach the Torah. Their major concern was with spiritual matters and they were the teachers of Israel.

Apart from the tribe of Levi, there was the rest of the nation. They were not reserved for spiritual matters. Instead of spending their time in the pursuit of holy activities, they were to work the land, fight, and develop the physical side of the nation (See the Chapter on *Bemidbar*, "Nationality and Divinity").

Both of these objectives were essential. Without the Leviim, the nation would collapse due to a lack of ideology. However, if all that remained was an ideal but the nation was physically incapable of defending this idea, then it would not endure.

Am Yisrael is God's messenger in the world. We come to herald the fact that an entire nation can serve God in this world. Both sides of the nation served God. It was obvious that the Leviim served God; after all, that was their entire purpose. They did not receive land or other worldly possessions in order that they might devote their whole time to Divine service. But it is a revelation that the rest of the nation were also involved in activities that were *kadosh*, that were imbued with a Divinity and were God's will.

Indeed, the whole nation worshipped God each in their own way. Some in the *Beit Hamikdash* and some in the fields, in the banks, and in politics. But the nation had to be comprised of both in order to be just that—a nation.

Obviously, there is a great chasm between the ideal and setting it into practice. To learn and dream in the detached atmosphere of the desert is one thing. But to translate that rather sterile theoretical setting into everyday life in the land of Israel is a daunting prospect.

Therefore, at this juncture, *Am Yisrael* was worried. Would they succeed in this God-given task of forming a nation from diverse parts? Would they be able to fuse the Divine with the mundane to such a degree that the mundane was elevated to the level of *kedusha*? Would the pressures of everyday life lead them to forget that politics and banking were also service of God in the national arena?

Such was the atmosphere at the time. Excitement at entering *Eretz Yisrael* after the forty-year trek in the desert was mixed with apprehension at the responsibility that this demanded of the whole nation. Moshe reassured them that "God is the One who will lead you." God was going to take them into the land and, as such, He would help and ensure that they would succeed in His task. God was going to do to the nations in Israel as He had done to the tribes of Emor, Sichon, and Og. He was going to fight with the Jewish people in their conquest of the land of Israel.

This was of great consequence. God was present in their wars. The wars that *Am Yisrael* fought were essential to their future, and they would only win on one condition: that God would "fight" with them. If the war was only a physical fight, the nation was not guaranteed success. But if the war was a fusion of the Divine and the national ideals of the Jewish people, then they would win. In the words of the Mishnah: "You are not like the other nations because 'God goes with you to fight for you'" (*Sotah* 8:1).

The Mishnah attributes this difference to the fact that the nation went into battle together with priests who held the *Aron*, the Ark. When the nation went to war, the whole nation was a part of the national struggle. It was inconceivable that the tribe of Levi would ignore the rest of the tribes and carry on business as usual. Nor was it credible that the nation could fight while disregarding the spiritual nature of the war.

The need to defend ourselves against other nations took on a new meaning. War was not a show of strength nor the last resort of a weak nation. War was also part of God's will. We are allowed to fight some wars and others are forbidden. This is also covered by halacha, because war was part of the national objective. We had to defend ourselves in order to fulfill our Divine task. If we refused to fight, we would be rejected and fail in our responsibilities to the Almighty. Such a war was a Divine imperative.

Moshe taught the nation that they were not to worry as they entered the land of Israel. Forty years previously, the princes of the nations had balked at the idea of entering the land and had convinced the people not to enter (See Chapter on *Sh'lach*, "Spies, Politics, and God"). Because of that, the nation had wandered in the desert for an extra forty years. Now, all of the people who had left Egypt had died and their children were ready to enter the land of Israel.

Moshe's final message was that they should seize the opportunity and enter the land. God would fight for them and, thus, the war would be part of the Divine will.

If the people could understand this concept, they were ready to enter Israel and live a national life. God was not only present at times of war but also at times of peace. In the same way that war was part of the national element of *Am Yisrael*, so were agriculture, economics, and politics. As much as God would fight with them, He would also plow the fields with them, trade with them, and govern with them. God was present in every national activity that the Jewish people engaged in. Politics became sanctified, an expression of sanctity and *kedusha*.

This was what the nation needed to hear to alleviate their fears. Now they were ready to enter the land of Israel and form a nation.

Ha'azinu
Song of the Heart

Whoever has a soul of song should know his nature and spiritual inner desire, and the special holy food that he needs to fulfill his spiritual appetite like a breath of air. This delicate soul of song sees the great wonders.
(*Orot Hakodesh*, Volume III, p. 215)

Singing is an expression of spiritual elevation at its greatest heights. The soul is naturally drawn to spirituality and, therefore, at the peak of spirituality, it proclaims a song. Man has to work so that the physical body may be drawn to the soul's song.
(*Ein Iyah, Berachot*, Chapter 6, note 2)

Every single word that is currently spoken with regard to the building of the Jewish people is not secular, rather it is a song—the song of the world, the song of the great human redemption that precedes the coming of the Messiah.
(*Ma'amrei HaRiyah*, p. 481)

"**M**oshe came and spoke all of the words of this song to the entire people." Moshe was about to die and leave the Jewish people just as they were to enter the land of Israel. His last two acts were to bless the people and sing them this song. The song was to endure throughout the subsequent history of *Am Yisrael*. The people would take the song with them and it would guide them on their path. It was the song of Jewish history and contained all they needed to know.

> The deeds of God are perfect, for all His ways are justice.
> He is a God of faith, never unfair, righteous and moral.
> He is your Father, your Master, who made and established you.
> Remember days gone by, ponder the years of the generations,
> Ask your father, and he will tell you, your grandfather will explain.
>   (*Devarim* 32:4–7).

These lines seem to be addressed to another generation, not the age of the desert journeys. The listeners are extolled to ask their forefathers to explain what God did when He took the children of Israel out of Egypt, how He kept them alive in the desert and brought them to the Promised Land. It foretells that *Am Yisrael* will sin sometime in the future and that God will hide His face from them. This is in complete contrast to the close relationship that the generation of the desert had with their Maker. He spoke to them, sent them daily sustenance, and guided them through the perils of the desert.

> Yeshurun (Israel) became fat and rebelled, you became fat, thick, gross.
> They left God who made them and spurned the Almighty, their support.
> They provoked His jealousy with alien practices and angered Him with vile deeds.
> They sacrificed to demons, who were not gods, to deities that they never knew,
> New things from nearby that their fathers never considered.
> You ignored the Almighty who bore you and forgot God your deliverance.
> God saw and was offended, provoked by His sons and daughters.
> He said "I will hide My face from them and let us see what will be with them.
> They are a contradictory generation, untrustworthy sons."
>   (*ibid*., 15–20).

This was the song that Moshe related to *Am Yisrael* immediately before his death. It was harsh and brutal, but it was a picture of reality. If the nation paid close attention to the words and spirit of the song, they would be armed to encounter the future in the land. If they recognized the dangers that entering the land posed, they would be in a better position to ensure that the worst did not happen.

The danger was that on leaving the Divine atmosphere of the desert camp that was surrounded on all sides by Clouds of Divine Glory and entering the Land of Israel, they would forget God. They would work the land and raise crops. They would trade with the surrounding nations. They would defend themselves from attack and create a thriving economy. They would do all this and forget that God was the force behind their success. They would proclaim "my strength and power caused all of this" (*Devarim* 8:17). They would become what Moshe called "fat"; they would become complacent and forget God. When this happened, Moshe assured them that they would suffer severe calamities. God would stop protecting them, and they would have to fend for themselves and would ultimately fail. The song was designed to enlighten them to the pitfalls and serve as a warning to all future generations.

How did Moshe know that this was going to happen? How could he be so certain, that he closed the Torah on this note? When was the content of this song revealed to Moshe?

The answer to all of these questions is contained in the essence of the song itself. The song is not just a medium to convey a message. *Shira*, song, is in itself a form of prophecy. In fact, prophecy is only achieved through song. All prophets sang and played music in order to enter the state of mind in which they received their prophetic visions. This is seen in the words of the prophet Shmuel to Shaul, "You will come to the hill of the Lord. There you will meet a band of prophets led by a harp, a drum, a flute, and a lyre, and they are prophesying" (*Shmuel* I 10:5). The *Gemara* states that music and a feeling of joy were a prerequisite for a prophet to receive prophecy. "The *Shechinah* does not rest [on a person] through sadness, nor sorrows, nor lightheadedness, nor conversation, nor idle chatter. But only through holy joy" (*Shabbat* 30b). The *Gemara* learns this from the verse used to describe David, who came to play the harp for Shaul to alleviate his melancholy. "'Take for me a musician.' And when he played, the hand of God was upon him" (*Melachim* II 3:15).

The fact that Moshe received prophecy is not a novel concept. Moshe was the ultimate prophet. He was the prototype of all the prophets, "those that came before him and those that will be after him" (*Thirteen Principles of Faith of the Rambam*, Principle 7). God informed Aharon and Miriyam that "Moshe My servant is trusted throughout My house. I speak to him face to face, in a true vision and not through metaphor, he sees the face of God" (*Bemidbar* 12:7–8).

Therefore, it was certain that Moshe should speak of the entire span of Jewish history in his song. A more extraordinary fact is that the entire nation had sung a song of tremendous prophetic proportions forty years earlier, just after leaving Egypt.

When the Jewish people left Egypt, they escaped in the direction of the Red Sea. After travelling for three days, they arrived at the banks of the sea, looked back, and saw the Egyptians following them. They were trapped on both sides and prayed for a miracle. God drew back the waters and the Jews passed through on the dry land. The Egyptians saw this and followed *Am Yisrael* into the sea, whereupon God let the sea revert back to its original form. The Egyptians were all drowned and the nation was saved.

At that juncture, the nation also sang a song of praise to God for performing this miracle.

> I will sing to God for His great victory,
> He threw horse and rider into the sea.
> God is my strength and song and my salvation.
> God is the Master of war, God is His name.
> He cast Paro's chariots and soldiers into the sea,
> His best officers drowned in the Red Sea.
>
> (*Shemot* 15:1–4).

However, later on in the song, we find verses that do not relate to this miracle at all but talk about very different events.

> Bring them and plant them on the mountain of Your inheritance.
> The place that You dwell in You have made, O God.
> Your hands formed the Temple of God.
> God will reign forever and ever.
>
> (*ibid.*, 17–18).

These verses are clearly talking about the *Beit Hamikdash* that will be built in Jerusalem some 480 years later (see *Melachim* I 6:1). This new nation of recently released slaves was singing about a Temple that was to be built many years later and had not yet even been commanded. The midrash informs us that "a regular maidservant saw a prophetic vision that was greater than the vision of the prophet Yechezkel Ben Buzi" (*Mechilta, B'shalach* 2). Each and every person who witnessed the miracle and joined in the song achieved an extraordinary level of prophecy.

All this was due to the incredible power of *shira*. Song brings with it prophecy because it overrides the resistance that people have to experiencing the Divine. Were we able to remove the layers that we have built around ourselves to deaden the voice of God, we would also achieve prophecy. Yet we remain incapable of baring our soul and ignore the prophetic voice. *Shira* comes to reveal the song of the heart, the cry of the inner recesses of the soul. Through *shira*, the individual enters the inner chambers of existence and reveals the Divine self. In so doing, they achieve a level of prophecy, each according to their own spiritual level.

Therefore, Moshe sang to the children of Israel a song of prophecy just before he died. This is the way that he wanted to leave *Am Yisrael*—with a song of prophecy that came straight from the heart. "Words that come out of the heart enter the heart" (colloquial saying).

Vezot HaBeracha
The End and a New Beginning

Moshe was great in his own right and also in relation to Am Yisrael.
*Due to his intense love of Israel, he agreed that all his achievements
would be linked to Israel's fate. Therefore, even though, on his own
merit, he should have continued living and taken them into the land of
Israel. However, because his name was synonymous with Israel's, and
they were unworthy of such a leader to lead them into the land, he had
to die in the desert.*

(*Ein Iyah, Berachot*, Chapter 5, Note 60)

*When one prays with only oneself and one's own needs in mind, the
prayer is not yet complete. The highest possible standard is that one
should see oneself swallowed into the collective and pray on their behalf.*

(*ibid.*, Chapter 6, Note 41)

*Moshe established the blessing "Who sustains all," for their individual
physical realm. Through the miraculous events, the future was
illuminated. Afterwards, we had to enter the land of Israel and we
entered a new stage, that was concerned with the physical welfare of
the collective, and so Yehoshua established the blessing "for the Land."*

(*ibid.*, Chapter 7, Note 31)

This is the last *parsha* of the Torah and it is the *parsha* in which Moshe dies.
The *parsha* itself contains the blessings that Moshe bestowed on each and
every tribe. The narrative then relates the final scene of Moshe's life. He

ascended the mountain of Nevo from where he could see the whole of the land of Israel just before he died. This was the closest that he could get to entering the land, and this was the last thing that he saw in this world. "God said to him: 'This is the Land that I swore to Avraham, Yitzchak, and Ya'akov, and promised it to their descendants. Look at it with your own eyes, but you will not enter it'" (*Devarim* 34:4). Moshe died on that spot and was buried in an unknown location in the area.

The Torah extols the virtues of the ultimate Jewish leader, the greatest that ever lived. "No other prophet in Israel has arisen like Moshe, who knew God face to face. [No one else did] all of the signs and miracles that God sent him to perform in Egypt" (*ibid.*, 10–11). The entire Torah was the work of Moshe; he performed all of the miracles, not only those in Egypt, but throughout the Torah. Moshe was also instrumental in forming and sustaining the new nation. It was he who first brought God's message of salvation to the elders of Israel in Egypt. It was he who approached Paro with the courageous demand that he let the Jewish people leave Egypt to go and worship God in the desert. It was he who led them out and led them for forty years in the desert.

On numerous occasions, when the people had angered God so much that He threatened to destroy them, Moshe came to their rescue and pleaded on their behalf. Were it not for him, they would never have survived the trials and tribulations of forty years in the desert. Without Moshe to intercede on our behalf, we would have been annihilated before we even reached the Promised Land.

Moshe was the initiator and facilitator of the continued meeting between *Am Yisrael* and God. He brought them to *Har Sinai* and ensured that no one ascended the mountain who was not supposed to. He remained there for forty days and nights, learning and transcribing the Torah for the benefit of mankind. "Moshe received the Torah and passed it on to Yehoshua. Yehoshua passed it to the Elders, and so forth" (*Avot* 1:1). Moshe gave the whole Torah that he had learned to the nation of Israel, teaching it to them a number of times (see *Eruvin* 54b). Moshe also erected and dedicated the *Mishkan*. This was so that the meeting of God could be sustained as long as the *Mishkan* and *Beit Hamikdash* stood.

The midrash goes even further in evaluating Moshe's worth. There is a well-known midrash that explains the verse: "The children of Israel were fertile and their population increased greatly" (*Shemot* 1:7) to mean that "each Jewish woman gave birth to six children at a time" (*Shemot Rabba* 1:8). This may sound incredible but it is completely eclipsed by another midrash. This one states that "one woman gave birth to 600,000 children at one time!" This is even considered incredible by the standards of the midrash, so the midrash itself offers an explanation. "That woman was Yocheved, who gave birth to Moshe, and he was as precious as the 600,000 members of *Am Yisrael*. Therefore, the verse states 'then Moshe and the children of Israel sang'" (*Shemot* 15:1). (*Shir Hashirim Rabba* 1:3).

The midrash suggests that Moshe alone was worth the entire people. The verse that the midrash brings as "proof" implies that, when the nation sang and Moshe sang, his song was equivalent to the 600,000 songs and praises of the rest of the nation.

The number 600,000 is the number of *Clal Yisrael*, the congregation of Israel. The midrash tells us that Moshe was *Clal Yisrael*; he was, in essence, a microcosm of the Jewish people.

If this was the case, that Moshe was not only the one who enabled the nation to evolve and form, but he *was* the nation, then a huge question arises out of the events of this week's *parsha*. How could the Jewish people possibly survive without Moshe? If he was the nation, at his demise, the nation would be finished.

However, this was far from the case and the Torah explains to us why this did not happen. Within the description of Moshe's death, the Torah informs us that "Yehoshua Ben Nun was imbued with a wise spirit because Moshe had ordained him. The children of Israel listened to him as God had commanded Moshe" (*Devarim* 34:9). The Jewish people were not doomed. Even though there would never be another prophet like Moshe, the nation had a leader, Yehoshua, who had earned the right to lead through his devotion to his rabbi and teacher, Moshe. "Yehoshua, his servant, never left the tent" (*Shemot* 33:11). This means that Yehoshua remained faithful to the teachings and ways of Moshe, never deviating from his path. For this reason, he was deemed to be fit to replace Moshe on his death.

The idea of finding a replacement for Moshe was of utmost importance to one person in particular, to Moshe himself. The midrash brings an exchange of thoughts that took place sometime before Moshe died. At one point, God said to Moshe: "Climb up the mountain of Avarim and espy the land that I will give to the children of Israel. See it and you will die in the same manner as your brother, Aharon" (*Bemidbar* 27:12–13). Immediately after these verses, the Torah says, "Moshe spoke to God: 'God should appoint a leader for the community. He will lead them, so that they should not be like sheep that have no shepherd.' God said to Moshe: 'Take Yehoshua Ben Nun, a man who is imbued with the Divine spirit, and ordain him. Set him before Elazar the Cohen and before the entire community and command him in front of all of them. Put some of your glory on him, in order that the community will listen to him'" (*ibid.*, 15–20).

The midrash explains that this passage is recorded "in order to praise the righteous that, when they die, they ignore their own needs and are concerned with the needs of the congregation" (*Sifrei, Pinchas* 138). Moshe's concern was solely with finding a replacement for himself before he died. When God informed him that his death was imminent, his primary concern was to ordain the next leader of the people. In the words of the midrash, he asked God: "Inform me if You are to appoint a leader or not" (*ibid.*). Moshe was not satisfied until God commanded him to ordain Yehoshua.

The midrash even explains that Moshe was not only to appoint Yehoshua to replace him after his death. Moshe was to "appoint him to ask and answer and to teach and decide halachic decisions during your lifetime. So that when you die the people should not say that he refrained from deciding and now he suddenly decides [on halachic matters]. Moshe immediately sat him down next to him" (*ibid.*). Thus, Yehoshua partly replaced Moshe during his own lifetime.

This would affront the pride of another leader. After all, Moshe was the outright leader of *Am Yisrael* and their very existence was to his credit. How could be share the platform of leadership with another individual? The answer is that Moshe was totally unconcerned with himself and his own welfare. He was totally committed to the nation. He *was* the nation. All that mattered to him was that *Am Yisrael* survived and thrived. Everything else was irrelevant.

Such was Moshe, an individual who was really 600,000 souls in one body, a representation of *Clal Yisrael*. Even the site of his burial was unknown. He simply passed on the leadership to Yehoshua. Then, and only then, was he ready to die.

The *parsha* is not an end, in the same way that the Torah is not the end of Jewish history, only the beginning. *Am Yisrael Chai*—even though Moshe died, his nation continues to live and flourish to this day.

Appendix I
Glossary of Hebrew Terms

Achoti Kalla—a kabbalistic expression literally meaning my sister is my wife, it expresses the close affinity a man and wife should feel for each other.

adanim—silver blocks used to steady the *Mishkan*.

Adar—the twelfth month of the Jewish calendar.

alma d'itgalya—a kabbalistic term for the revealed world.

alma d'itkasya—a kabbalistic term for the hidden world.

Am—A People.

Am Yisrael—the Jewish people.

Am Yisrael Chai—the nation of Israel lives!

Amida—the standing prayer, composed of nineteen blessings, the crux of the daily services.

Arei Miklat—cities of refuge for someone who had killed someone accidentally and wanted to escape the revenge of the family.

Aron—the Ark of the Covenant that contained the tablets of the Ten Commandments and was placed in the Holy of Holies in the Temple.

Arvit—the evening prayer.

Av—the fifth month of the Jewish calendar.

Av Hatumah—the highest form of *tumah*, spiritual impurity.

Avot—Fathers, one of the tractates of the Mishnah that deals with moral behavior.

Ba'al Keri—state of impurity caused by ejaculation.

Ba'al Teshuvah—a returnee, one who repents and returns to Judaism.

bamah/bamot—private altar(s) that were initially permitted until the time that the Temple was built.

Beit Din—the Jewish courts.

Beit Hamidrash—House of Study, usually the study hall of a yeshivah.

Beit Hamikdash—the Holy Temple.

bikkurim—the first fruits that were required to be consumed in the Temple.

bracha/brachot—blessing/ blessings.

brit—covenant, often used in context of the covenant of circumcision.

ceruvim—cherubs on top of the Ark of the Covenant.

Chazan—the reader or leader of prayers.

chet haegel—the sin of the Golden Calf.

chilazon—a snail that produced the *techelet* dye.

Chillul Hashem—a desecration of God's name.

chol—not holy; also, the weekday as opposed to *Shabbat*.

Chorev—another name for *Har Sinai*.

choshen—the breastplate worn by the *Cohen Gadol*.

chutz la'aretz—the Diaspora.

cohen/cohanim—priest / priests who served in the Temple.

Cohen Gadol—the high priest.

demama—silence.

emunah—faith.

Eretz Yisrael—the land of Israel.

erev rav—the mixed multitude of converts that left Egypt together with the Jewish people.

eshel—either a plant or an inn.

Ever HaYarden—the other side of the Jordan river, lands belonging to Amon and Moav.

Galut—the exile.

goy—nation or non-Jew.

haftara—portion of the prophets read on *Shabbat* and festivals in the synagogue after the reading of the Torah, corresponding to the Torah portion.

HaKhel—Ceremony of the Assembly, held once every seven years, when all the nation assembled in the Temple to hear the Torah being read by the king.

halacha—a law.

hasid—righteous person, also a follower of the Ba'al Shem Tov.

kabalat haTorah—receiving the Torah on *Har Sinai*.

kaddish—prayer recited by mourners.

karet—Divine punishment of being cut off, either dying young or dying childless.

kedusha—sanctity, holiness.

ketoret—incense offered in the Temple.

Ketuba/ot—marriage contract/s.

Kiseh Hakavod—the Divine throne of Glory.

Knesset—aggregation, or congregation.

Kodesh Kodashim—the Holy of Holies, the innermost chamber in the Temple that was entered by the *Cohen Gadol* once a year on Yom Kippur.

lashon hara—evil speech, a severe crime in the Torah.

levi/ levi'im—member(s) of the tribe of Levi that served in the Temple.

ma'amad Har Sinai—all the events on *Har Sinai* surrounding receiving the Torah.

ma'asrot—tithes of a tenth of one's produce that was to be given to members of the tribe of Levi.

Maccabees—fighters against the Greeks and against the Hellenistic influences on the Jewish settlement in Israel toward the end of the Second Temple period.

metzorah—someone afflicted by *tzara'at*.

midot—(good) character traits.

mikvah—ritual bath that removes spiritual impurity.

milah—circumcision, performed on every Jewish male on the eighth day after birth, or thereafter.

mincha—the afternoon prayer.

Mishkan—the Sanctuary, the temporary Temple that served the Jewish people until the Temple itself was built in Jerusalem.

mitzva/ mitzvot—commandment(s); also, a good deed not necessarily commanded in the Torah explicitly.

mitzvot hateluyot ba'aretz—commandments that are dependent on the land of Israel and cannot be performed in the Diaspora, such as *Sh'mittah*.

motzi shem ra—inventing damaging stories about another.

nidda—the impure state of a menstruating woman.

Parah Adumah—the red cow whose ashes were needed in order to ritually purify someone who had become impure through contact (even indirectly) with a corpse.

parsha/ parshiot—portion(s) of the Torah read weekly in the synagogue.

Pesach—the festival of Passover.

Rosh Hashanah—the festival of the New Year.

Sanhedrin—the highest court that convened in a chamber underneath the Temple.

Sefer Torah—the Torah scrolls.

sha'atnez—forbidden combination of wool and linen.

Shabbat—the Sabbath day.

Shacharit—the morning prayer.

shalem—complete.

shalom—peace, a word that comes from the root *shalem*.

Shavuot—the festival of Pentecost.

Shechinah—the Divine Presence that exists in this world.

shechita—the method by which meat is slaughtered and prepared for consumption.

shira—song.

shlamim—the peace offerings in the Temple.

Sh'ma—a central prayer of the morning and evening services, meaning "Listen."

Sh'mittah—the seventh year of the agricultural cycle when the land of Israel must lie fallow.

shofar—the ram's horn that is used as part of the service on Rosh Hashanah and at other times.

Succot—the Festival of Tabernacles.

taharah—spiritual purity (noun).

tahor—spiritually pure (adjective).

tallit—the four-cornered garment that must have *tzitziot* on each corner, usually worn for prayer.

talmid chacham—Torah scholar.

tamei—spiritually impure (adjective).

Tanach—the Bible consisting of the Torah, the Prophets, and the Writings. The latter two are called the *Nevi'im* and the *Chetuvim*, hence the acronym TaNaCh.

techelet—blue thread tied into the *tzitzit*.

tephillin—phylacteries, worn by grown Jewish males on the arm and the head.

terumah/ terumot—tithe(s) of produce to be given to the cohen.

Teshuva—return, repentance.

tevillah—immersion in a *mikvah* in order to achieve spiritual purity.

Tisha B'Av—the ninth day of the month of Av, the saddest day of the Jewish year.

tumah—spiritual impurity.

tzadik/tzadikkim—a righteous person/people.

tzara'at—spiritual skin disease often mistakenly translated as leprosy; a result of evil speech.

tzitzit/ tzitziot—the fringes on the corners of four-cornered garments.

Ur Kasdim—Ur of the Chaldees, Abraham's birthplace, or where he spent his early years before leaving to go to live in the land of Israel.

Urim and Tumim—the device worn on the breastplate of the *Cohen Gadol* that enabled him to communicate with God.

Yamim Noraim—the days of Awe, Rosh Hashanah and Yom Kippur.

Yerushalayim—Jerusalem.

yeshiva/ yeshivot—religious educational institution(s) dedicated mostly to the study of the Talmud.

yetzer harah—the evil inclination.

Yom haShoah—Holocaust Remembrance Day.

Yom Kippur—the Day of Atonement.

Yovel—fiftieth year of produce in the land of Israel.

Zechut Avot—the merits of the forefathers.

Appendix II
List of Names and Books
Mentioned in the Text

Aharon—Aaron, Moses' brother and the first high priest of Israel.

Akiva, Rabbi—one of the most prominent of the sages in Israel during the period of the Mishnah.

Amalek—the king and tribe that attacked the Jewish people throughout their history, beginning immediately after the Exodus from Egypt.

Ashi, Rav—the Babylonian scholar who was one of the final compilers of the *Talmud Bavli*.

Avraham [Avinu]—Abraham [our forefather].

Avram—Abraham's name before it was changed to Avraham.

Avihu—Aharon's son.

Avodah Zarra—idol worship, also a tractate of the Talmud that deals with idolatry.

Avot DeRabbi Natan—a volume of tannaic material accompanying *Avot* composed in Israel by the Tanna, Rabbi Natan.

Ba'al Shem Tov—(5460–5520/1700–1760). Founder of the hasidic movement in Europe. He emphasized the individual and emotion in serving God as opposed to pure intellectual study. The hasidic movement put cleaving to the tzaddik, the rebbe, at the center of its philosophy. It attracted many followers and had an influence on all Jews, not only the followers of the Ba'al Shem Tov.

Babba Batra—tractate of the Talmud dealing with property and estates.

Babba Kamma—tractate of the Talmud that deals with ownership and civil law.

Balak—King of Moav at the time the Jewish people were about to enter the land of Israel.

Bemidbar—*"In the Desert,"* the *Book of Numbers*.

Bemidbar Rabba—a collection of midrashic material related to the *Book of Bemidbar*, mostly based on *Midrash Tanchuma* (circa 4760, 10th century C.E.).

Ben Azzai—Israeli Tanna, contemporary of the famed Rabbi Akiva.

Ben Yehoyada—an explanation of the aggadic sections of the Talmud written by Rabbi Yosef Chayim (5595–5669/1835–1909), known as the Ben Ish Chai after his most famous halachic work. He was the Chief Rabbi of Baghdad.

Berachot—Tractate of the Talmud that deals with blessings and prayer.

BeReishit—*"In the Beginning,"* the *Book of Genesis*.

BeReishit Rabba—an Israeli collection of midrashic material related to the *Book of BeReishit*. It was composed by, or based on the teachings of, Rabbi Moshe HaDarshan (circa 4810/1050 C.E.). Other opinions claim that it dates from several centuries earlier, making it the most ancient of the existing midrashim.

Betzalel—a member of the tribe of Yehudah who designed and fashioned the *Mishkan* when the Jews wandered the desert for forty years after leaving Egypt.

Bila'am—a Midiyanite prophet who was hired by the king of Moav to curse the Jewish people after the Exodus from Egypt before entering the land of Israel.

Binyamin—Benjamin, Jacob and Rachel's son; also one of the tribes of Israel made up of his descendants.

Bnei Yisrael—the children of Israel.

Calev—Miriyam's husband, and thus Moshe's brother-in-law. He was the spy from the tribe of Yehudah, who entered the land and came back with a favorable report.

Chafetz Chayim—(5599–5693/1839–1933), Rabbi Yisrael Meir Cohen (Kagan). Born in Poland, he founded a yeshivah in Radin and lived there most of his life. He refused to occupy any rabbinic position and, instead, earned a living from a small shop and the sale of his numerous halachic and ethical works. He wrote the most authoritative commentary on the first section of the *Shulchan Aruch* (*Orach Chayim*), called the *Mishnah Berura*, and a work on the laws of Lashon Harah named *Chafetz Chayim*, after which he is known.

Chagiga—a tractate of the Talmud dealing with the laws of the festival sacrifice.

Charlap, Rabbi Ya'akov Moshe—(5643–5712/1883–1952). One of the closest of Rav Kook's students, Rabbi Charlap was the rabbi of the Sha'arei Chesed section of Jerusalem. He was a great scholar in all sections of the Torah including kabbala.

Chava—Eve, the first woman.

Chizkiyahu—the king of Israel during the period of kings, at the time of the First Temple. He was the son of the wicked king, Achaz, and attempted to rectify the evil state that he inherited from him.

Chulin—a tractate of the Talmud that deals with *kashrut*.

Dayeinu—"it would have been enough," the name of a song sung on Passover to thank God for the numerous miracles He performed for us on our exodus from Egypt.

Eli—*Cohen Gadol* at the end of the Shilo period, a generation before Saul was anointed as the first king of Israel.

Eliezer Ben Dordia—a Jew living in Israel at the time of the Tannaim who performed a tremendous act of repentance.

Eliyahu of Vilna / the Gaon of Vilna / the Gra—(5480–5558/1720–1797). The leader of European non-hasidic Jewry, and one of the most outstanding Torah personalities of the last few centuries. His entire life was devoted to Torah; he slept, ate, spoke, and wrote little. He mastered all branches of Torah study, halacha, and kabbala. He also wrote a book on algebra and encouraged the study of science. Many of his students emigrated to Israel on his insistence and established the original settlement in Jerusalem of the modern era. The Gra was the epitome of Lithuanian Jewry, who propounded an analytical approach to Torah study and were strongly opposed to the Ba'al Shem Tov and the Hasidic movement. Much of his teachings were recorded in writing by his students.

Em Habanim Semeicha—a work written by Rabbi Yissachar Teichtal during the Second World War. Rabbi Teichtal was an anti-Zionist Satmar Hasid in Hungary. During the war, he was in hiding and reconsidered his views on secular building in the land of Israel. This book is his revised conclusion. Written entirely from memory, it is a powerful argument for the need to establish a state in the land, drawing from a wide range of sources. Rabbi Teichtal himself was murdered by the Nazis, but the book survived.

Ephraim—the son of Joseph and the name of the tribe made up of his descendants.

Erchin—a tractate of the Talmud dealing with evaluation of dedications to the Temple.

Eruvin—a tractate of the Talmud dealing with definitions of the public and the private domain.

Even Haezer—see *Shulchan Aruch*.

Ezra—the Jewish leader in the time of the Second Temple. It was his efforts that encouraged the Jews to return to the land. He went on a mission to all of the existing Jewish communities, urging them to return to Israel. Many answered his call, but many remained in the Diaspora.

Gad—the son of Jacob; also the name of one of the tribes that were his descendants.

Gamliel, Rabbi—a leader of Israel during the period of the Mishnah, he was part of a long dynasty of rulers leading back to King David.

Gemara—the Talmud.

Gur Aryeh—an elucidation of Rashi's commentary on the Torah written by the famed Maharal of Prague, Rabbi Yehudah Loew (5285–5369/1525–1609). He is well known for having made a golem to defend the Jews of Prague, but was also a great philosopher and prolific writer.

Haggadah—the prayer book of the seder on the first night of Pesach.

HaEmek Davar—a commentary on the Torah by Rabbi Naphtali Tzvi Yehudah Berlin, known as the Netziv.

HaLevi, Rabbi Yehudah—(4834–4901/1074–1141). A foremost poet and philosopher in the Golden Age of Spanish Jewry. His most famous philosophical work is *Sefer haKuzari*, which describes conversations between the king of the Khozar tribe and religious leaders, in an attempt to establish the validity of the various traditions. Eventually, the king turns to the *Chacham*, the Jewish sage, who convinces him of the truth of Judaism. The king and all his nation converted. Most of the book is a philosophical argument for Judaism against Greek philosophy and a Karaite rejection of the Oral law. The book stresses the centrality of the land of Israel. Rabbi Yehudah HaLevi himself emigrated to Israel toward the end of his life.

Hamoadim BeHalacha—The Festivals in Jewish Law, a book on the festivals written by Rabbi Shlomo Zevin (5645–5738/1885–1978), the founder and editor of *The Talmudic Encyclopedia*.

Hilchot Avodah Zarra—The Laws of Idolatry, in the Mishneh Torah.

Hilchot Bikkurim—The Laws of the First Fruits in the Mishneh Torah.

Hilchot Deyot—The Laws of Wisdom (philosophy and credo) in the Mishneh Torah.

Hilchot Issurei Biyah—The Laws of Forbidden (and permissible) Sexual Relationships in the Mishneh Torah.

Hilchot Melachim—The Laws of Kings in the Mishneh Torah.

Hilchot Sh'mittah VeYovel—The Laws of the Seventh Fallow Year in the Land of Israel and the Jubilee (fiftieth) Year in the Mishneh Torah.

Hilchot Talmud Torah—The Laws of Torah Study in the Mishneh Torah.

Hilchot Temidim u'Musaphim—The Laws of (certain types) Sacrifices in the Mishneh Torah.

Hilchot Tumat Met—The Laws of Spiritual Impurity Connected with a Corpse in the Mishneh Torah.

Hilchot Tumat Tzara'at—The Laws of Spiritual Impurity Connected with *Tzara'at* in the Mishneh Torah.

Hillel—one of the sages of the first generation of the Mishnaic, Tannaic period, during the second Temple period. He was born in Babylon and studied in Jerusalem with the foremost scholars of his day. He was appointed head of the rabbinic courts a century before the destruction of the second Temple. He founded the School of Hillel (Beit Hillel) that argued with the School of Shammai (Beit Shammai), his contemporary.

Horaiyot—a tractate of the Talmud dealing with the laws appertaining to a mistake made by the *Beit Din*, the Jewish courts.

Hoshea—a prophet during the First Temple period, contemporary of Yeshiyahu.

Huna, Rav—second generation of Babylonian Amoraim, scholars of the Talmud, post-Mishnah period.

Ikkar Siftei Chachamim—see *Siftei Chachamim*.

Kagan, Rabbi Yisrael Meir—see Chafetz Chayim.

Kaplan, Rabbi Aryeh—(5694–5753/1934–1983). An American rabbi who revealed, taught, and translated many kabbalistic and hasidic works for a general English-speaking audience. He was a noted physicist and a prolific writer. In his eleven-year writing career, he wrote almost fifty books on a wide variety of subjects, as well as numerous articles.

Ketubot—a tractate of the Talmud dealing with the laws of the marriage contract.

Kiddushin—a tractate of the Talmud dealing with the laws of marriage.

Kohelet—*Ecclesiastes, Book of the Tanach*, written by King Shlomo, discussing the purpose of life and existence.

Kook, Rabbi Avraham Yitzchak—(1865–1935). Rav Kook was born in Latvia, studied in Lithuanian yeshivot, most notably Volozhin, under the tutelage of the Netziv. He held various rabbinic posts before emigrating to Israel and being appointed the Rabbi of Yafo (Jaffa). He left Israel for a conference in 1914, was caught by the First World War and was forced to remain for two years in Switzerland. Later, he spent a few years as a rabbi in London. On returning to Israel after the war, he was appointed Rabbi of Jerusalem and was made the first Chief Rabbi of Israel. He was a prolific writer on many subjects, most particularly a kabbalistic understanding of the redemption process that was being revealed before his eyes. He tried to draw the irreligious pioneers nearer to Torah and the Torah leaders nearer to the pioneers. This won him many enemies and he was subjected to fierce opposition. He died of cancer in Jerusalem.

Korach—a cousin of Moshe who rebelled against him and against Aharon in the desert, after leaving Egypt.

Lecha Dodi—the song sung on Friday night as part of the service in the synagogue, composed by the kabbalist Rabbi Shlomo Alkavetz (5265–5344/1505–1584) in Safed.

Levi—the son of Jacob, and one of the tribes made up of his descendants.

Maharasha, Chiddushei Aggadot—Rabbi Shmuel Idelish (5315–5392/1555–1632). The Maharasha wrote two works on the Talmud, one a halachic work, *Chiddushei Halachot*, and the other on the aggadic sections, known as *Chiddushei Aggadot*. Both are printed at the back of all standard editions of the Talmud.

Makot—a tractate of the Talmud that deals with corporal punishment.

Mechilta—the halachic midrash on the *Book of Shemot*, composed in Israel during the Tannaic period by the School of Rabbi Yishmael.

Megilla—a tractate of the Talmud dealing with the laws of Purim.

Meir, Rabbi—a sage of the mishnaic period, a student of Rabbi Akiva. The Talmud says that if a Mishnah brings a law without mentioning who said it, then it refers to Rabbi Meir (*Sanhedrin* 86a).

Melachim—*The Book of Kings*, one of the books of the *Tanach*, the Bible.

Menachot—a tractate in the Talmud dealing with flour offerings in the Temple.

Menashe—one of Joseph's sons, also the name of a wicked king during the first Temple period.

Midrash Rabba—the generic term for the several volumes of the *Aggadic Midrash*, the *Rabba*, for example, *BeReishit Rabba* on the *Book of BeReishit*. These were composed in Israel during the period of the Mishnah.

Midrash Shmuel—a collection of midrashic literature on the book of Shmuel (Samuel), the only midrash on a book of the early prophets. It was probably written in Israel (circa 4760, tenth century C.E.) and is based on many earlier midrashim.

Midrash Tanchuma—a collection of midrashic material composed in Israel, mostly based on the exegeses of Rabbi Tanchum bar Abba (fourth century).

Midrash Y'lamdeinu—a collection of midrashic literature that is synonymous with *Midrash Tanchuma*.

Mishlei—*Proverbs*, one of the books of the *Tanach*, written by King Shlomo.

Mishnah—a collection of statements of the Tannaim, compiled by Rabbi Yehudah haNasi (circa 3984/188 C.E.) The Mishnah was the first comprehensive codification of the Oral Law

Mishnah Berura—see Chafetz Chayim.

Mishneh Torah—see Rambam.

Moshe—Moses

Nadav—one of Aaron's son.

Nedarim—a tractate of the Talmud dealing with the laws of vows.

Netziv—Rabbi Naphtali Tzvi Yehudah Berlin (5576–5653/1816–1893). He married the granddaughter of Rabbi Chayim of Volozhin, the founder of the famous Volozhin Yeshivah. He succeeded his father-in-law as the Rosh Yeshivah of Volozhin and held the position for forty years. He closed the yeshivah in protest against the pressure of the Russian government to allow secular studies in the yeshivah. Many great people passed through the yeshivah, including Rabbi Kook, many of the Zionist leaders, and such thinkers as the poet Bialik.

Nezikin—the order of the Mishnah that deals with damages and civil law.

Niddah—a tractate of the Talmud dealing with the laws of menstruation and spiritual purity.

Onkelos—translator of the Torah into Aramaic (circa 3850, 90 C.E.). His interpretive translation appears alongside the text in most editions of the Torah. He was a convert to Judaism during the second Temple period.

Orach Chayim—see *Shulchan Aruch*.

Otzar HaMidrashim—a modern collection of midrashic literature collected by Rabbi Yehudah David Eisenstein (5614–5716/1854–1956), an American encyclopedist and author.

Parah—a tractate of the Talmud that deals with the laws of the *parah adumah*, the red cow.

Paro—pharoah, the ruler of Egypt.

Peah—a tractate of the Talmud that deals with the requirement to leave the corners of the field unharvested for the poor to gather.

Pinchas—the grandson of Aharon who achieved fame by killing the prince of the tribe of Shimon, Zimri Ben Salu.

Pirkei deRabbi Eliezer—midrash traditionally composed by Rabbi Eliezer Ben Horkinos, or by his school in Israel (circa 3860, 100 C.E.). It starts with a number of sayings in his name. The collection is more aggadic in nature than a regular midrash in that it relates events from the Creation to the wanderings in the desert.

Rabbeinu Nissim—(4760–4810/1000–1050). A North African scholar and student of Rav Hai Gaon of the Gaonic period, subsequent to the completion of the Talmud. He wrote an explanation of the entire Talmud, only part of which survives to the present day.

Rambam—Maimonides, Rabbi Moshe Ben Maimon (4895–4964/1135–1204). Born in Cordova, Spain, he was educated in Torah, philosophy, Greek, Arabic, and science. His family had to flee from Spain and eventually settled in Egypt. During these journeys, the Rambam continued his studies and writing. When his brother was killed at sea, he was forced to take up a trade and became a doctor. He was appointed chief physician to the sultan and wrote a number of important medical works. He wrote many Torah works; a commentary of the Mishnah, the *Mishneh Torah*, a complete compendium of all the laws (not only those that are applicable to our times but also the laws of sacrifices, Temple worship, and government administration) and the *Moreh Nevuchim*, the *Guide to the Perplexed*, an important philosophical work. He was the leader of the entire Jewish world and many letters remain that he wrote to various communities.

Ramban—Nachmanides, Rabbi Moshe Ben Nachman (4954–5030/1194–1270). Born in Geronda, Spain, he served as the Rabbi of Barcelona. He wrote many works, most notably a commentary on the Torah that popularized the kabbala to the masses. Today, it is one of the basic Torah commentaries. He was forced to leave Spain by the church, after winning a theological debate, and arrived in Jerusalem where he built a synagogue that is still active today.

Rashi—Rabbi Shlomo Yitzchaki (3800–3865/1040–1105) in Worms, on the Franco-German border. He was the foremost commentator on the *Tanach* and the Talmud. His explanations of the text were designed to aid the learner to understand the basic run of the story or halacha. When he arrived at difficult words, he translated them into Old French. His commentary is so widely accepted that it is impossible to learn a text without consulting "the Rashi."

Rebbe of Kotzk—(5549–5619/1789–1859). The brilliant and complex leader of the Hasidim of Kotzk, which later developed into the Gerer (Gur) dynasty. He spent many years secluded in his study, searching for the truth and for Divine revelation.

Rebbi—Rabbi Yehudah haNasi (the Prince). The last Israeli Tanna, scholar of the Mishnaic period, he lived during the second and third century C.E. (circa 4000). He was the compiler of the Mishnah, which he did in order to prevent the Oral Law from being lost forever.

Rechavam—the son of King Shlomo, who became king on his father's death. During his unsuccessful reign, the kingdom was divided into two: the lower kingdom of Yehudah (Judea), which he controlled; and the Northern kingdom of Israel, initially ruled by Yerovam.

Reishit Chochma—a kabbalistic ethical work written by Rabbi Eliyahu De Vidas in the sixteenth century C.E. He was a member of the kabbalistic school in Tzfat, Safed, and wrote the work to instruct the masses through the kabbala.

Reuven—Ya'akov's first-born, the son of Leah, also the name of the tribe made up of his descendants.

Ruach HaChayim—an explanation of tractate *Avot* by Rabbi Chayim of Volozhin (5509–5581/1749–1821), the foremost student of the Gaon of Vilna and the founder of the famous yeshivah in Volozhin.

Sanhedrin—a tractate of the Talmud that deals with laws pertaining to the Sanhedrin, the High Court.

Sefer haKuzari—see Rabbi Yehudah HaLevi.

Selichot—prayers recited leading up to and during the Days of Awe and on fast days. They beseech God for forgiveness and call for the final redemption.

Shabbat—a tractate of the Talmud that deals with the laws of the Sabbath.

Shaul—King Saul, the first king of Israel.

Shekalim—a tractate of the Talmud dealing with the shekel coin that was donated to the Temple once a year.

Shemot Rabba—a collection of midrashic material on the *Book of Shemot*, an Israeli Midrash based on *Midrash Tanchuma*.

Shimon—the son of Jacob, and one of the tribes that was made up of his descendants.

Shir HaShirim—the *Song of Songs*, a book of the *Tanach* composed by King Shlomo.

Shir HaShirim Rabba—a collection of midrashic material based on the verses of the *Shir HaShirim,* the Song of Songs. It is one of the earlier midrashim and was composed somewhere in the fifth century C.E.

Shlomo—King Solomon.

Shmuel—the prophet Samuel, also the name of a book in the *Tanach* dealing with events during his leadership of the Jewish people.

Shoftim—the *Book of Judges*, one of the books of the *Tanach* that deals with the events that occurred during the period of the judges, that is, from the death of Yehoshua until the anointing of the first king, Shaul (Saul).

Shulchan Aruch—the definitive code of Jewish law written by Rabbi Yosef Karo (5248–5335/1488–1575) in Tzfat (Safed), Israel. It contains four sections: *Orach Chayim*, dealing with everyday laws; *Yoreh Deah*, dealing with that which is permitted and forbidden; *Even Haezer*, family law; and *Choshen Mishpat*, judicial law.

Sifra—a halachic midrash on the *Book of Vayikra*, otherwise known as *Torat Cohanim*. Composed sometime after the completion of the Mishnah by the school of Rabbi Akiva.

Sifrei—a halachic midrash on the *Book of Bemidbar*, composed in Israel by the school of Rabbi Yishmael, a contemporary of Rabbi Akiva.

Siftei Chachamim—an elucidation of Rashi's commentary on the Torah written by Rabbi Shabtai Bess (5401–5478/1641–1718). It is printed in many editions of the Torah in its shortened form, known as *Ikkar Siftei Chachamim* (the *Essential Siftei Chachamim*).

Sotah—a tractate of the Talmud dealing with cases of adultery.

Succah—a tractate of the Talmud dealing with the laws of the Feast of Tabernacles.

Talmud Yerushalmi—the Jerusalem Talmud, written at the same time as the *Talmud Bavli*, the Babylonian Talmud, but completed some one hundred years previous to the completion of the *Bavli*, in the fourth century. Written in Tiveria (Tiberias) it was called the

Jerusalem Talmud out of respect for Jerusalem and was completed by the Israeli sage, Rabbi Yochanan.

Tanna Devei Eliyahu Rabba/Zuta—a collection of midrashic material that was taught by the prophet Eliyahu (Elijah) to one of the Israeli Ammoraim sages of the talmudic period. It is divided into two parts: the *Rabba* (major part) and the *Zuta* (minor part), both written by the same author.

Targum—a translation, usually referring to the Aramaic translation of the Torah by Onkelos.

Tehillim—*Psalms*, one of the books of the *Tanach*, the Bible, traditionally composed by King David.

Torah Shleima—an encyclopedic collection of midrashic literature that follows the verses of the Torah and presents all of the midrashim on each verse. It has run to some thirty volumes and is still incomplete. It was edited by Rabbi Menachem Kasher (5655–5743/1895–1983). Born in Poland, he emigrated to Israel, where he headed a yeshivah, developing and making major contributions to many halachic and talmudic projects.

Torat Hacohanim—see *Sifra*.

Tosephta—a collection of mishnaic material not included in the Mishnah, it was collected and edited by Rabbi Chiyah, a contemporary of Rabbi Yehudah the Prince, the editor of the Mishnah. The *Tosephta* was a parallel work to the Mishnah.

U'Netaneh Tokef—the central prayer of the High Holiday services, composed by Rabbi Amnon of Mainz, Germany (circa tenth century C.E.) as an act of repentance for having considered conversion to Christianity.

Vayikra—"and He called," the *Book of Leviticus*.

Vayikra Rabba—a midrash on the *Book of Vayikra*. It is one of the earlier midrashic works, composed in Israel during the fifth century (circa 4250).

Ya'akov—Jacob.

Yafe Toar—a classic commentary on the *Midrash Rabba*, written by Rabbi Shmuel Ashkenazi (5285–5355/1525–1595), who lived in Constantinople.

Yechezkel—a prophet in Israel during the First Temple period; also name of one of the books of the *Tanach* that contains his prophecies.

Yehoshua—Joshua, the leader after Moses, also the name of the book in the *Tanach*, the Bible, that relates the events of his reign.

Yehuda—Judah, son of Jacob and Leah, also the name of one of the tribes.

Yerovam—king of the splinter state of Israel, that split from the Davidic dynasty that ruled Yehudah—(Judea), he was of the generation after Shlomo.

Yerushalmi—see *Talmud Yerushalmi*.

Yeshiyahu—the prophet Isaiah; also name of the book of the *Tanach* that contains his prophecies. He was the son of the prophet Amos and came from Jerusalem. He prophesied destruction, and later, comfort and rebirth. This duality has lead to a theory that the book was composed by two distinct people.

Yevamot—a tractate in the Talmud dealing with levirate marriages. This is a case when a brother dies without children. The living brother is required to marry his sister-in-law, and the offspring are thought of as descendants of the deceased brother. If the brother refuses his obligation, he must undergo a ceremony called *Chalitza*. This is what is always enacted and levirate marriage is unknown today.

Yisrael—Israel; also the God-given name of Jacob.

Yitro—Jethro, Moses' father in law.

Yitzchak—Isaac.

Yocheved—Moshe's mother, the daughter of Levi, granddaughter of Ya'akov.

Yoma—a tractate of the Talmud dealing with Yom Kippur, the Day of Atonement.

Yosef—Joseph, one of Jacob's sons from his wife Rachel.

Zecharia—one of the last prophets; also the name of one of the books of the *Tanach* containing his prophecies. He was one of the three prophets to accompany the people from exile in Babylon to Jerusalem, and he testified as to the location of the altar.

Zera'im—the order of the Mishnah that deals with agricultural commandments.

Zevachim—a tractate of the Talmud that deals with certain types of sacrifices.

Zohar—the *Book of Illumination*, the classic kabbalistic work, traditionally thought to be composed by Rabbi Shimon Bar Yochai, the student of Rabbi Akiva. Scrolls of the work were stored for many years. It was finally edited and published by Rabbi Moshe de Leon (4998–5065/1238–1305).

Appendix III
Works by Rav Kook

Rav Kook wrote many works, articles, and essays during his life. Many have been published and a large number remain in manuscript form. Many of the names of the books and collections have the word *Or* (light) in them, which was a major theme in his writings and contain his acronym, *Riyah*; literally the visionary.

Books published by Mossad HaRav Kook, the Rabbi Kook Institute

The Author thanks Rabbi Katzenelebogen for permission to use the quotes from these books in this work.

Eder Hayakar—a work written in memory of his father-in-law, Rabbi Eliyahu David Rabinowitz-Teomim, known by his acronym, the Aderet (5602–5665/1842–1905), the Rabbi of Jerusalem. The work is partly biographical and partly ethical.

Igrot HaRiyah—the collected letters of Rav Kook. Thus far, four volumes have been published, spanning many years of Rav Kook's correspondence.

Midot HaRiyah—an evaluation of a variety of character traits, *midot*, and their relevance and significance today.

Olat Riyah—an explanation and commentary on the *Siddur*, the prayerbook. Much of the work was collected from other places, particularly *Ein Iyah*.

Orot—a major work by Rav Kook dealing with the land of Israel, the people of Israel, and the connection between the two. A collection of different articles written at different periods.

Orot HaKodesh—a four-volume collection of Rav Kook's philosophical writings and a major attempt to categorize his thought. It was edited by one of his main disciples, Rabbi David HaCohen, known as the Nazir, due to his Nazerite vow.

Orot HaRiyah—a collection of poems, and small pieces, from different periods.

Orot Hateshuva—*The Lights of Repentance*, a work on the essence, nature, and particular problems of return and repentance in our generation.

Orot HaTorah—a short work on the nature of Torah and Torah study. It also deals with the difference between the Torah of the land of Israel and that of the Diaspora.

Rosh Milin—a kabbalistic explanation of the meaning behind the Hebrew letters of the Alef Bet. It was written while Rav Kook was in Switzerland during the First World War and was completed in three days.

Shabbat Ha'aretz—a work on the laws and concept of the *Sh'mittah*, the seventh year when the land of Israel must lay fallow. Rav Kook wrote it in order to explain his position with regard to the halachic loophole that was created whereby the land was sold to a non-Jew. Thus work was permitted during the *Sh'mittah* year. Rav Kook saw this as a necessity, due to the vulnerable position of the *yishuv*, the settlement in Israel, at the time.

Other Books Quoted in this Work

Ein Iyah—an elucidation of the aggadic portions of the Talmud. Thus far, three volumes have been published; two on *Berachot* and one on *Shabbat*.

Ma'amrei HaRiyah—a collection of articles and published essays that span most of Rav Kook's career.

Index

existence of, 88–90
four cubits of halacha and, 201
as God of the Jews, 92–94
justice and, 108–109, 141
on lighting of menorah, 198–201
meeting with (*see* Divine Meeting)
Moshe and, 68, 83–85, 247–248
Noach and, 15
ownership of *Am Yisrael* and, 257
plagues brought on Egypt, 87–90, 91–94, 95–98
power of, 96–99
Red Sea miracle, 98–99
tower of Bavel and, 15–16, 246
visits to Earth, 16
watchfulness of, 94
God's Name, desecration of, 226–227
Gold, menorah and, 112
Golden Calf, 104, 119–123, 257, 258
Good will, 157
Goshen, 62
Goy, 185
Grape vines. *See* Vineyards

Ha'azinu, 291–294
Hagar, 37
Haggadah, 87
Hail, plague of, 97
HaKhel, 194
Halacha
civil justice and, 108
comprehensiveness of, 89–90
consequences of exile and, 201
deciding before one's rabbi, 148–149, 150
significance of, 22–23
transmission of, 150
Halachic literature, 201

HaLevi, R. Yehuda, 92, 121
Half-shekel coins, 126, 127
Hamon, 34
Hanukkah, 199, 201
Har Habayit, 279
Harmony, in *shalom*, 141
Har Sinai, 69. *See also Ma'amad Har Sinai*
reception of Ten Commandments on, 101–104
Sh'mittah and, 171
significance of name, 258, 259
Hasid, 108
Hasidim, practice of *tumah* and *taharah*, 170
Hebrew, Yosef and, 74
Hefker, 172
Hevel, 8–9, 11, 246
Hidden world, 46, 47. *See also* Alma d'itkasya
High Court, 193
High Priest. *See Cohen Gadol*
Hillel, R., 172, 179
History, respect for, 83
Holiness. *See also Kedusha*
of *Am Yisrael*, 136
Holocaust, 204
silence of Aharon and, 161–162
Holy of Holies, 164, 169
Homosexuality, 14
Horev. *See Har Sinai*
Hoshea, 66
Humility, of Moshe, 83
Huna, Rav, 14

Idol worship(ers)
Avraham's conversion of, 21
Avraham's father and, 32
characteristics of, 89, 90, 92, 121

on *Beit Hamikdash*, 262
on *BeReishit*, 246–247
birth of Jewish nation and,
77–79
census of *Am Yisrael*, 126, 187–
188
cities of refuge and, 232–233
clothing of *cohanim* and, 116
as *Cohen Gadol*, 132
as the congregation of Israel,
296–297, 298
death of, 295–296
on Divine order, 272, 275
in Egypt, 88, 89, 90, 92, 93
Eretz Yisrael and, 241, 242, 249–
251, 252–253, 288, 290
Ever HaYarden and, 231–232
on female war hostages, 272
on fusion of heaven and earth,
249
God and, 68, 83–85, 247–248
God's covenant and, 283–286
Golden Calf and, 104, 120, 122
humility of, 83
justice and, 141, 267–268
Korach and, 210–212
leadership qualities and, 81–85
the miracle of rock giving water
and, 250
Mishkan and, 112, 125–126, 131–
132, 296
ordination of Yehoshua,
297–298
parah adumah and, 216
as prophet, 293
sacrifices of the princes and, 192
song of, 291–294
spies sent to *Eretz Yisrael*, 204,
205

Torah and, 68, 242–243, 245,
296–297
on universal responsibility, 256–
259
Zimri Ben Salu and, 226, 227
Moshe ben Maimon, R. (Rambam)
on bribes, 268
on changing status, 228–229
on David, 67
on *dror*, 175
on *kedusha*, 164
on Levi, 52
on "strange fire," 149
on *techelet*, 10
on Torah transmission, 51
on woodcutters and water
carriers, 285
Motzi Shem Ra, 156
Murder, unintentional, cities of
refuge and, 232–233

Nadav, 148–150, 160, 161, 162
Naphtali (tribe of), 236, 237
Naso, 191–195
Nation(s). *See also* Am Yisrael
characteristics of, 188–189
origin of term, 78, 102–103
relevance of Torah to, 258–259
National ideals, fusion with spiri-
tual ideals, 193–195, 279–281,
288–290
Negative commandments, trans-
gressions and, 226
Nidda, 151
Nile River, 89, 252
Nimrod, 32–33
Ninth of Av, 203–204
Nitzavim, 283–286
Noach, 13, 15

Taharah. See also Purity *(continued)*
  parah adumah and, 216–218
  during pregnancy, 153
  as proximity to God, 152
  tzara'at and, 158
Tallit, 210–211
Talmid chacham, clothing of, 116–117
Tanach, 66, 67
Tazria, 151–154
Techelet, 10, 20, 22
  choshen and, 117, 118
  Korach and, 210–211, 212, 213
Temple, second
  ninth of Av and, 204
  rededication of, 199, 201
Temple, the. *See also Beit Hamikdash; Mishkan*
  Ark of the Covenant in, 131
  cherubs in, 131
  clothing of *cohanim*, 116–118
  destruction, cause of, 207
  as Divine meeting, 113, 118
  Divine Order and, 146
  miracles of, 145, 164
  ninth of Av and, 204
  pilgrimages to, 130–131
  shalom and, 145
  tribe of Levi and, 66–67, 279
Temple Mount, 279
Temple service
  intoxication and, 163–164
  kings of Israel and, 194
  purity of *Cohen Gadol* and, 168–170
  tribe of Levi and, 66–67, 279
  on Yom Kippur, 164
Ten Commandments, reception of, 101–104

Tephillin, 20, 22
Terach, 32, 33
Terumot, 111–114, 207, 251
Teshuvah, 158
  free will and, 180
  R. Eliezer Ben Dordia and, 179–180
  sin of *chillul hashem* and, 226, 227
Tetzaveh, 115–118
Tevillah, 216
Thieves, Torah law and, 106–107
Time, wasting, 44
Tisha B'Av, 203–204
Tithes, 207. *See also* Terumot
Toldot, 37–42
Torah. *See also* Torah, guarding of; Torah, spreading of
  on *Am Yisrael's* strength, 127
  consideration for soldiers in war, 273
  exile and, 200, 201
  intellect and, 169
  major principle of, 34–35
  Moshe and, 68, 242–243, 245, 296–297
  on peace, 141
  reception of, 101–104
  significance of civil law in, 106–108
  synthesis of *alma d'itkasya* and *alma d'itgalya*, 69
  tamei and, 169
  universal relevance of, 258–259
Torah, guarding of. *See also Alma d'itkasya*
  sons of Leah and, 56
  Ya'akov and, 50–53
  Yosef's brothers and, 58, 62
Torah, spreading of. *See also Alma d'itgalya*

About the Author

Rabbi Gideon Weitzman was born in Britain and spent many years studying in Yeshivat Bet-El, Israel. He devoted much time to researching Rav Kook's philosophy. He was ordained by the Israeli Chief Rabbinate and has published articles on various halachic issues. He is a popular lecturer in Israel, Britain, and America. He is married to Rivka and they have four children.